The Criminal Justice System

The Criminal Justice System

Politics and Policies

Tenth Edition

GEORGE F. COLE
University of Connecticut

MARC G. GERTZ
Florida State University

WADSWORTH
CENGAGE Learning·

Australia • Brazil • Japan • Korea • Mexico • Singapore • Spain • United Kingdom • United States

WADSWORTH
CENGAGE Learning

The Criminal Justice System:
Politics and Policies,
Tenth Edition
George F. Cole, Marc G. Gertz

Editor-in-Chief: Linda Ganster

Acquisitions Editor: Carolyn Henderson Meier

Editorial Assistant: Casey Lozier

Media Editor: Ting Jian Yap

Marketing Manager: Michelle Williams

Manufacturing Planner: Judy Inouye

Rights Acquisitions Specialist: Thomas McDonough

Design Direction, Production Management, and Composition: PreMediaGlobal

Cover Designer: Riezebos Holzbaur/Brieanna Hattey

Cover Image: © Paul Chesley/Photodisc/Gettyimages

Library of Congress Control Number: 2012942362

ISBN-13: 978-1-111-34663-8

ISBN-10: 1-111-34663-1

Wadsworth
20 Davis Drive
Belmont, CA 94002–3098
USA

Cengage Learning is a leading provider of customized learning solutions with office locations around the globe, including Singapore, the United Kingdom, Australia, Mexico, Brazil, and Japan. Locate your local office at **www.cengage.com/global.**

Cengage Learning products are represented in Canada by Nelson Education, Ltd.

To learn more about Wadsworth, visit **www.cengage.com/Wadsworth**

Purchase any of our products at your local college store or at our preferred online store **www.cengagebrain.com.**

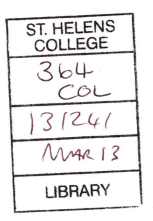
Printed in the United States of America
1 2 3 4 5 6 7 16 15 14 13 12

Contents

Preface

Entering into the fourth decade of publication with this Tenth Edition, we see scholarship further supporting this book's fundamental premise: The link between law, politics, and public policy must be understood to accurately grasp the workings of the criminal justice system. Since our last edition, new policies and research in the justice system have affirmed and deepened our belief in this premise. Media attention on everything from duct tape to airport security and schoolyards has yet again refocused our citizens on crime. The public continues to express high levels of fear and worry about crime. Citizens react strongly to events like child abductions, school shootings, and terrorism, despite data that our crime rate is declining. Crime continues to be listed as an important public problem, although it has fallen somewhat when compared to the state of the economy in recent years. Therefore, politicians respond with "tough on crime" campaigns and legislation. We also see increased funds for homeland security—which is criminal justice by a different name. Culture, public opinion, and public interest campaigns and interest groups are becoming more educated and more vocal. We see more public participation in crime legislation in the wake of 9/11, as evidenced by Amber Alerts, sex offender registration, trying juveniles as adults, and the impact of race and science on the imposition of the death penalty.

Our goal remains to offer you the classics that help illustrate the nexus between policy and politics, and reconcile some of these works with a sampling of the latest research. Survey and foundational courses remain our target audience, and we feel a deep responsibility to a collection of classics. Many of you will take issue with our definition of a classic, but our aim is to provide works that have had staying power, or works whose impact on politics or society was so influential that the works framed scholarly debate for years to come. We walk the reader through the seminal works that established the links between criminal justice and law, politics, and culture. That path reveals times when the empirical tools of social science debunk or demystify many of our publicly held assumptions. In exhibiting some of today's most contemporary criminal justice debates, like gun control, immigration, the growing number of prison inmates, and terrorism, our journey shows how popular opinion, or possibly legislative reaction to popular opinion, can lead to laws and choices that are at odds with the experts. Expert opinion has also changed over time, and our selection of readings demonstrates this as well. No longer is expert opinion limited to academia, but it is increasingly conducted also by members of government agencies, nonprofit organizations, and private research companies.

We are pleased by the widespread attention this collection has received, and encourage its continued use in criminal justice, political science, public administration, and sociology courses. We limit jargon and extensive discussions of methodologies to make this book accessible and user friendly for undergraduates, as well as to provide an efficient introduction to graduate students who have the skills to go to those original works if need be. Our duty is to stay abreast of present-day work, but we would be remiss to not provide the undergirdings of current research—those scholars who blazed trails on works of race and sentencing or culture, for example, and an array of works that scholars may still argue against.

In this Tenth Edition, our introductory sections address new research in the criminal justice fields, as well as the role politics play in the justice system. This book is more than a collection of works, and we continue to integrate the individual articles. There are 21 readings new to this edition, including Spelman's "Mass Incarceration: Money and Policy"; Tyler's "Legitimacy: Promoting Support and Cooperation"; Mears's "Criminal Justice Policy without Theory or Research"; Kraska's "Militarizing the Police"; Alpert, MacDonald, and Dunham's "Suspicion and Discretion: Decision Making During Citizen Stops"; Decker, Lewis, Provine, and Varsanyi's "Policing Immigration: Federal Laws and Local Police"; Clarke and Newman's "Terrorism and Local Police"; Waters and Ussery's "Enforcing the Law: The Stress of Being a Police Officer"; Vilke and Chan's "Less Than Lethal Use of Force"; Bjerk's "Prosecutorial Discretion: Making the Crime Fit the Penalty"; Gershowitz and Killinger's "The State (Never) Rests"; Galanter's "The Vanishing Trial"; Rikard and Rosenberg's "The Aging Inmate"; Lukemeyer and McCorkle's "The Privatization of Incarceration"; Markowitz's "Mental Illness, Crime, and Violence: Risk, Context, and Social Control"; Baker, Bedard, and Gertz's "The Unique Experience of Female Prisoners"; Xu, Fiedler, and Flaming's "Discovering the Impact of Community Policing"; Grabosky and Shover's "The Problem of White-Collar Crime, and Forestalling Future Epidemics"; Beaver's "Prevention and Treatment from a Biosocial Perspective"; Quinn's "Specialized Courts"; and Weisburd, Mastrofski,

Greenspan, and Willis's "The Growth of COMPSTAT." Although we keep some classics, our new selections maintain our tradition of understanding and viewing the criminal justice system as exactly that, a system, which can best be understood as a relationship between politics and policy. We provide discussion questions at the end of each section, which serve this synthetic goal, and provide useful tools for class discussion stressing critical thinking, essay exam preparations, and comprehensive overviews.

Special thanks are extended to Thomas Baker and Wanda Leal for their help in the creation of this edition. We also thank our colleagues, both at our respective universities, and from our professional time in criminal justice agencies, as well as the many faculty currently using this text, who took the time and energy to give us feedback.

George F. Cole
Marc G. Gertz

Author Biographies

George F. Cole is Professor Emeritus of Political Science at the University of Connecticut. A specialist in the administration of criminal justice, he has published extensively on such topics as prosecution, courts, and corrections. Cole developed and directed the graduate corrections program at the University of Connecticut and was a Fellow at the National Institute of Justice. Among his other accomplishments, he has been granted two awards under the Fulbright–Hays Program to conduct criminal justice research in England and the former Yugoslavia. In 1995 Cole was named Fellow of the Academy of Criminal Justice Sciences for distinguished teaching and research.

Marc G. Gertz is a professor of Criminology and Criminal Justice at Florida State University, where he has been a member of the faculty since 1976. Gertz received his Ph.D. from The University of Connecticut, Storrs. His interests include public law/judicial process and behavior, administration of criminal justice, public administration/organization theory, public policy in the criminal justice system, American politics, and research methods.

PART I

❂

Politics and the Administration of Justice

The close relationship between law, policy, and politics has been recognized since ancient times. Our country's founders imagined a society in which crime control is balanced with due process protections for individuals, later asserting that if the 'constable blundered' the criminal should go free. In "Two Models of the Criminal Process," Herbert Packer examines crime control and due process protections within our criminal justice system, discussing how they often compete for priority.

The social conflicts of the second half of the twentieth century have made it clear that the way criminal justice is allocated reflects the values of those who hold the power in the political system. Consider how recent changes to policies about crime and justice that were enacted in an era focused on harsh punishment have shifted, along with the attitudes of the American public, towards a less punitive approach. Governments and legislators are reacting to what they think the public wants, and in effect have increased the power that the state has over individuals.

The 1960s saw the start of a "get tough on crime" attitude in the United States, which seemed to get tougher with time. Politicians continuously debated what to do with criminals, and how harsh punishments should be; however, with the economic crisis our country is currently facing, the debate is shifting. All across the political spectrum, the views on criminal justice are starting to become uniformly less punitive.

CHANGING ATTITUDES TOWARD
CRIMINAL JUSTICE POLICY

Criminality and fear of crime are not new phenomena; they have always been part of the American experience. Public opinion polls have long indicated that Americans remained steadfast in identifying crime as one of the top five public problems to be addressed by government; however, in recent years, with the state of the economy, crime is no longer one of these top five problems. This does not mean that Americans no longer fear crime, simply that other problems have taken center stage. With this belief, attitudes on crime and punishment are starting to change from "tough on crime" to "right on crime."

The "get tough on crime" movement began in the 1960s in response to increasing crime rates. At this time, politicians were all competing over who could take the toughest view on crime. For example, in 1968, Republican presidential candidate Richard Nixon consistently claimed throughout his campaign that "the solution to the crime problem is not the quadrupling of funds for any governmental war on poverty, but more convictions." Once elected, President Nixon launched the "war on drugs," and called drug abuse "public enemy number one." After President Nixon, both Republicans and Democrats continued to fight over who could take the toughest stance on crime, forcing each successive president to continue expanding the harsh penalties for crime. The punitive movement brought new policies such as mandatory minimums, 3-strike laws, and severe penalties for drug offenses.

The current debate over the "tough on crime" policies is directly related to the effects of these laws. Because of these policies, the prison population rose more than 500 percent from 1972 to 1997. Also, the number of state inmates incarcerated for a drug offense rose 1,000 percent from 1980 to 1995, with one out of every four inmates having been incarcerated for a drug offense. As expected, this huge growth in prisons and incarceration cost a substantial amount of money. It was recently estimated that the prison boom cost taxpayers more than $38 billion. In his chapter "Mass Incarceration: Money and Policy," William Spelman discusses the growth of prisons and the best predictors for prison populations. Not only have these punitive policies resulted in a dramatic increase in rates of incarceration, but they also disproportionately affected minorities. Studies have shown that even though blacks and whites have similar rates of drug use, blacks are arrested for drug crimes at a significantly higher rate than whites. Blacks make up 38 percent of all drug arrestees, despite only making up 12 percent of the U.S. population. In addition to being arrested more frequently, blacks are also given harsher sentences than whites. Several studies have found that blacks are sentenced to prison more than whites. Michael Tonry further discusses the disparities facing blacks in the criminal justice system, and what part the war on drugs has played in creating these disparities in his chapter "Racial Politics, Racial Disparities, and the War on Crime." Beyond these effects of the harsh crime policies is the concern that they do not work in reducing recidivism,

and instead have a revolving door effect. Many prisoners, aft
recidivate and end up back in prison. Daniel Mears sugg
"Criminal Justice Policy Without Theory or Research" th
in the fact that many criminal justice policies lack a th
and empirical support.

In recent years, attitudes about the "tough on cr'
been changing. New laws are being passed to counteract the
by these punitive laws. For example, the recently-passed Second Cha..
offers services to help inmates re-enter society. Additionally, more and more
states that are deeply in debt are shifting away from their harsh policies. Take
New York's recent repeal of their Rockefeller laws, which were once known
as being the strictest drug laws in the country. In the same year, at least 16
other states have changed their "tough on crime" laws.

In recent primary elections, Republican candidates have been discussing their views on crime and punishment, and for the first time in decades
they are not worried about sounding tough on crime. In fact, conservative
reformers launched the "right on crime" movement, which was endorsed by
Republican presidential candidate Newt Gingrich, as well as other Republican
leaders including Jeb Bush, Bill Bennett, and Ralph Reed. In addition,
other Republicans have a track record of enacting less punitive policies. For
example, Republican presidential candidate Mitt Romney enacted policies
that provided inmates with better re-entry service during his term as governor
of Massachusetts. In Florida, Republican Governor Rick Scott has proposed
budget cuts for state correction agencies that will close seven state prisons.

THE FIRST BLACK PRESIDENT AND CRIME

The historic election of Barack Obama, the first black President of the
United States, raised expectations for significant change, and indeed his
election has had measurable impact on the criminal justice system. President
Obama's criminal policies focus on reducing disparities in criminal sentencing and promoting fairness in the criminal justice system. For example, he
reduced the disparity between sentencing for crack cocaine and powder
cocaine. The Fair Sentencing Act reduced the weight disparity for crack
cocaine to powder cocaine from 100 to 1 to 18 to 1. This large disparity that
President Obama eliminated was disproportionately affecting minorities and
the impoverished. President Obama also expanded the federal hate crime
laws, making it a felony to assault anyone based on their sexual orientation or
gender identity. Prior to the President's expansion, federal hate crime laws
covered offenses motivated by the victim's race, religion, color, or national
origin. Along with the reduction of the crack/powder cocaine sentencing
disparity, the expansion of hate crime laws shows that President Obama has
enacted policies to reduce disparities and unfair treatment throughout the
criminal justice system.

The Continuing Crime Drop

It has long been thought that there is a connection between crime and the economy. When the economy is good, more people have jobs, and there is less crime; when the economy is bad, fewer people have jobs, and there is more crime. Under this logic, after the latest economic collapse most people expected an upswing in crime; however, that rise in crime never occurred. In fact, homicide rates in black communities—which disproportionately suffer from greater unemployment, low wages, and crime—have declined. Why haven't crime rates increased along with unemployment rates? Some experts think that the relationship between unemployment and crime is more complex than a simple correlation, so that even though unemployment is high, there may be other factors that are keeping crime down, such as better policing. A similar thought endorsed by some experts is simply that there is no real relationship between unemployment and crime.

Another explanation that is gaining momentum among the criminological community is that the election of President Obama had a direct effect on the decreasing homicide rates in black communities. Some experts believe that the election of President Obama has provided inspiration to some potential criminals in these communities. Studies show that after President Obama was elected, the residents of these black communities have felt more optimistic about their economic future than they have in the past, implying that the more secure they feel about their future, the less likely they are to engage in criminal behavior. This argument goes off of legitimacy theory, which asserts that the stronger the people's belief in the legitimacy of their government, the more likely they are to obey the laws. Legitimacy is discussed further in Tom Tyler's chapter, "Legitimacy, Trust and Confidence: Promoting Support and Cooperation," where he explains the importance of public support and cooperation for the legitimacy of the police.

The "tough on crime" movement began because of a small upswing in crime that politicians used as a platform for debate over who could be more punitive. With the decline in crime and the failure of these harsh laws, attitudes about criminal justice policies have changed. Recently, politicians have been supporting criminal justice policies that are not as harsh, leading to a less punitive approach to the administration of justice.

WRITING ASSIGNMENTS

1. There is a dynamic and constant tension between due process, equal protection, the use of discretion, and the preservation of public order in the criminal justice system. What are some examples of these competing values?

2. Discuss how politics are involved in the criminal justice system. Should we attempt to have a justice system that is free of politics?

3. With a struggling economy, the United States is still spending a substantial amount of money on

the criminal justice system. What areas of our system might be altered in order to spend less money?

4. A significant number of criminal justice policies are not created with a strong theoretical base or empirical support. Discuss whether or not our system should strive to create policies that are empirically supported by research.

1

✵

Two Models of the Criminal Process

Herbert L. Packer

In one of the most important contributions to systematic thought about the administration of criminal justice, Herbert Packer articulates the values supporting two models of the justice process. He notes the gulf existing between the "Due Process Model" of criminal administration, with its emphasis on the rights of the individual, and the "Crime Control Model," which sees the regulation of criminal conduct as the most important function of the judicial system.

Two models of the criminal process will let us perceive the normative antinomy at the heart of the criminal law. These models are not labeled Is and Ought, nor are they to be taken in that sense. Rather, they represent an attempt to abstract two separate value systems that compete for priority in the operation of the criminal process. Neither is presented as either corresponding to reality or representing the ideal to the exclusion of the other. The two models merely afford a convenient way to talk about the operation of a process whose day-to-day functioning involves a constant series of minute adjustments between the competing demands of two value systems and whose normative future likewise involves a series of resolutions of the tensions between competing claims.

I call these two models the Due Process Model and the Crime Control Model. . . . As we examine the way the models operate in each successive stage, we will raise two further inquiries: first, where on a spectrum between the extremes represented by the two models do our present practices seem approximately to fall; second, what appears to be the direction and thrust of current and foreseeable trends along each such spectrum?

There is a risk in an enterprise of this sort that is latent in any attempt to polarize. It is, simply, that values are too various to be pinned down to yes-or-no answers. The models are distortions of reality. And, since they are normative in character, there is a danger of seeing one or the other as Good or Bad. The reader will have his preferences, as I do, but we should not be so rigid as to demand consistently polarized answers to the range of questions posed in the criminal process. The weighty questions of public policy that inhere in any attempt to discern where on the spectrum of normative choice the "right" answer lies are beyond the scope of the present inquiry. The attempt here is primarily to clarify the terms of discussion by isolating the assumptions that underlie competing policy claims, and examining the conclusions that those claims, if fully accepted, would lead to.

VALUES UNDERLYING THE MODELS

Each of the two models we are about to examine is an attempt to give operational content to a complex of values underlying the criminal law. As I have suggested earlier, it is possible to identify two competing systems of values, the tension between which accounts for the intense activity now observable in the development of the criminal process. The actors in this development— lawmakers, judges, police, prosecutors, defense lawyers—do not often pause to articulate the values that underlie the positions that they take on any given issue. Indeed, it would be a gross oversimplification to ascribe a coherent and consistent set of values to any of these actors. Each of the two competing schemes of values we will be developing in this section contains components that are demonstrably present some of the time in some of the actors' preferences regarding the criminal process. No one person has ever identified himself as holding all of the values that underlie these two models. The models are polarities, and so are the schemes of values that underlie them. A person who subscribed to all of the values underlying the other would be rightly viewed as a fanatic. The values are presented here as an aid to analysis, not as a program for action.

Some Common Ground

However, the polarity of the two models is not absolute. Although it would be possible to construct models that exist in an institutional vacuum, it would not serve our purposes to do so. We are postulating, not a criminal process that operates in any kind of society at all, but rather one that operates within the framework of contemporary American society. This leaves plenty of room for polarization, but it does require the observance of some limits. A model of the criminal process that left out of account relatively stable and enduring features of the American legal system would not have much relevance to our central inquiry. For convenience, these elements of stability and continuity can be roughly equated with minimal agreed limits expressed in the Constitution of the United States and, more importantly, with unarticulated assumptions that can be perceived to underlie those limits. Of course, it is true that the Constitution is constantly appealed to by proponents and opponents of many measures that affect the criminal process. And only the naive would deny that there are few conclusive positions that can be reached by appeal to the Constitution. Yet there are assumptions about the criminal process that are widely shared and that may be viewed as common ground for the operation of any model of the criminal process. Our first task is to clarify these assumptions.

First, there is the assumption, implicit in the ex post facto clause of the Constitution, that the function of defining conduct that may be treated as criminal is separate from and prior to the process of identifying and dealing with persons as criminals. How wide or narrow the definition of criminal conduct must be is an important question of policy that yields highly variable results depending on the values held by those making the relevant decisions.

But that there must be a means of definition that is in some sense separate from and prior to the operation of the process is clear. If this were not so, our efforts to deal with the phenomenon of organized crime would appear ludicrous indeed (which is not to say that we have by any means exhausted the possibilities for dealing with that problem within the limits of this basic assumption).

A related assumption that limits the area of controversy is that the criminal process ordinarily ought to be invoked by those charged with the responsibility for doing so when it appears that a crime has been committed and that there is a reasonable prospect of apprehending and convicting its perpetrator.

Although police and prosecutors are allowed broad discretion for deciding not to invoke the criminal process, it is commonly agreed that these officials have no general dispensing power. If the legislature has decided that certain conduct is to be treated as criminal, the decision makers at every level of the criminal process are expected to accept that basic decision as a premise for action. The controversial nature of the occasional case in which the relevant decision makers appear not to have played their appointed role only serves to highlight the strength with which the premise holds. This assumption may be viewed as the other side of the ex post facto coin. Just as conduct that is not proscribed as criminal may not be dealt with in the criminal process, so conduct that has been denominated as criminal must be treated as such by the participants in the criminal process acting within their respective competences.

Next, there is the assumption that there are limits to the powers of government to investigate and apprehend persons suspected of committing crimes. I do not refer to the controversy (settled recently, at least in broad outline) as to whether the Fourth Amendment's prohibition against unreasonable searches and seizures applies to the states with the same force with which it applies to the federal government. Rather, I am talking about the general assumption that a degree of scrutiny and control must be exercised with respect to the activities of law-enforcement officers, that the security and privacy of the individual may not be invaded at will. It is possible to imagine a society in which even lip service is not paid to this assumption. Nazi Germany approached but never quite reached this position. But no one in our society would maintain that any individual may be taken into custody at any time and held without any limitation of time during the process of investigating his possible commission of crimes, or would argue that there should be no form of redress for violation of at least some standards for official investigative conduct. Although this assumption may not appear to have much in the way of positive content, its absence would render moot some of our most hotly controverted problems. If there were not general agreement that there must be some limits on police power to detain and investigate, the highly controversial provisions of the Uniform Arrest Act, permitting the police to detain a person for questioning for a short period even though they do not have grounds for making an arrest, would be a magnanimous concession by the all-powerful state rather than, as it is now perceived, a substantial expansion of police power.

Finally, there is a complex of assumptions embraced by terms such as "the adversary system," "procedural due process," "notice and an opportunity to be heard," and "day in court." Common to them all is the notion that the alleged criminal is not merely an object to be acted upon but an independent entity in the process who may, if he so desires, force the operators of the process to demonstrate to an independent authority (judge and jury) that he is guilty of the charges against him. It is a minimal assumption. It speaks in terms of "may" rather than "must." It permits but does not require the accused, acting by himself or through his own agent, to play an active role in the process. By virtue of that fact the process becomes or has the capacity to become a contest between, if not equals, at least independent actors. As we shall see, much of the space between the two models is occupied by stronger or weaker notions of how this contest is to be arranged, in what cases it is to be played, and by what rules. The Crime Control Model tends to de-emphasize this adversary aspect of the process; the Due Process Model tends to make it central.

The common ground, and it is important, is the agreement that the process has, for everyone subjected to it, at least the potentiality of becoming to some extent an adversary struggle.

So much for common ground. There is a good deal of it, even in the narrowest view. Its existence should not be overlooked, because it is, by definition, what permits partial resolutions of the tension between the two models to take place.

The rhetoric of the criminal process consists largely of claims that disputed territory is "really" common ground: that, for example, the premise of an adversary system "necessarily" embraces the appointment of counsel for everyone accused of crime, or conversely, that the obligation to pursue persons suspected of committing crimes "necessarily" embraces interrogation of suspects without the intervention of counsel. We may smile indulgently at such claims; they are rhetoric, and no more. But the form in which they are made suggests an important truth: that there *is* a common ground of value assumption about the criminal process that makes continued discourse about its problems possible.

Crime Control Values

The value system that underlies the Crime Control Model is based on the proposition that the repression of criminal conduct is by far the most important function to be performed by the criminal process. The failure of law enforcement to bring criminal conduct under tight control is viewed as leading to the breakdown of public order and thence to the disappearance of an important condition of human freedom. If the laws go unenforced—which is to say, if it is perceived that there is a high percentage of failure to apprehend and convict in the criminal process—a general disregard for legal controls tends to develop. The law-abiding citizen then becomes the victim of all sorts of unjustifiable invasions of his interests. His security of person and property is sharply diminished, and, therefore, so is his liberty to function as a member of society. The claim ultimately is that the criminal process is a positive guarantor of social freedom. In order to achieve this high purpose, the Crime Control Model requires that primary attention be paid to the efficiency with which the criminal process operates to screen suspects, determine guilt, and secure appropriate dispositions of persons convicted of crime.

Efficiency of operation is not, of course, a criterion that can be applied in a vacuum. By "efficiency" we mean the system's capacity to apprehend, try, convict, and dispose of a high proportion of criminal offenders whose offenses become known. In a society in which only the grossest forms of antisocial behavior were made criminal and in which the crime rate was exceedingly low, the criminal process might require the devotion of many more man-hours of police, prosecutorial, and judicial time per case than ours does, and still operate with tolerable efficiency. A society that was prepared to increase even further the resources devoted to the suppression of crime might cope with a rising crime rate without sacrifice of efficiency while continuing to maintain an elaborate and time-consuming set of criminal processes. However, neither of these possible characteristics corresponds with social reality in this country. We use the criminal sanction to cover an increasingly wide spectrum of behavior thought to be antisocial, and the amount of crime is very high indeed, although both level and trend are hard to assess. At the same time, although precise measures are not available, it does not appear that we are disposed in the public sector of the economy to increase very drastically the quantity, much less the quality, of the resources devoted to the suppression of criminal activity through the operation of the criminal process. These factors have an important bearing on the criterion of efficiency, and therefore on the nature of the Crime Control Model.

The model, in order to operate successfully, must produce a high rate of apprehension and conviction, and must do so in a context where the magnitudes being dealt with are very large and the resources for dealing with them are very limited. There must then be a premium on speed and finality. Speed, in turn, depends on informality and on uniformity; finality depends on minimizing the occasions for challenge. The process must not be cluttered up with ceremonious rituals that do not advance the progress of a case.

Facts can be established more quickly through interrogation in a police station than through the formal process of examination and cross-examination in a court. It follows that extrajudicial processes should be preferred to judicial processes, informal operations to formal ones. But informality is not enough; there must also be uniformity. Routine, stereotyped procedures are essential if large numbers are being handled. The model that will operate successfully on these presuppositions must be an administrative, almost a managerial, model. The image that comes to mind is an assembly-line conveyor belt down which moves an endless stream of cases, never stopping, carrying the cases to workers who stand at fixed stations and who perform on each case as it comes by the same small but essential operation that brings it one step closer to being a finished product, or, to exchange the metaphor for the reality, a closed file.

The criminal process, in this model, is seen as a screening process in which each successive state—prearrest investigation, arrest, postarrest investigation, preparation for trial, trial or entry of plea, conviction, disposition—involves a series of routinized operations whose success is gauged primarily by their tendency to pass the case along to a successful conclusion.

What is a successful conclusion? One that throws off at an early stage those cases in which it appears unlikely that the person apprehended is an offender and then secures, as expeditiously as possible, the conviction of the rest, with a minimum of occasions for challenge, let alone post-audit. By the application of administrative expertness, primarily that of the police and prosecutors, an early determination of the probability of innocence or guilt emerges. Those who are probably innocent are screened out. Those who are probably guilty are passed quickly through the remaining stages of the process. The key to the operation of the model regarding those who are not screened out is what I shall call a presumption of guilt. The concept requires some explanation, since it may appear startling to assert that what appears to be the precise converse of our generally accepted ideology of a presumption of innocence can be an essential element of a model that does correspond in some respects to the actual operation of the criminal process.

The presumption of guilt is what makes it possible for the system to deal efficiently with large numbers, as the Crime Control Model demands. The supposition is that the screening processes operated by police and prosecutors are reliable indicators of probable guilt. Once a man has been arrested and investigated without being found to be probably innocent, or, to put it differently, once a determination has been made that there is enough evidence of guilt to permit holding him for further action, then all subsequent activity directed toward him is based on the view that he is probably guilty. The precise point at which this occurs will vary from case to case; in many cases it will occur as soon as the suspect is arrested, or even before, if the evidence of probable guilt that has come to the attention of the authorities is sufficiently strong.

But in any case the presumption of guilt will begin to operate well before the "suspect" becomes a "defendant." The presumption of guilt is not, of course, a thing. Nor is it even a rule of law in the usual sense. It simply is the consequence of a complex of attitudes, a mood. If there is confidence in the reliability of informal administrative fact-finding activities that take place in the early stages of the criminal process, the remaining stages of the process can be relatively perfunctory without any loss in operating efficiency. The presumption of guilt, as it operates in the Crime Control Model, is the operational expression of that confidence.

It would be a mistake to think of the presumption of guilt as the opposite of the presumption of innocence that we are so used to thinking of as the polestar of the criminal process and that, as we shall see, occupies an important position in the Due Process Model. The presumption of innocence is not its opposite; it is irrelevant to the presumption of guilt; the two concepts are different rather than opposite ideas. The difference can perhaps be epitomized by an example. A murderer, for reasons best known to himself, chooses to shoot his victim in plain view of a large number of people. When the police arrive, he hands them his gun and says, "I did it and I'm glad." His account of what happened is corroborated by several eyewitnesses. He is placed under arrest and led off to jail. Under these circumstances, which may seem extreme but which in fact characterize with rough accuracy the evidentiary situation in a large proportion of criminal cases, it would be plainly absurd to maintain that more probably than not the suspect did not commit the killing. But that is not what the presumption of innocence means. It means that until there has been an adjudication of guilt by an authority legally competent to make such an adjudication, the suspect is to be treated, for reasons that have nothing whatever to do with the probable outcome of the case, as if his guilt is an open question.

The presumption of innocence is a direction to officials about how they are to proceed, not a prediction of outcome. The presumption of guilt, however, is purely and simply a prediction of outcome. The presumption of innocence is, then, a direction to the authorities to ignore the presumption of guilt in their treatment of the suspect. It tells them, in effect, to close their eyes to what will frequently seem to be factual probabilities. The reasons why it tells them this are among the animating presuppositions of the Due Process Model, and we will come to them shortly. It is enough to note at this point that the presumption of guilt is descriptive and factual; the presumption of innocence is normative and legal. The pure Crime Control Model has no truck with the presumption of innocence, although its real-life emanations are, as we shall see, brought into uneasy compromise with the dictates of this dominant ideological position. In the presumption of guilt this model finds a factual predicate for the position that the dominant goal of repressing crime can be achieved through highly summary processes without any great loss of efficiency (as previously defined), because of the probability that, in the run of cases, the preliminary screening process operated by the police and the prosecuting officials contains adequate guarantees of reliable fact-finding. Indeed, the model takes an even stronger position. It is that subsequent processes, particularly those of a formal adjudicatory nature, are unlikely to produce as reliable fact-finding as the expert administrative process that precedes them is capable of. The criminal process thus must put special weight on the quality of administrative fact-finding. It becomes important, then, to place as few restrictions as possible on the character of the administrative fact-finding processes and to limit restrictions to such as enhance reliability, excluding those designed for other purposes. As we shall see, this view of restrictions on administrative fact-finding is a consistent theme in the development of the Crime Control Model.

In this model, as I have suggested, the center of gravity of the process lies in the early, administrative fact-finding stages. The complementary proposition is that the subsequent stages are relatively unimportant and should be truncated as much as possible. This, too, produces tensions with presently dominant ideology.

The pure Crime Control Model has very little use for many conspicuous features of the adjudicative process, and in real life works out a number of ingenious compromises with them. Even in the pure model, however, there have to be devices for dealing with the suspect after the preliminary screening process has resulted in a determination of probable guilt. The focal device, as we shall see, is the plea of guilty; through its use, adjudicative fact-finding is reduced to its barest essentials and operating at its most successful pitch, it offers two possibilities: an administrative fact-finding process leading (1) to exoneration of the suspect, or (2) to the entry of a plea of guilty.

Due Process Values

If the Crime Control Model resembles an assembly line, the Due Process Model looks very much like an obstacle course. Each of its successive stages is designed to present formidable impediments to carrying the accused any further along in the process. Its ideology is not the converse of that underlying the Crime Control Model. It does not rest on the idea that it is not socially desirable to repress crime, although critics of its application have been known to claim so. Its ideology is composed of a complex of ideas, some of them based on judgments about the efficacy of crime control devices, others having to do with quite different considerations. The ideology of due process is far more deeply impressed on the formal structure of the law than is the ideology of crime control; yet an accurate tracing of the strands that make it up is strangely difficult. What follows is only an attempt at an approximation.

The Due Process Model encounters its rival on the Crime Control Model's own ground in respect to the reliability of fact-finding processes. The Crime Control Model, as we have suggested, places heavy reliance on the ability of investigative and prosecutorial officers, acting in an informal setting in which their distinctive skills are given full sway, to elicit and reconstruct a tolerably accurate account of what actually took place in an alleged criminal event. The Due Process Model rejects this premise and substitutes for it a view of informal, nonadjudicative fact-finding that stresses the possibility of error. People are notoriously poor observers of disturbing events—the more emotion-arousing the context, the greater the possibility that recollection will be incorrect; confessions and admissions by persons in police custody may be induced by physical or psychological coercion so that the police end up hearing what the suspect thinks they want to hear rather than the truth; witnesses may be animated by bias or interest that no one would trouble to discover except one specially charged with protecting the interests of the accused (as the police are not). Considerations of this kind all lead to a rejection of informal fact-finding processes as definitive of factual guilt and to an insistence on formal, adjudicative, adversary fact-finding processes in which the factual case against the accused is publicly heard by an impartial tribunal and is evaluated only after the accused has had a full opportunity to discredit the case against him. Even then, the distrust of fact-finding processes that animates the Due Process Model is not dissipated. The possibilities of human error being what they are, further scrutiny is necessary, or at least must be available, in case facts have been overlooked or suppressed in the heat of battle.

How far this subsequent scrutiny must be available is a hotly controverted issue today. In the pure Due Process Model the answer would be: at least as long as there is an allegation of factual error that has not received an adjudicative hearing in a fact-finding context. The demand for finality is thus very low in the Due Process Model.

This strand of due process ideology is not enough to sustain the model. If all that were at issue between the two models was a series of questions about the reliability of fact-finding processes, we would have but one model of the criminal process, the nature of whose constituent elements would pose questions of fact not of value. Even if the discussion is confined, for the moment, to the question of reliability, it is apparent that more is at stake than simply an evaluation of what kinds of fact-finding processes, alone or in combination, are likely to produce the most nearly reliable results. The stumbling block is this: How much reliability is compatible with efficiency? Granted that informal fact-finding will make some mistakes that can be remedied if backed up by adjudicative fact-finding, the desirability of providing this backup is not affirmed or negated by factual demonstrations or predictions that the increase in reliability will be x percent or x plus n percent. It still remains to ask how much weight is to be given to the competing demands of reliability (a high degree of probability in each case that factual guilt has been accurately determined) and efficiency (expeditious handling of the large numbers of cases that the process ingests). The Crime Control Model is more optimistic about the improbability of error in a significant number of cases: but it is also, though only in part therefore, more tolerant about the amount of error that it will put up with. The Due Process Model insists on the prevention and elimination of mistakes to the extent possible; the Crime Control Model accepts the probability of mistakes up to the level at which they interfere with the goal of repressing crime, either because too many guilty people are escaping or, more subtly, because general awareness of the unreliability of the process leads to a decrease in the deterrent efficacy of the criminal law. In this view, reliability and efficiency are not polar opposites but rather complementary characteristics. The system is reliable *because* efficient; reliability becomes a matter of independent concern only when it becomes so attenuated as to impair efficiency.

All of this the Due Process Model rejects. If efficiency demands shortcuts around reliability, then absolute efficiency must be rejected. The aim of the process is at least as much to protect the factually innocent as it is to convict the factually guilty. It is a little like quality control in industrial technology;

tolerable deviation from standard varies with the importance of conformity to standard in the destined uses of the product. The Due Process Model resembles a factory that has to devote a substantial part of its input to quality control. This necessarily cuts down on quantitative output.

All of this is only the beginning of the ideological difference between the two models. The Due Process Model could disclaim any attempt to provide enhanced reliability for the fact-finding process and still produce a set of institutions and processes that would differ sharply from those demanded by the Crime Control Model. Indeed, it may not be too great an oversimplification to assert that in point of historical development the doctrinal pressures emanating from the demands of the Due Process Model have tended to evolve from an original matrix of concern for the maximization of reliability into values quite different and more far-reaching. These values can be expressed in, although not adequately described by, the concept of the primacy of the individual and the complementary concept of limitation on official power.

The combination of stigma and loss of liberty that is embodied in the end result of the criminal process is viewed as being the heaviest deprivation that government can inflict on the individual. Furthermore, the processes that culminate in these highly afflictive sanctions are seen as in themselves coercive, restricting, and demeaning. Power is always subject to abuse—sometimes subtle, other times, as in the criminal process, open and ugly. Precisely because of its potency in subjecting the individual to the coercive power of the state, the criminal process must, in this model, be subjected to controls that prevent it from operating with maximal efficiency. According to this ideology, maximal efficiency means maximal tyranny. And, although no one would assert that minimal efficiency means minimal tyranny, the proponents of the Due Process Model would accept with considerable equanimity a substantial diminution in the efficiency with which the criminal process operates in the interest of preventing official oppression of the individual.

The most modest-seeming but potentially far-reaching mechanism by which the Due Process Model implements these antiauthoritarian values is the doctrine of legal guilt. According to this doctrine, a person is not to be held guilty of a crime merely on a showing that in all probability, based upon reliable evidence, he did factually what he is said to have done. Instead, he is to be held guilty if and only if these factual determinations are made in procedurally regular fashion and by authorities acting within competences duly allocated to them. Furthermore, he is not to be held guilty, even though the factual determination is or might be adverse to him, if various rules designed to protect him and to safeguard the integrity of the process are not given effect: the tribunal that convicts him must have the power to deal with his kind of case ("jurisdiction") and must be geographically appropriate ("venue"); too long a time must not have elapsed since the offense was committed ("statute of limitations"); he must not have been previously convicted or acquitted of the same or a substantially similar offense ("double jeopardy"); he must not fall within a category of persons, such as children or the insane, who are legally immune to conviction ("criminal responsibility"); and so on. None of these requirements has anything to do with the factual question of whether the person did or did not engage in the conduct that is charged as the offense against him; yet favorable answers to any of them will mean that he is legally innocent. Wherever the competence to make adequate factual determination lies, it is apparent that only a tribunal that is aware of these guilt-defeating doctrines and is willing to apply them can be viewed as competent to make determinations of legal guilt.

The police and the prosecutors are ruled out by lack of competence, in the first instance, and by lack of assurance of willingness, in the second. Only an impartial tribunal can be trusted to make determinations of legal as opposed to factual guilt.

In this concept of legal guilt lies the explanation for the apparently quixotic presumption of innocence of which we spoke earlier. A man who, after police investigation, is charged with having committed a crime can hardly be said to be presumptively innocent, if what we mean is factual innocence. But if what we mean is that it has yet to be determined if any of the myriad legal doctrines that serve in one way or another the end of limiting official power through the observance of certain substantive and procedural regularities may be appropriately invoked to exculpate the accused man, it is apparent that as a matter of prediction it cannot be said with confidence that more probably than not he will be found guilty.

Beyond the question of predictability this model posits a functional reason for observing the presumption of innocence: by forcing the state to prove its case against the accused in an adjudicative context, the presumption of innocence serves to force into play all the qualifying and disabling doctrines that limit the use of the criminal sanction against the individual, thereby enhancing his opportunity to secure a favorable outcome. In this sense, the presumption of innocence may be seen to operate as a kind of self-fulfilling prophecy. By opening up a procedural situation that permits the successful assertion of defenses having nothing to do with factual guilt, it vindicates the proposition that the factually guilty may nonetheless be legally innocent and should therefore be given a chance to qualify for that kind of treatment.

The possibility of legal innocence is expanded enormously when the criminal process is viewed as the appropriate forum for correcting its own abuses. This notion may well account for a greater amount of the distance between the two models than any other. In theory the Crime Control Model can tolerate rules that forbid illegal arrests, unreasonable searches, coercive interrogations, and the like. What it cannot tolerate is the vindication of those rules in the criminal process itself through the exclusion of evidence illegally obtained or through the reversal of convictions in cases where the criminal process has breached the rules laid down for its observance. And the Due Process Model, although it may in the first instance be addressed to the maintenance of reliable fact-finding techniques, comes eventually to incorporate prophylactic and deterrent rules that result in the release of the factually guilty even in cases in which blotting out the illegality would still leave an adjudicative fact-finder convinced of the accused person's guilt. Only by penalizing errant police and prosecutors within the criminal process itself can adequate pressure be maintained, so the argument runs, to induce conformity with the Due Process Model.

Another strand in the complex of attitudes underlying the Due Process Model is the idea—itself a shorthand statement for a complex of attitudes—of equality. This notion has only recently emerged as an explicit basis for pressing the demands of the Due Process Model, but it appears to represent, at least in its potential, a most powerful norm for influencing official conduct. Stated most starkly, the ideal of equality holds that "there can be no equal justice where the kind of trial a man gets depends on the amount of money he has." The factual predicate underlying this assertion is that there are gross inequalities in the financial means of criminal defendants as a class, that in an adversary system of criminal justice an effective defense is largely a function of the resources that can be mustered on behalf of the accused, and that the very large proportion of criminal defendants who are, operationally speaking, "indigent" will thus be denied an effective defense. This factual premise has been strongly reinforced by recent studies that in turn have been both a cause and an effect of an increasing emphasis upon norms for the criminal process based on the premise.

The norms derived from the premise do not take the form of an insistence upon governmental responsibility to provide literally equal opportunities for all criminal defendants to challenge the process. Rather, they take as their point of departure the notion that the criminal process, initiated as it is by the government and containing as it does the likelihood of severe deprivations at the hands of government, imposes some kind of public obligation to ensure that financial inability does not destroy the capacity of an accused to assert what may be meritorious challenges to the processes being invoked against him. At its most gross, the norm of equality would act to prevent situations in which financial inability forms an absolute barrier to the assertion of a right that is in theory generally available, as where there is a right to appeal that is, however, effectively conditional upon the filing of a trial transcript obtained at the defendant's expense. Beyond this, it may provide the basis for a claim whenever the system theoretically makes some kind of challenge available to an accused who has the means to press it. If, for example, a defendant who is adequately represented has the opportunity to prevent the case against him from coming to the trial stage by forcing the state to its proof in a preliminary hearing, the norm of equality may be invoked to assert that the same kind of opportunity must be available to others as well. In a sense the system, as it functions for the small minority whose resources permit them to exploit all its defensive possibilities, provides a benchmark by which its functioning in all other cases is to be tested: not, perhaps, to guarantee literal identity but rather to provide a measure of whether the process as a whole is recognizably of the same general order. The demands made by a norm of this kind are likely by their very nature to be quite sweeping.

Although the norm's imperatives may be initially limited to determining whether in a particular case the accused was injured or prejudiced by his relative inability to make an appropriate challenge, the norm of equality very quickly moves to another level on which the demand is that the process in general be adapted to minimize discriminations rather than that a mere series of post hoc determinations of discriminations be made or makeable.

It should be observed that the impact of the equality norm will vary greatly depending upon the point in time at which it is introduced into a model of the criminal process. If one were starting from scratch to decide how the process ought to work, the norm of equality would have nothing very important to say on such questions as, for example, whether an accused should have the effective assistance of counsel in deciding whether to enter a plea of guilty. One could decide, on quite independent considerations, that it is or is not a good thing to afford that facility to the generality of persons accused of crime. But the impact of the equality norm becomes far greater when it is brought to bear on a process whose contours have already been shaped. If our model of the criminal process affords defendants who are in a financial position to do so the right to consult a lawyer before entering a plea, then the equality norm exerts powerful pressure to provide such an opportunity to all defendants and to regard the failure to do so as a malfunctioning of the process of whose consequences the accused is entitled to be relieved. In a sense, this has been the role of the equality norm in affecting the real-world criminal process. It has made its appearance on the scene comparatively late and has therefore encountered a system in which the relative financial inability of most persons accused of crime results in treatment very different from that accorded the small minority of the financially capable. For this reason, its impact has already been substantial and may be expected to be even more so in the future.

There is a final strand of thought in the Due Process Model that is often ignored but that needs to be candidly faced if thought on the subject is not to be obscured. This is a mood of skepticism about the morality and utility of the criminal sanction, taken either as a whole or in some of its applications. The subject is a large and complicated one, comprehending as it does much of the intellectual history of our times. It is properly the subject of another essay altogether. To put the matter briefly, one cannot improve upon the statement by Professor Paul Bator:

> In summary we are told that the criminal law's notion of just condemnation and punishment is a cruel hypocrisy visited by a smug society on the psychologically and economically crippled; that its premise of a morally autonomous will with at least some measure of choice whether to comply with the values expressed in a penal code is unscientific and outmoded; that its reliance on punishment as an educational and deterrent agent is misplaced, particularly in the case of the very members of society most likely to engage in criminal conduct; and that its failure to provide for individualized and humane rehabilitation of offenders is inhuman and wasteful.[1]

This skepticism, which may be fairly said to be widespread among the most influential and articulate contemporary leaders of informed opinion, leads to an attitude toward the processes of the criminal law that, to quote Mr. Bator again, engenders "a peculiar receptivity toward claims of injustice which arise within the traditional structure of the system itself; fundamental disagreement and unease about the very bases of the criminal law has, inevitably, created acute pressure at least to expand and liberalize those of its processes and doctrines which serve to make more tentative its judgments or limit its power." In short, doubts about the ends for which power is being exercised create pressure to limit the discretion with which that power is exercised.

The point need not be pressed to the extreme of doubts about or rejection of the premises upon which the criminal sanction in general rests. Unease may be stirred simply by reflection on the variety of uses to which the criminal sanction is put and by a judgment that an increasingly large proportion of those uses may represent an unwise invocation of so extreme a sanction. It would be an interesting irony if doubts about the propriety of certain uses of the criminal sanction prove to contribute to a restrictive trend in the criminal process that in the end requires a choice among uses and finally an abandonment of some of the very uses that stirred the original doubts, but for a reason quite unrelated to those doubts.

There are two kinds of problems that need to be dealt with in any model of the criminal process. One is what the rules shall be. The other is how the rules shall be implemented. The second is at least as important as the first, as we shall see time and again in our detailed development of the models. The distinctive difference between the two models is not only in the rules of conduct that they lay down but also in the sanctions that are to be invoked when a claim is presented that the rules have been breached and, no less importantly, in the timing that is permitted or required for the invocation of those sanctions.

As I have already suggested, the Due Process Model locates at least some of the sanctions for breach of the operative rules in the criminal process itself. The relation between these two aspects of the process—the rules and the sanctions for their breach—is a purely formal one unless there is some mechanism for bringing them into play with each other. The hinge between them in the Due Process Model is the availability of legal counsel. This has a double aspect. Many of the rules that the model requires are couched in terms of the availability of counsel to do various things at various stages of the process—this is the conventionally recognized aspect; beyond it, there is a pervasive assumption that counsel is necessary in order to invoke sanctions for breach of any of the rules. The more freely available these sanctions are, the more important is the role of counsel in seeing to it that the sanctions are appropriately invoked. If the process is seen as a series of occasions for checking its own operation, the role of counsel is a much more nearly central one than is the case in a process that is seen as primarily concerned with expeditious determination of factual guilt. And if equality of operation is a governing norm, the availability of counsel is seen as requiring it for all. Of all the controverted aspects of the criminal process, the right to counsel, including the role of government in its provision, is the most dependent on what one's model of the process looks like, and the least susceptible of resolution unless one has confronted the antinomies of the two models.

I do not mean to suggest that questions about the right to counsel disappear if one adopts a model of the process that conforms more or less closely to the Crime Control Model, but only that such questions become absolutely central if one's model moves very far down the spectrum of possibilities toward the pure Due Process Model. The reason for this centrality is to be found in the assumption underlying both models that the process is an adversary one in which the initiative in invoking relevant rules rests primarily on the parties concerned, the state, and the accused. One could construct models that placed central responsibility on adjudicative agents such as committing magistrates and trial judges. And there are, as we shall see, marginal but nonetheless important adjustments in the role of the adjudicative agents that enter into the models with which we are concerned. For present purposes it is enough to say that these adjustments are marginal, that the animating presuppositions that underlie both models in the context of the American criminal system relegate the adjudicative agents to a relatively passive role, and therefore place central importance on the role of counsel.

One last introductory note: . . . What assumptions do we make about the sources of authority to shape the real-world operations of the criminal process?

Recognizing that our models are only models, what agencies of government have the power to pick and choose between their competing demands? Once again, the limiting features of the American context come into play. Ours is not a system of legislative supremacy. The distinctively American institution of judicial review exercises a limiting and ultimately a shaping influence on the criminal process. Because the Crime Control Model is basically an affirmative model, emphasizing at every turn the existence and exercise of official power, its validating authority is ultimately legislative (although proximately administrative).

Because the Due Process Model is basically a negative model, asserting limits on the nature of official power and on the modes of its exercise, its validating authority is judicial and requires an appeal to supralegislative law, to the law of the Constitution. To the extent that tensions between the two models are resolved by deference to the Due Process Model, the authoritative force at work is the judicial power, working in the distinctively judicial mode of invoking the sanction of nullity. That is at once the strength and the weakness of the Due Process Model: its strength because in our system the appeal to the Constitution provides the last and overriding word; its weakness because saying no in specific cases is an exercise in futility unless there is a general willingness on the part of the officials who operate the process to apply negative prescriptions across the board. It is no accident that statements reinforcing the Due Process Model come from the courts, while at the same time facts denying it are established by the police and prosecutors.

DISCUSSION QUESTIONS

1. Discuss the common ground between the crime control model and the due process model. Why is this common ground so important?
2. Compare and contrast the crime control model and the due process model.

3. The crime control model and the due process model represent the extreme ends of the spectrum. Where on the spectrum do the practices of our current criminal process fall?

4. Packer indicates that there are two types of problems that need to be addressed in any models of the criminal process. The first is what the rules are, and the second is how the rules are going to be implemented. Discuss what the rules of both of the models would be and how they would be implemented.

NOTE

1. Paul Bator, "Finality in Criminal Law and federal Habeas Corpus for State Prisoners," *Harvard Law Review* 76 (1963): 441–442.

2

✸

Racial Politics, Racial Disparities, and the War on Crime

Michael Tonry

African Americans make up more than 50 percent of the prison population but only 12 percent of all U.S. residents. When all punishments—probation, intermediate sanctions, incarceration—are taken into account, one in three African-American men in their twenties are currently under correctional supervision. Michael Tonry believes that racial disparities are a reflection of racial politics, especially the War on Drugs.

Racial disparities in arrests, jailing, and imprisonment steadily worsened after 1980 for reasons that have little to do with changes in crime patterns and almost everything to do with two political developments. First, conservative Republicans in national elections "played the race card" by using anticrime slogans (remember Willie Horton?) as a way to appeal to anti-Black sentiments of White voters. Second, conservative politicians of both parties promoted and voted for harsh crime control and drug policies that exacerbated existing racial disparities.

The worsened disparities might have been ethically defensible if they had been based on good faith beliefs that some greater policy good would thereby have been achieved. Sometimes unwanted side effects of social policy are inevitable. Traffic accidents and fatalities are a price we pay for the convenience of automobiles. Occupational injuries are a price we pay for engaging in the industries in which they occur.

The principal causes of worse racial disparities have been the War on Drugs launched by the Bush and Reagan administrations, characterized by vast increases in arrests and imprisonment of street-level drug dealers, and the continuing movement toward harsher penalties. Policies toward drug offenders are a primary cause of recent increases in jail and prison admissions and populations. Racial disparities among drug offenders are worse than among other offenders.

It should go without saying in the late 20th century that governments detest racial injustice and desire racial justice, and that racial disparities are tolerable only if they are unavoidable or are outweighed by even more important social gains. There are no offsetting gains that can justify the harms done to Black Americans by recent drug and crime control policies.

This article presents data on racial trends in arrests, jailing, and imprisonment; examines the rationales for the policies that have produced those trends; and considers whether the adoption of policies known to have disparate adverse effects on Blacks can be ethically justified. First, the evidence concerning the effectiveness of recent drug and crime control policies that have exacerbated racial disparities is examined. Next, data on arrests, jail, and imprisonment trends are presented and demonstrate that racial disparities have worsened, but not because Blacks are committing larger proportions of the serious offenses (homicide, rape, robbery, aggravated assault) for which offenders were traditionally sent to prison. Finally, the reasons why recent policies were adopted and whether they can be ethically justified are considered.

CRIME REDUCTION EFFECTS OF CRIME CONTROL POLICY

There is no basis for a claim that recent harsh crime control policies or the enforcement strategies of the War on Drugs were based on good faith beliefs that they would achieve their ostensible purposes. In this and other countries, practitioners and scholars have long known that manipulation of penalties has few, if any, effects on crime rates.

Commissions and expert advisory bodies have been commissioned by the federal government repeatedly over the last 30 years to survey knowledge of the effects of crime control policies, and consistently they have concluded that there is little reason to believe that harsher penalties significantly enhance public safety. In 1967, the President's Commission on Law Enforcement and Administration of Justice observed that crime control efforts can have little effect on crime rates without much larger efforts being directed at crime's underlying social and economic causes. "The Commission . . . has no doubt whatever that the most significant action that can be taken against crime is action designed to eliminate slums and ghettos, to improve education, to provide jobs. . . .We shall not have dealt effectively with crime until we have alleviated the conditions that stimulate it."

In 1978, the National Academy of Sciences Panel on Research on Deterrent and Incapacitative Effects, funded by President Ford's department of justice and asked to examine the available evidence on the crime-reductive effects of sanctions, concluded: "In summary, we cannot assert that the evidence warrants an affirmative conclusion regarding deterrence" (Blumstein, Cohen, and Nagin 1978). Fifteen years later, the National Academy of Sciences Panel on the Understanding and Control of Violent Behavior, created and paid for with funds from the Reagan and Bush administration departments of justice, surveyed knowledge of the effects of harsher penalties on violent crime (Reiss and Roth 1993). A rhetorical question and answer in the panel's final report says it all: "What effect has increasing the prison population had on violent crime? Apparently very little. . . . If tripling the average length of sentence of incarceration per crime [between 1976 and 1989] had a strong preventive effect," reasoned the panel, "then violent crime rates should have declined" (p. 7). They had not.

I mention that the two National Academy of Sciences panels were created and supported by national Republican administrations to demonstrate that skepticism about the crime-preventive effects of harsher punishments is not a fantasy of liberal Democrats. Anyone who has spent much time talking with judges or corrections officials knows that most, whatever their political affiliations, do not believe that harsher penalties significantly enhance public safety.

Likewise, outside the United States, conservative governments in other English-speaking countries have repudiated claims that harsher penalties significantly improve public safety. In Margaret Thatcher's England, for example, a 1990 White Paper (an official policy statement of the government), based on a 3-year study, expressed its skepticism about the preventive effects of sanctions:

> Deterrence is a principle with much immediate appeal. . . . But much crime is committed on impulse, given the opportunity presented by an open window or an unlocked door, and it is committed by offenders who live from moment to moment: their crimes are as impulsive as the rest of their feckless, sad, or pathetic lives. It is unrealistic to construct sentencing arrangements on the assumption that most offenders will weigh up the possibilities in advance and base their conduct on rational calculation. (Home Office 1990)

Canada is the other English-speaking country that has recently had a conservative government. In Brian Mulroney's Canada, the Committee on Justice and the Solicitor General (in American terms, the judiciary committee) proposed in 1993 that Canada shift from an American-style crime control system to a European-style preventive approach. In arguing for the shift in emphasis, the committee observed that "the United States affords a glaring example of the limited effect that criminal justice responses may have on crime. . . . If locking up those who violate the law contributed to safer societies then the United States should be the safest country in the world" (Standing Committee on Justice and the Solicitor General 1993). Six years earlier, the Canadian Sentencing Commission (1987) had reached similar conclusions: "Deterrence cannot be used, with empirical justification, to guide the imposition of sanctions."

There is no better evidentiary base to justify recent drug control policies. Because no other western country has adopted drug policies as harsh as those of the United States, a bit of background may be useful before I show why there was no reasonable basis for believing recent policies would achieve their ostensible goals. In drug policy jargon, the United States has adopted a prohibitionistic rather than a harm-reduction strategy and has emphasized supply-side over demand-side tactics (Wilson 1990). This strategic choice implies a preference for legal threats and moral denunciation of drug use and users instead of a preference for minimizing net costs and social harms to the general public, the law enforcement system, and drug users. The tactical choice is between a law enforcement emphasis on arrest and punishment of dealers, distributors, and importers, interdiction, and source-country programs or a prevention emphasis on drug treatment, drug-abuse education in schools, and mass media programs aimed at public education. The supply-side bias in recent American policies was exemplified throughout the Bush administration by its insistence that 70% of federal antidrug funds be devoted to law enforcement and only 30% to treatment and education (Office of National Drug Control Policy 1990).

It has been a long time since most researchers and practitioners believed that current knowledge justifies recent American drug control policies. Because the potential income from drug dealing means that willing aspirants are nearly always available to replace arrested street-level dealers, large-scale arrests have repeatedly been shown to have little or no effect on the volume of drug trafficking or on the retail prices of drugs (e.g., Chaiken 1988; Sviridoff, Sadd, Curtis, and Grinc 1992). Because the United States has long and porous borders, and because an unachievably large proportion of attempted smuggling would have to be stopped to affect drug prices significantly, interdiction has repeatedly been shown to have little or no effect on volume or prices (Reuter 1988). Because cocaine, heroin, and marijuana can be grown in many parts of the world in which government controls are weak and peasant farmers' incentives are strong, source-country programs have seldom been shown to have significant influence on drug availability or price in the United States (Moore 1990).

The evidence in support of demand-side strategies is far stronger. In December 1993, the President's Commission on Model State Drug Laws, appointed by President Bush, categorically concluded, "Treatment works." That conclusion is echoed by more authoritative surveys of drug treatment evaluations by the U.S. General Accounting Office (1990), the National Institute of Medicine (Gerstein and Jarwood 1990), and in *Crime and Justice* by Anglin and Hser (1990). Because drug use and offending tend to coincide in the lives of drug-using offenders, the most effective and cost-effective way to deal with such offenders is to get and keep them in well-run treatment programs.

A sizable literature now also documents the effectiveness of school-based drug education in reducing drug experimentation and use among young people (e.g., Botvin 1990; Ellickson and Bell 1990). Although there is no credible literature that documents the effects of mass media campaigns on drug use, a judge could take judicial notice of their ubiquity. It is not unreasonable to believe that such campaigns have influenced across-the-board declines in drug use in the United States since 1980 (a date, incidentally, that precedes the launch of the War on Drugs by nearly 8 years).

That the preceding summary of our knowledge of the effectiveness of drug control methods is balanced and accurate is shown by the support it receives from leading conservative scholars. Senator-scholar Daniel Patrick Moynihan (1993) has written, "Interdiction and 'drug busts' are probably necessary symbolic acts, but nothing more." James Q. Wilson (1990), for two decades America's leading conservative crime control scholar, observed that "significant reductions in drug abuse will come only from reducing demand for those drugs. . . . The marginal product of further investment in supply reduction is likely to be small" (p. 534). He reports that "I know of no serious law-enforcement official who disagrees with this conclusion. Typically, police officials tell interviewers that they are fighting either a losing war or, at best, a holding action" (p. 534).

Thus a fair-minded survey of existing knowledge provides no grounds for believing that the War on Drugs or the harsh policies exemplified by "three strikes and you're out" laws and evidenced by a tripling in America's prison population since 1980 could achieve their ostensible purposes. If such policies cannot be explained in instrumental terms, how can they be explained? The last section answers that question, but first a summary of recent data on racial trends in arrests, jailing, and incarceration.

RACIAL DISPARITIES
IN ARRESTS, JAIL, AND PRISON

Racial disparities, especially affecting Blacks, have long bedeviled the criminal justice system. Many hundreds of studies of disparities have been conducted and there is now widespread agreement among researchers about causes. Racial bias and stereotyping no doubt play some role, but they are not the major cause. In the longer term, disparities in jail and prison are mainly the result of racial differences in offending patterns. In the shorter term, the worsening disparities since 1980 are not primarily the result of racial differences in offending but were foreseeable effects of the War on Drugs and the movement toward increased use of incarceration. These patterns can best be seen by approaching the recent increases in racial disparities in imprisonment as a mystery to be solved. (Because of space limitations, jail data are not discussed here at length, but the trends parallel those for prisons. Between 1980 and 1991, e.g., the percentage of jail inmates who were Black increased from 40% to 48%.)

Figure 1, showing the percentages of prison inmates who were Black or White from 1960 to 1991, reveals two trends. First, for as long as prison population data have been compiled, the percentage of inmates who are Black has

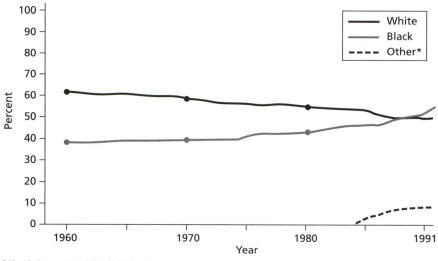

* Hispanics in many states, Asians, Native Americans.

FIGURE 1 Prisoners in State and Federal Prisons on Census Data by Race, 1960–1991

Sources: For 1960, 1970, 1980: Cahalan 1986, table 3.31; for 1985–1991: Bureau of Justice Statistics 1993, 1991a, 1991b, 1989a, 1989b, 1987.

by several times exceeded the percentage of Americans who are Black (10% to 13% during the relevant period). Second, since 1980 the Black percentage among prisoners has increased sharply.

Racial disproportions among prison inmates are inherently undesirable, and considerable energy has been expended on efforts to understand them. In 1982, Blumstein showed that around 80% of the disproportion could be explained on the basis of racial differences in arrest patterns. Of the unexplained 20%, Blumstein argued, some might represent bias and some might reflect racial differences in criminal history or arguably valid case-processing differences. Some years earlier, Hindelang (1976, 1978) had demonstrated that racial patterns in victims' identifications of their assailants closely resembled racial differences in arrests. Some years later, Langan (1985) skipped over the arrest stage altogether and showed that racial patterns in victims' identifications of their assailants explained about 80% of disparities in prison admissions. In 1990, Klein, Petersilia, and Turner showed that, after criminal history and other legitimate differences between cases were taken into account, the offender's race had no independent predictive effect in California on whether he was sent to prison or for how long. There the matter rests. Blumstein (1993a) updated his analysis and reached similar conclusions (with one important exception that is discussed below).

Although racial crime patterns explain a large part of racial imprisonment patterns, they do not explain why the Black percentage rose so rapidly after 1980. Table 1 shows Black and White percentages among people arrested for the eight

Table 1 Percentage Black and White Arrests for Index 1 Offenses, 1976–1991 (3-year intervals)*

	1976		1979		1982		1985		1988		1991		1992	
	White	Black	White	Black	White	Black	White	Black	White	Black	White	Black	White	Black
Murder and nonnegligent manslaughter	45.0	53.5	49.4	47.7	48.8	49.7	50.1	48.4	45.0	53.5	43.4	54.8	43.5	55.1
Forcible rape	51.2	46.6	50.2	47.7	48.7	49.7	52.2	46.5	52.7	45.8	54.8	43.5	55.5	42.8
Robbery	38.9	59.2	41.0	56.9	38.2	60.7	37.4	61.7	36.3	62.6	37.6	61.1	37.7	60.9
Aggravated assault	56.8	41.0	60.9	37.0	59.8	38.8	58.0	40.4	57.6	40.7	60.0	38.3	59.5	38.8
Burglary	69.0	29.2	69.5	28.7	67.0	31.7	69.7	28.9	67.0	31.3	68.8	29.3	67.8	30.4
Larceny-theft	65.7	32.1	67.2	30.2	64.7	33.4	67.2	30.6	65.6	32.2	66.6	30.9	66.2	31.4
Motor vehicle theft	71.1	26.2	70.0	27.2	66.9	31.4	65.8	32.4	58.7	39.5	58.5	39.3	58.4	39.4
Arson	—	—	78.9	19.2	74.0	24.7	75.7	22.8	73.5	25.0	76.7	21.5	76.4	21.9
Violent crime†	50.4	47.5	53.7	44.1	51.9	46.7	51.5	47.1	51.7	46.8	53.6	44.8	53.6	44.8
Property crime‡	67.0	30.9	68.2	29.4	65.5	32.7	67.7	30.3	65.3	32.6	66.4	31.3	65.8	31.8
Total crime index	64.1	33.8	65.3	32.4	62.7	35.6	64.5	33.7	62.4	35.7	63.2	34.6	62.7	35.2

*Because of rounding, the percentages may not add to total.

†Violent crimes are offenses of murder, forcible rape, robbery, and aggravated assault.

‡Property crimes are offenses of burglary, larceny-theft, motor vehicle theft, and arson.

SOURCES: *Sourcebook of Criminal Justice Statistics.* Various years. Washington, DC: U.S. Department of Justice, Bureau of Justice Statistics; FBI 1993, Table 43.

serious FBI Index Crimes at 3-year intervals from 1976 to 1991 and for 1992. Within narrow bands of fluctuation, racial arrest percentages have been stable since 1976. Comparing 1976 with 1992, for example, Black percentages among people arrested for murder, robbery, and burglary were slightly up and Black percentages among those arrested for rape, aggravated assault, and theft were slightly down. Overall, the percentage among those arrested for violent crimes who were Black fell from 47.5% to 44.8%. Because prison sentences have traditionally been imposed on people convicted of violent crimes, Blumstein's and the other analyses suggest that the Black percentage among inmates should be flat or declining. That, however, is not what Figure 1 shows. Why not?

Part of the answer can be found in prison admissions. Figure 2 shows racial percentages among prison admissions from 1960 to 1992. Arrests of Blacks for violent crimes may not have increased since 1980, but the percentage of Blacks among those sent to prison has increased starkly, reaching 54% in 1991 and 1992. Why? The main explanation concerns the War on Drugs.

Table 2 shows racial percentages among persons arrested for drug crimes between 1976 and 1992. Blacks today make up about 13% of the U.S. population and, according to National Institute on Drug Abuse (1991) surveys of Americans' drug use, are no more likely than Whites ever to have used most drugs of abuse. Nonetheless, the percentages of Blacks among drug arrestees were in the low 20% range in the late 1970s, climbing to around 30% in the early 1980s and peaking at 42% in 1989. The number of drug arrests of Blacks more than doubled between 1985 and 1989, whereas White drug arrests increased only by 27%. Figure 3 shows the stark differences in drug arrest trends by race from 1976 to 1991.

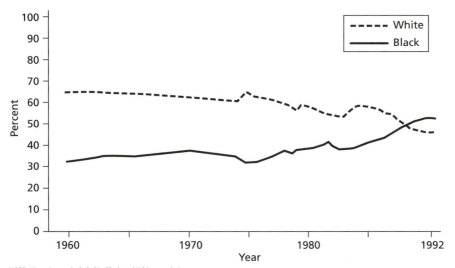

NOTE: Hispanics are included in Black and White populations.

FIGURE 2 Admissions to Federal and State Prisons by Race, 1960–1992

Source: Langan 1991; Gilliard 1992; Perkins 1992, Perkins and Gilliard 1992.

Table 2 U.S. Drug Arrests by Race, 1976–1992

Year	Total Violations	White	White %	Black	Black %
1976	475,209	366,081	77	103,615	22
1977	565,371	434,471	77	122,594	22
1978	592,168	462,728	78	127,277	21
1979	516,142	396,065	77	112,748	22
1980	531,953	401,979	76	125,607	24
1981	584,776	432,556	74	146,858	25
1982	562,390	400,683	71	156,369	28
1983	615,081	423,151	69	185,601	30
1984	560,729	392,904	70	162,979	29
1985	700,009	482,486	69	210,298	30
1986	688,815	463,457	67	219,159	32
1987	809,157	511,278	63	291,177	36
1988	844,300	503,125	60	334,015	40
1989	1,074,345	613,800	57	452,574	42
1990	860,016	503,315	59	349,965	41
1991	763,340	443,596	58	312,997	41
1992	919,561	546,430	59	364,546	40

SOURCES: FBI 1993, Table 43; *Sourcebook of Criminal Justice Statistics*—1978–1992. Various tables. Washington, DC: U.S. Department of Justice, Bureau of Justice Statistics.

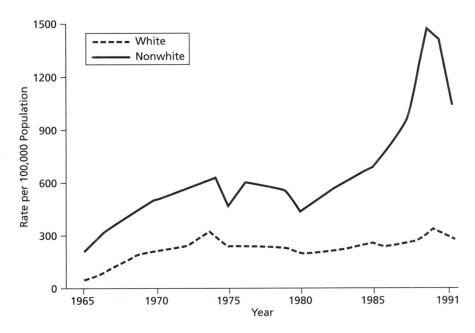

FIGURE 3 Arrest Rates for Drug Offenses by Race, 1965–1991

Source: Blumstein 1993b.

Drug control policies are a major cause of worsening racial disparities in prison. In the federal prisons, for example, 22% of new admissions and 25% of the resident population were drug offenders in 1980. By 1990, 42% of new admissions were drug offenders and in 1992 were 58% of the resident population. In state prisons, 5.7% of inmates in 1979 were drug offenders, a figure that by 1991 had climbed to 21.3% to become the single largest category of prisoners (robbers, burglars, and murderers were next at 14.8%, 12.4%, and 10.6%, respectively) (Beck et al. 1993).

The effect of drug policies can be seen in prison data from a number of states. Figure 4 shows Black and White prison admissions in North Carolina from 1970 to 1990. White rates held steady; Black rates doubled between 1980 and 1990, rising most rapidly after 1987. Figure 5 shows prison admissions for drug crimes in Virginia from 1983 to 1989; the racial balance flipped from two-thirds White, one-third non-White in 1983 to the reverse in 1989. Similarly, in Pennsylvania, Clark (1992) reports, Black male prison admissions for drug crimes grew four times faster (up 1,613%) between 1980 and 1990 than did White male admissions (up 477%). In California, according to Zimring and Hawkins (1994), the number of males in prison for drug crimes grew 15 fold between 1980 and 1990 and "there were more people in prison in California for drug offences in 1991 than there were for *all* offences in California at the end of 1979" (p. 89; emphasis in original).

Why, if Blacks in their lives are no more likely than Whites to use illicit drugs, are Blacks so much more likely to be arrested and imprisoned? One possible answer, which is almost certainly wrong, is that Blacks are

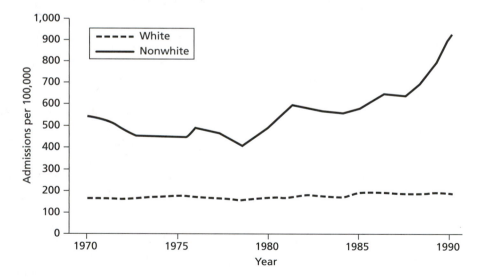

FIGURE 4 Prison Admissions per 100,000 General Population, North Carolina, by Race, 1970–1990

Source: Clarke 1992.

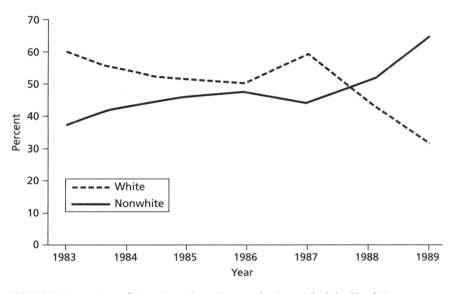

FIGURE 5 Percentage of New Drug Commitments by Race, Virginia, Fiscal Years 1983–1989

Source: Austin and McVey 1989.

proportionately more likely to sell drugs. We have no representative surveys of drug dealers and so cannot with confidence paint demographic pictures. However, there is little reason to suspect that drug crimes are more interracial than are most other crimes. In addition, the considerations that make arrests of Black dealers relatively easy make arrests of White dealers relatively hard.

Drug arrests are easier to make in socially disorganized inner-city minority areas than in working- or middle-class urban or suburban areas for a number of reasons. First, although drug sales in working- or middle-class areas are likely to take place indoors and in private spaces where they are difficult to observe, drug sales in poor minority areas are likely to take place outdoors in streets, alleys, or abandoned buildings, or indoors in public places like bars. Second, although working- or middle-class drug dealers in stable areas are unlikely to sell drugs to undercover strangers, dealers in disorganized areas have little choice but to sell to strangers and new acquaintances. These differences mean that it is easier for police to make arrests and undercover purchases in urban minority areas than elsewhere. Because arrests are fungible for purposes of both the individual officer's personnel file and the department's year-to-year statistical comparisons, more easy arrests look better than fewer hard ones. And because, as ethnographic studies of drug trafficking make clear (Fagan 1993; Padilla 1992), arrested drug dealers in disadvantaged urban minority communities are generally replaced within days, there is a nearly inexhaustible potential supply of young minority Americans to be arrested.

There is another reason why the War on Drugs worsened racial disparities in the justice system. Penalties for drug crimes were steadily made harsher since the mid-1980s. In particular, purveyors of crack cocaine, a drug used primarily by poor urban Blacks and Hispanics, are punished far more severely than are purveyors of powder cocaine, a pharmacologically indistinguishable drug used primarily by middle-class Whites. The most notorious disparity occurs under federal law, which equates 1 gram of crack with 100 grams of powder. As a result, the average prison sentence served by Black federal prisoners is 40% longer than the average sentence for Whites (McDonald and Carlson 1993). Although the Minnesota Supreme Court and two federal district courts have struck down the 100-to-1 rule as a denial of constitutional equal protection to Blacks, at the time of writing, every federal court of appeals that had considered the question had upheld the provision.

The people who launched the drug wars knew all these things—that the enemy troops would mostly be young minority males, that an emphasis on supply-side antidrug strategies, particularly use of mass arrests, would disproportionately ensnare young minority males, that the 100-to-1 rule would disproportionately affect Blacks, and that there was no valid basis for believing that any of these things would reduce drug availability or prices.

Likewise, as the first section showed, there was no basis for a good faith belief that the harsher crime control policies of recent years—more and longer mandatory minimum sentences, tougher and more rigid sentencing guidelines, and three-strikes-and-you're-out laws—would reduce crime rates, and there was a good basis for predicting that they would disproportionately damage Blacks. If Blacks are more likely than Whites to be arrested, especially for drug crimes, the greater harshness of toughened penalties will disproportionately be borne by Blacks. Because much crime is intraracial, concern for Black victims might justify harsher treatment of Black offenders if there were any reason to believe that harsher penalties would reduce crime rates. Unfortunately, as the conservative national governments of Margaret Thatcher and Brian Mulroney and reports of National Academy of Sciences Panels funded by the administrations of Republican Presidents Ford, Reagan, and Bush all agree, there is no reason to believe that harsher penalties significantly reduce crime rates.

JUSTIFYING THE UNJUSTIFIABLE

There is no valid policy justification for the harsh drug and crime control policies of the Reagan and Bush administrations, and for their adverse differential effect on Blacks. The justification, such as it is, is entirely political. Crime is an emotional subject and visceral appeals by politicians to people's fears and resentments are difficult to counter.

It is easy to seize the low ground in political debates about crime policy. When one candidate campaigns with pictures of clanging prison gates and grief-stricken relatives of a rape or murder victim, and with disingenuous promises that newer, tougher policies will work, it is difficult for an opponent to explain that crime is a complicated problem, that real solutions must be long term, and that simplistic toughness does not reduce crime rates. This is why, as a result, candidates often compete to establish which is tougher in his views about crime. It is also why less conservative candidates often try to preempt their more conservative opponents by adopting a tough stance early in the campaign. Finally, it is why political pundits congratulate President Clinton on his acumen in proposing federal crime legislation as or more harsh than his opponents. He has, it is commonly said, "taken the crime issue away from the Republicans."

Conservative Republican politicians have, since the late 1960s, used welfare, especially Aid to Families with Dependent Children, and crime as symbolic issues to appeal to anti-Black sentiments and resentments of White voters, as Thomas and Mary Edsall's *Chain Reaction: The Impact of Race, Rights, and Taxes on American Politics* (1991) makes clear. The Edsalls provide a history, since the mid-1960s, of "a conservative politics that had the effect of polarizing the electorate along racial lines." Anyone who observed Ronald Reagan's portrayal in several campaigns of Linda Evans, a Black Chicago woman, as the "welfare queen" or George Bush's use of Black murderer Willie Horton to caricature Michael Dukakis's criminal justice policies knows of what the Edsalls write.

The story of Willie Horton is the better known and makes the Edsalls' point. Horton, who in 1975 had been convicted of the murder of a 17-year-old boy, failed to return from a June 12, 1986, furlough. The following April, he broke into a home in Oxon Hill, Maryland, where he raped a woman and stabbed her companion.

Lee Atwater, Bush's campaign strategist, after testing the visceral effects of Willie Horton's picture and story on participants in focus groups, decided a year later to make Horton a wedge issue for Republicans. Atwater reportedly told a group of Republican activists that Bush would win the presidency "if I can make Willie Horton a household name." He later told a Republican gathering in Atlanta, "there's a story about a fellow named Willie Horton who, for all I know, may end up being Dukakis's running mate." Atwater for a time denied making both remarks but in 1991, dying of cancer, recanted: "In 1988, fighting Dukakis, I said that I would . . . make Willie Horton his running mate. I am sorry."

The sad reality is that tragedies like the crimes of Willie Horton are inevitable. So are airplane crashes, 40,000 to 50,000 traffic fatalities per year, and defense department cost overruns. Every person convicted of a violent crime cannot be held forever. Furloughs are used in most corrections systems as a way to ease offenders back into the community and to test their suitability for eventual release on parole or commutation. Horton had successfully completed nine previous furloughs, from each of which he had returned without incident, under a program established in 1972 not by Michael Dukakis but by Governor Francis Sargent, a Republican.

Public discourse about criminal justice issues has been debased by the cynicism that made Willie Horton a major participant in the 1988 presidential election. That cynicism has made it difficult to discuss or develop sensible public policies, and that cynicism explains why conservative politicians have been able year after year successfully to propose ever harsher penalties and crime control and drug policies that no informed person believes can achieve their ostensible goals.

Three final points, arguments that apologists for current policies sometimes make, warrant mention. First, it is sometimes said to be unfair to blame national Republican administrations for the failures and disparate impacts of recent crime control policies. This ignores the efforts of the Reagan and Bush administrations to encourage and, through federal mandates and funding restrictions, to coerce states to follow the federal lead. Attorney General William Barr (e.g., 1992) made the most aggressive efforts to compel state adoption of tougher criminal justice policies, and the Bush administration's final proposed crime bills restricted eligibility for federal funds to states that, like the federal government, abolished parole release and adopted sentencing standards no less severe than those in the federal sentencing guidelines. In any case, as the Edsalls' book makes clear, the use of crime control issues (among others including welfare reform and affirmative action) to elicit anti-Black sentiments from White voters has long been a stratagem of both state and federal Republican politicians.

Second, sometimes it is argued that political leaders have merely followed the public will; voters are outraged by crime and want tougher policies (DiIulio 1991). This is a half-truth that gets the causal order backwards. Various measures of public sentiment, including both representative surveys like Gallup and Harris polls and work with focus groups, have for many years consistently shown that the public is of two minds about crime (Roberts 1992). First, people are frustrated and want offenders to be punished. Second, people believe that social adversity, poverty, and a troubled home life are the principal causes of crime, and they believe government should work to rehabilitate offenders. A number of surveys have found that respondents who would oppose a tax increase to pay for more prisons would support a tax increase to pay for rehabilitative programs. These findings of voter ambivalence about crime should not be surprising. Most people have complicated views about complicated problems. For example, most judges and corrections officials have the same ambivalent feelings about offenders that the general public has. Conservative politicians have seized upon public support of punishment and ignored public support of rehabilitation and public recognition that crime presents complex, not easy, challenges. By presenting crime control issues only in emotional, stereotyped ways, conservative politicians have raised [crime's] salience as a political issue but made it impossible for their opponents to respond other than in the same stereotyped ways.

Third, sometimes it is argued that disparate impacts on Black offenders are no problem and that, because much crime is intraracial, failure to adopt tough policies would disserve the interests of Black victims. As former Attorney General Barr (1992) put it, perhaps in ill-chosen words, "the benefits of increased incarceration would be enjoyed disproportionately by Black Americans" (p. 17). This argument also is based on a half-truth. No one wants to live in unsafe neighborhoods or to be victimized by crime, and in a crisis, people who need help will seek it from the police, the public agency of last resort. Requesting help in a crisis and supporting harsh policies with racially disparate effects are not the same thing. The relevant distinction is between acute and chronic problems. A substantial body of public opinion research (e.g., National Opinion Research Center surveys conducted throughout the 1980s summarized in Wood 1990) shows that Blacks far more than Whites support establishment of more generous social welfare policies, full employ-ment programs, and increased social spending. The congressional Black and Hispanic caucuses have consistently opposed bills calling for tougher sanctions and supported bills calling for increased spending on social programs aimed at improving conditions that cause crime. Thus, in claiming to be concerned about Black victims, conservative politicians are responding to natural human calls for help in a crisis while ignoring evidence that Black citizens would rather have government support efforts to ameliorate the chronic social conditions that cause crime and thereby make calls for help in a crisis less necessary.

The evidence on the effectiveness of recent crime control and drug abuse policies, as the first section demonstrated, cannot justify their racially disparate effects on Blacks, nor, as this section demonstrates, can the claims that such policies merely manifest the people's will or respect the interests of Black vic-tims. All that is left is politics of the ugliest kind. The War on Drugs and the set of harsh crime control policies in which it was enmeshed were adopted to achieve political, not policy, objectives, and it is the adoption for political pur-poses of policies with foreseeable disparate impacts, the use of disadvantaged Black Americans as means to the achievement of White politicians' electoral ends, that must in the end be justified. It cannot.

DISCUSSION QUESTIONS

1. Discuss whether or not harsh drug and crime control policies can be justified, knowing they have disproportionately adverse effects on Blacks.

2. Tonry says that Blacks are no more likely than Whites to use illicit drugs, but they are much more likely to be arrested and imprisoned for drug use. What are possible reasons for this trend?

3. Several studies that were funded by Republican administrations found that harsher penalties had little effect on crime. Why were such harsh policies created when research shows that they are not effective?

4. Given the research that this article uses, restructure our current policies in order to create policies that may actually have an effect on crime rates.

REFERENCES

Anglin, M. Douglas, and Yih-Ing Hser (1990). "Treatment of Drug Abuse." In M. Tonry and J. Q. Wilson (eds.), *Drugs and Crime*. Chicago: University of Chicago Press.

Austin, James, and Aaron David McVey (1989). *The Impact of the War on Drugs*. San Francisco: National Council on Crime and Delinquency.

Barr, William P. (1992). "The Case for More Incarceration." Washington, D.C.: U.S. Department of Justice, Office of Policy Development.

Blumstein, Alfred (1982). "On the Racial Disproportionality of United States' Prison Populations." *Journal of Criminal Law and Criminology* 73:1259–81.

——— (1993a). "Racial Disproportionality of U.S. Prison Populations Revisited." *University of Colorado Law Review* 64:743–60.

——— (1993b). "Making Rationality Relevant—The American Society of Criminology 1992 Presidential Address." *Criminology* 31:1–16.

Blumstein, Alfred, Jacqueline Cohen, and Daniel Nagin (1978). *Deterrence and Incapacitation*. Report of the National Academy of Sciences Panel on Research on Deterrent and Incapacitative Effects. Washington, D.C.: National Academy Press.

Botvin, Gilbert J. (1990). "Substance Abuse Prevention: Theory, Practice, and Effectiveness." In M. Tonry and J. Q. Wilson (eds.), *Drugs and Crime*. Chicago: University of Chicago Press.

Bureau of Justice Statistics (1987). *Correctional Populations in the United States, 1985*. Washington, D.C.: U.S. Department of Justice, Bureau of Justice Statistics.

——— (1989a). *Correctional Populations in the United States, 1987*. Washington,

D.C.: U.S. Department of Justice, Bureau of Justice Statistics.

——— (1989b). *Correctional Populations in the United States, 1986*. Washington, D.C.: U.S. Department of Justice, Bureau of Justice Statistics.

——— (1991a). *Correctional Populations in the United States, 1989*. Washington, D.C.: U.S. Department of Justice, Bureau of Justice Statistics.

——— (1991b). *Correctional Populations in the United States, 1988*. Washington, D.C.: U.S. Department of Justice, Bureau of Justice Statistics.

——— (1993). *Correctional Populations in the United States, 1991*. Washington, D.C.: U.S. Department of Justice, Bureau of Justice Statistics.

Cahalan, Margaret Werner (1986). *Historical Corrections Statistics in the United States, 1850–1984*. Washington, D.C.: U.S. Department of Justice, Bureau of Justice Statistics.

Canadian Sentencing Commission (1987). *Sentencing Reform: A Canadian Approach*. Ottawa: Canadian Government Publishing Centre.

Chaiken, Marcia, ed. (1988). *Street Level Enforcement: Examining the Issues*. Washington, D.C.: U.S. Government Printing Office.

Clark, Stover (1992). "Pennsylvania Corrections in Context." *Overcrowded Times* 3:4–5.

Clarke, Stevens H. (1992). "North Carolina Prisons Growing." *Overcrowded Times* 3:1, 11–13.

DiIulio, John J. (1991). *No Escape: The Future of American Corrections*. New York: Basic Books.

Edsall, Thomas, and Mary Edsall (1991). *Chain Reaction: The Impact of Race, Rights, and Taxes on American Politics*. New York: Norton.

Ellickson, Phyllis L., and Robert M. Bell (1990). *Prospects for Preventing Drug Use*

Among Young Adolescents. Santa Monica, Calif.: RAND.

Fagan, Jeffrey (1993). "The Political Economy of Drug Dealing Among Urban Gangs." In R. C. Davis, A. J. Lurigio, and D. P. Rosenbaum (eds.), *Drugs and the Community.* Springfield, Ill.: Charles C. Thomas.

Federal Bureau of Investigation (1993). *Uniform Crime Reports for the United States—1992.* Washington, D.C.: U.S. Government Printing Office.

Gerstein, Dean R., and Henrik J. Jarwood, eds. (1990). *Treating Drug Problems.* Report of the Committee for Substance Abuse Coverage Study, Division of Health Care Services, National Institute of Medicine. Washington, D.C.: National Academy Press.

Gilliard, Darrell K. (1992). *National Corrections Reporting Program, 1987.* Washington, D.C.: U.S. Department of Justice, Bureau of Justice Statistics.

Hindelang, Michael. (1976). *Criminal Victimization in Eight American Cities: A Descriptive Analysis of Common Theft and Assault.* Washington, D.C.: Law Enforcement Assistance Administration.

———— (1978). "Race and Involvement in Common Law Personal Crimes." *American Sociological Review* 43:93–108.

Home Office (1990). *Protecting the Public.* London: H. M. Stationery Office.

Klein, Stephen, Joan Petersilia, and Susan Turner (1990). "Race and Imprisonment Decisions in California." *Science* 247: 812–16.

Langan, Patrick A. (1985). "Racism on Trial: New Evidence to Explain the Racial Composition of Prisons in the United States." *Journal of Criminal Law and Criminology* 76:666–83.

———— (1991). *Race of Persons Admitted to State and Federal Institutions, 1926–86.*

Washington, D.C.: U.S. Department of Justice, Bureau of Justice Statistics.

McDonald, Douglas, and Ken Carlson (1993). *Sentencing in the Federal Courts: Does Race Matter?* Washington, D.C.: U.S. Department of Justice, Bureau of Justice Statistics.

Moore, Mark H. (1990). "Supply Reduction and Drug Law Enforcement." In M. Tonry and J. Q. Wilson (eds.), *Drugs and Crime.* Chicago: University of Chicago Press.

Moynihan, Daniel Patrick (1993). "Iatrogenic Government—Social Policy and Drug Research." *American Scholar* 62:351–62.

National Institute on Drug Abuse (1991). *National Household Survey on Drug Abuse: Population Estimates 1990.* Washington, D.C.: U.S. Government Printing Office.

Office of National Drug Control Policy (1990). *National Drug Control Strategy—January 1990.* Washington, D.C.: Author.

Padilla, Felix (1992). *The Gang as an American Enterprise.* New Brunswick, N.J.: Rutgers University Press.

Perkins, Craig (1992). *National Corrections Reporting Program, 1989.* Washington, D.C.: U.S. Department of Justice, Bureau of Justice Statistics.

Perkins, Craig, and Darrell K. Gilliard (1992). *National Corrections Reporting Program, 1988.* Washington, D.C.: U.S. Department of Justice, Bureau of Justice Statistics.

Reiss, Albert J., Jr., and Jeffrey Roth (1993). *Understanding and Controlling Violence, Report of the National Academy of Sciences Panel on the Understanding and Control of Violence.* Washington, D.C.: National Academy Press.

Reuter, Peter (1988). "Can the Borders Be Sealed?" *Public Interest* 92:51–65.

Roberts, Julian V. (1992). "Public Opinion, Crime, and Criminal Justice." In M. Tonry (ed.), *Crime and Justice:*

A Review of Research, vol. 16. Chicago: University of Chicago Press.

Sourcebook of Criminal Justice Statistics (1978–1992). Washington, D.C.: Department of Justice, Bureau of Justice Statistics.

Standing Committee on Justice and the Solicitor General (1993). *Crime Prevention in Canada: Toward a National Strategy.* Ottawa: Canada Communication Group.

Sviridoff, Michele, Susan Sadd, Richard Curtis, and Randolph Grinc (1992). *The Neighborhood Effects of Street-Level Drug Enforcement.* New York: Vera Institute of Justice.

U.S. General Accounting Office (1990). *Drug Abuse: Research on Treatment May Not Address Current Needs.* Washington, D.C.: U.S. General Accounting Office.

Wilson, James Q. (1990). "Drugs and Crime." In M. Tonry and J. Q. Wilson (eds)., *Drugs and Crime.* Chicago: University of Chicago Press.

Wood, Floris W. (1990). *An American Profile: Opinions and Behavior, 1972–1989.* New York: Gale Research.

Zimring, Franklin E., and Gordon Hawkins (1994). "The Growth of Imprisonment in California." *British Journal of Criminology* 34:83–95.

3

✪

Mass Incarceration:
Money and Policy

William Spelman

An analysis of a state panel of prison populations from 1977 to 2005 shows that the best predictors of prison populations are crime, sentencing policy, prison crowding, and state spending. Prison populations grew at roughly the same rate and during the same periods as spending on education, welfare, health and hospitals, highways, parks, and natural resources. Current and lagged values of state spending on prison construction also accounted for a substantial amount of variation in subsequent prison populations. Public opinion, partisan politics, the electoral cycle, and social threats seem to have had little effect on the number of prisoners. The availability of publicly acceptable alternatives to incarceration may not be sufficient to reverse course. Federal funding of alternatives—but not prisons—would provide states with the financial incentive to reduce prison populations.

The United States houses a greater proportion of its citizens in prisons than any other country in the world—more than Russia and China, more than South Africa during apartheid, and maybe even more than North Korea (Walmsley, 2007). The direct costs of incarceration are in excess of $20,000 per prisoner. Many economists think the total social costs, which include legitimate income forgone by prisoners and reduced life prospects for their families, are roughly twice that (for example, Donohue, 2007; Kleykamp, Rosenfield, and Scotti, 2008). Evidence suggests that we have obtained some

Source: William Spelman "Crime, cash, and limited options: Explaining the prison boom," Criminology & Public Policy Vol 8:1, pp. 29–77. Copyright © 2009 American Society of Criminology. Reprinted with permission.

value for our money. Estimates vary widely, but the marginal prison bed seems to prevent somewhere between two and seven crimes, which saves potential victims between $4,000 and $19,000 per year (Levitt, 1996; Spelman, 2005; Western, 2006).

But note the details: If each prison bed reduces costs by no more than $19,000, but costs us $20,000 to $40,000, then do we need this many beds? Clearly not, and it is not (too) difficult to use current estimates of the crime-control effectiveness of prison, the costs of crime to victims and nonvictims, and the costs of prison to show that we overshot the mark sometime in the early 1990s. Enormous cutbacks—reductions of 50% or more in the prison population—are not difficult to justify and would probably save the U.S. public billions of dollars each year. Certainly, there is little economic justification for continuing to build.

How did we ever get to this point? Why is the prison population so high? No shortage of explanations is available. Some researchers view the prison boom as a straightforward response to the increase in crime during the 1970s and 1980s (although this seems to conflict with increasing prison populations during the crime decrease of the 1990s). Others view prison expansion as a response to demands of an increasingly conservative electorate or as a "wedge" issue that imparts a partisan political advantage to those who champion it. Still others argue that prison expansion is a means of shoring up failing social institutions such as the family and the public schools, an attempt at regaining control in an increasingly chaotic society.

It is fairly easy to document *how* we got to this point. The criminal justice system is in some sense a simple machine, in which the number of prisoners is equal to crime rates, times arrest rates per crime, times incarceration rates per arrest, times sentences served. This process makes it possible to break down annual changes in prison admissions into their component parts, and it has produced some clear findings. Prison growth during the 1980s was primarily caused by increases in incarceration rates among convicted offenders (Langan, 1991); later increases were mostly caused by increases in drug arrest rates and sentences served (Blumstein and Beck, 1999; Sabol, Rosich, Kane, Kirk, and Dubin, 2002). Although such findings tell us how prison populations increased, they beg the more important question: Why did incarceration rates and sentences served increase? Why did we become more punitive?

Some findings are consistent across studies: Prison populations seem to increase with the black population and the percentage of Republicans in the legislature and decrease as more is spent on welfare and education. But the effects of crime rates, public opinion, poverty and unemployment, and even sentencing policy are inconclusive, at best. It is difficult to tease a consistent narrative from these findings.

All studies attempted to connect prison populations to the economic, social, and political conditions prevailing at the time. For example, they measured the effects of Republican control of the state legislature in 1991 on the prison population in 1991. But the primary effect of Republican control (and other variables) may not have been immediate. The legislature may have authorized construction of a new prison, which could take years to complete. Even an immediate influx of prisoners will have long-lasting effects if prison populations are slow to shift over time.

This fact suggests that, in part at least, previous studies looked in the wrong place for their correlates. Today's unemployment, partisan political control, and per capita crime rates cannot be expected to be accurate predictors of capital spending and incarceration decisions made 5 years ago. It is also possible that the short-term, dynamic effects of changes in unemployment, politics, and crime are different from the long-term, equilibrium effects. To improve the accuracy of our explanations, we need to consider timing and to separate short-term results from long-term outcomes.

The analysis detailed below considers the same social, economic, and political variables as those examined in previous econometric studies. It includes more independent variables and uses current best practices to define the dependent variable and the model. More important, however, it considers timing in two ways. First, it includes capital spending as an intervening variable. As shown below, capital spending decisions are predictable and largely respond as expected to changes in current conditions and (arguably) to expectations of future prison needs; prison populations, in turn, seem to depend on previous capital decisions. Second, the analysis includes both dynamic and equilibrium elements, and it shows that these two effects differ, for some variables at least. The result is a remarkably simple explanation for what caused the prison boom of the last 30 years: persistently increasing crime rates, sentencing policies that put more offenders behind bars and kept them there longer, and sufficient state revenues to pay for it all.

DEPENDENT VARIABLES

Consistent with previous studies, let us measure the prison population as the jurisdictional population per 1,000 state residents. Thus, PRISON includes not only prisoners in state facilities (the custody population) but also convicted offenders doing state time in local jails, private correctional facilities, federal prisons, and facilities in other states.

Let us also measure P.CAPITAL, which is state spending on land and building acquisition and on new construction for the correctional system. These figures were taken from the Annual Survey of Governments conducted by the U.S. Bureau of the Census. Not all of this spending is on prisons; for the period 1987–2005, roughly 10% of spending was for noninstitutional purposes, mostly office space for administrators as well as probation and parole officers. Nevertheless, no breakdown is available for the 1977–1986 period, and 10% is sufficiently small that we can safely ignore it. As usual, we adjust for inflation by using the gross domestic product (GDP) price deflator.

Previous research has shown that the prison population is nonstationary; that is, it changes slowly over time, and the best predictor of prison in any given year is the value of prison for the previous year. The problem here is that any other variable that drifts up or down in the same way may seem to be correlated with prisons, even though these two variables are not related. This result is especially likely for variables such as GDP or state spending that, like PRISON, trend over time.

Independent Variables

Previous explanations for the prison boom can be roughly divided into five types: social threat, politics, crime control, crowding, and sentencing policy. More complete descriptions of each are provided elsewhere (e.g., Greenberg and West, 2001; Jacobs and Carmichael, 2001; Smith, 2004), and they are merely summarized here for completeness. A complete list of independent variables used, and their sources, is provided in Table 1.

The social threat argument states that society is likely to become more punitive when the social fabric is threatened. Threats include a sputtering economy, a growing underclass, or apparent weaknesses in such institutions of formal social control as the family, public schools, government, or mental health system.

Politics provides a simpler explanation for the prison boom: A conservative electorate and Republican-elected representatives are more likely to support prison expansion than others.

Timing may also be an issue. Prison populations may be higher or lower during gubernatorial or presidential election years, when elected officials may believe the public is paying greater attention.

Social and political threats extend well beyond the criminal justice system, but three alternative explanations lie closer to home. First, prison officials and policy makers may expand prisons in response to increasing crime rates. Because prison populations only increase when more convicted offenders enter the system than leave it, anything that increases the size of the incoming cohort can be expected to increase the prison population. All else equal, a 10% increase in crime should produce something like a 10% increase in the size of an incoming cohort.

Prison populations may also respond to crowding, which is measured by the number of convicted offenders who are serving time in local jails (Beck and Gilliard, 1995) or in private prisons, mental institutions, or prisons in other states. It may also respond to federal litigation to reduce overcrowding (Levitt, 1996). Crowding can be expected to decrease prison populations in the short run but increase prison capital spending, which makes larger populations possible in the long run.

Finally, intake and release choices may be constrained by previous sentencing policy choices. "Three strikes" and "truth-in-sentencing" laws mandate long sentences for some classes of offenders, which presumably increases prison populations (Turner, Greenwood, Chen, and Fain, 1999). Presumptive sentencing and decriminalization of minor drug offenses may reduce prison growth (Marvell, 1995).

All the independent variables described thus far measure objectives— variables that the state could reasonably hope to affect through prison

Table 1 List of variables used

Dependent Variables

PRISON	Prisoners under state jurisdiction per 1,000 resident population (National Prison Statistics, U.S. Bureau of Justice Statistics)
P.CAPITAL	Real state government spending per capita on capital outlays for corrections (Annual Survey of Governments [ASG], U.S. Census Bureau)

Independent Variables

Social Threats

The Economy

GDP	Real state gross domestic product over previous year (Regional Economic Accounts [REA], U.S. Bureau of Economic Analysis)
WAGE	Average real wage over previous year (REA)
UNEMP	Unemployment rate, averaged over calendar year (Local Area Unemployment Statistics, U.S. Bureau of Labor Statisics)
POVERTY	Proportion of persons under poverty threshold (Current Population Reports [CPR], U.S. Census Bureau)

The Underclass

DROPOUT	High-school graduates per 17-year-old resident, subtracted from 1 (Digest of Education Statistics [DES], National Center for Education Statistics)
UNWED	Proportion of all births to unwed mothers (National Vital Statistics Reports [NVSR], National Center for Health Statistics)
FOOD	Real state spending on U.S. Department of Agriculture Food Stamp program (REA)
BLACK	Black proportion of resident population (Annual Population Estimates [APE], U.S. Census Bureau)
HISPANIC	Spanish proportion of resident population, any race (APE)

Failing Institutions

DIVORCE	Divorces per 1,000 resident population (NVSR)
ENROLLED	Proportion of 5–17-year-olds enrolled in public primary and secondary schools (DES)
POLCHANGE	Absolute value of change in Republican proportion in legislature, next year (Klarner, 2003, 2007)
MHPOP	Number of inpatients in mental hospitals per 1,000 resident population (Raphael, 2000; Uniform Reporting System, Center for Mental Health Services, U.S. Substance Abuse and Mental Health Services Administration)

Public Opinion & Politics

CONSERV	Citizen ideology index (0 = liberal, 100 = conservative) (Berry, Ringquist, Fording, and Hanson, 1998; Fording, 2007)
REPGOV	Republican governor (1 = yes, 0 = no) (Klarner, 2007)

Table 1 (*continued*)

RCONTROL	Republican control of legislature (1 = yes, 0 = no) (Klarner)
MCONTROL	Mixed control of legislature, statehouse (1 = yes, 0 = no) (Klarner)
PCTREP	Percent of legislators who are Republicans (Klarner)

Electoral Cycle

GOVELEC	Gubernatorial election year (Klarner)
PRESELEC	Presidential election year

Crime

VIOLENT	Reported violent crimes per 1,000 resident population (Uniform Crime Reports [UCR], Federal Bureau of Investigation)
PROPERTY	Reported property crimes per 1,000 resident population (UCR)
DRUGS	Drug possession and trafficking arrests per 1,000 resident population (UCR)

Prison Crowding

JAIL	Number of convicted offenders doing time in local jails because of prison crowding, per 1,000 resident population (NPS)
OTHERINST	Number of convicted offenders doing time in institutions other than state prisons and local jails, per 1,000 resident population (NPS)
LITIGATION	State prison system facing litigation to reduce crowding (Levitt, 1996; *ACLU National Prison Project Journal*)

Sentencing Policy

HABITUAL	Habitual offender ("three strikes") law (1 = yes, 0 = no) (Zimring et al., 2001)
TRUTH	"Truth in sentencing" law (1 = yes, 0 = no) (Sabol et al., 2002)
PRESUMP	Presumptive sentencing guidelines (1 = yes, 0 = no) (Frase, 2005)
MJDECRIM	Marijuana decriminalized (1 = yes, 0 = no) (MacCoun and Reuter, 2001)

Institutional Capacity

T.SPENDING	Real state government spending per capita on operations and maintenance, capital outlays, and interest payments for all state functions (ASG)
MANDATORY	Real state government spending per capita on interest payments and on operations and maintenance for primary and secondary education, welfare, health, hospitals, and highways (ASG)
P.CAPMA	4-year moving average of P.CAPITAL, real capital spending on corrections, divided by PRISON lagged 1 year

expansion. Another class of variables measures constraints. No matter how appealing the objective, a state will find it difficult to build and operate more prisons if it has no money. Unfortunately, the simplest measure of financial capacity—state revenues—may be misleading by itself. Particularly in recent years, federal requirements and previously enacted statutes have mandated large expenditures in primary and secondary education, welfare, health care, and highways, all of which may squeeze out the correctional system; debt service is another such category of mandated expenditures. We can expect that total revenues will be positively associated with prison populations and capital spending, but that mandated expenditures will be negatively associated.

These suggestions do not by any means exhaust the possible explanations. For example, some researchers view prisons as a form of economic development, particularly if the potential sites of new prisons are in depressed rural areas (Cherry and Kunce, 2001; King, Mauer, and Huling, 2004). Because prisons are large-scale construction projects, they may be helpful in smoothing over temporary declines in demand for housing and commercial construction (Burns and Grebler, 1984). Criminologists have been arguing for years that crime control and overcrowding can be dealt with by increasing reliance on community corrections, so the number of offenders on, for example, intensive supervision probation or house arrest might be an indicator of how a state has chosen to deal with a particular threat. Nevertheless, the five categories described above cover the most frequently cited (and very likely the most important) explanations.

A MODEL OF PRISON POPULATION CHOICE

To parse these competing explanations, let us proceed in four steps. First, we must determine the proper form of the prison equation. A simple equilibrium model of prison population, which is based on perceived social benefits and costs, fills the bill handily. Because external conditions change faster than prison populations, states approach this long-run equilibrium but never reach it. The second step is to account for disequilibrium through a partial adjustment process. We then consider the effects of prison capacity; increases in capacity may reduce the social costs of putting a particular number of offenders behind bars, but the capacity increases respond to different social, economic, and political conditions than prison populations. Finally, let us consider how best to estimate this model given the statistical characteristics of prison population data.

Prison Benefits and Costs

The incarceration of each convicted offender provides some benefit to society. Justice is done. Future crimes are prevented through incapacitation and through general and specific deterrence. More generally, the exertion of formal control over the forces of disorder may reassure the public that

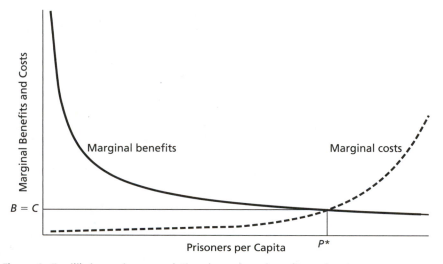

Figure 1. Equilibrium prison population depends on benefits and costs

other threats to the social order will be handled. We can reasonably expect that these benefits should be increasing at a diminishing rate as the number of imprisoned offenders increases. Thus, the marginal benefit of each new offender—the value of the next prison bed—should be decreasing with the number of prisoners.

Incarceration is also costly. Prisoners must be guarded, housed, fed, and clothed; the interest on prison construction bonds must be paid. Most prisoners had jobs in the legitimate economy before incarceration and their income will be lost; welfare payments to their dependents will increase to make up the difference. More generally, the removal of young men (particularly young black men) reduces the ability of all residents of urban neighborhoods to break the cycle of poverty and to achieve financial independence (Western, 2006).

These costs should be increasing but at an increasing rate with the number of prisoners. The simplest explanation for this expectation focuses on the financial costs. The first offenders imprisoned would be sent to those prisons that are the cheapest to operate and maintain; subsequent prisoners would be sent to more costly facilities, as we work our way up to the limits of current capacity. As we fill prisons beyond capacity or farm prisoners out to other states or institutions, we incur both higher financial costs (increased transportation costs, profit, an inconvenience premium) and higher inchoate political and administrative costs (these prisoners remain our responsibility, but we cannot control and take care of them directly). Thus, the marginal cost of each offender—the cost of the next prison bed—should be increasing with the number of prisoners.

Prison capacity is notoriously difficult to estimate accurately. We can, however, estimate changes in capacity through the proxy of capital spending on the prison system. Some of this spending will no doubt go into deferred maintenance or prison improvements but neither will go into prison

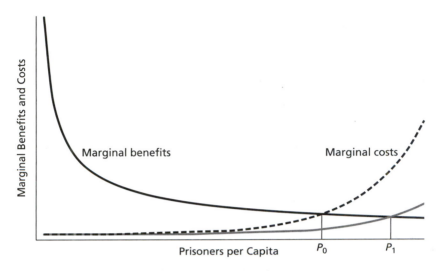

Figure 2 Value of capacity increase depends on cost function

expansion. It may take several years before a project is complete, but eventually most capital spending will shift the cost curve outward, which reduces marginal costs and allows for larger prison populations.

We can expect that the critical predictors of capital spending would be those associated with higher marginal costs: the number of state prisoners in county jails and other institutions, or litigation to decrease crowding in current facilities. A Republican-controlled legislature and a conservative electorate may be more willing to spend limited funds on prisons than on other state functions, which reduces opportunity costs. Capital spending should also depend on funding availability (measured by state revenues net of mandatory expenditures) as well as on expected future increases in prison demand (signaled by increases in crime or social threats or by strict sentencing policies that reduce the state's ability to control prison populations on a short-term basis).

The values of predictor variables can affect prison populations directly (through the prison equation) or indirectly (by affecting capital spending, which affects future prison populations through the prison equation). To estimate the full effect of each predictor variable, we need to take both the direct and the indirect effects into account.

Predictors of prison capital spending are generally consistent with expectations. States spend more when violent crime rates increase (but not property crimes or drug arrests) and when many prisoners are held in county jails and other institutions. Capital spending is lower for states that have decriminalized marijuana and (rather perversely) those that have adopted habitual offender statutes. Presumptive sentencing and truth-in-sentencing policies seem to have little effect on capital spending, however. Some evidence suggests, then, that legislatures respond to an apparent need for prison expansion by increasing capital spending.

Yet other predictors may be more important. Capital spending increases when the electorate is conservative and the legislature is controlled by Republicans (and, to a lesser extent, when one party controls each house). Spending also increases more during presidential election years, when the public presumably is paying more attention. By far, the largest effects are associated with resources. Capital spending increases dramatically with total state spending, and it decreases as more spending is required for education, welfare, and other mandatory functions.

Little evidence is available to suggest that other social threats matter much. None of the underclass and institutional threat variables is significant, and the significant increase in spending associated with higher unemployment rates is offset by an increase when GDP increases. The long-term expectations of resource availability may be more at issue here than responding to an economic threat.

Prison capital spending seems to respond to expectations of future but expectations of future need for prisons do not seem to be particularly important. The key categories are politics and state spending—not crime, crowding, or sentencing policy. The key expectations, then, are that more prisons will remain good politics, and that the resources needed to pay for them will continue to be available. This finding calls into question the claim that prison capacity increases in response to downstream need for prisons. More on this theory is discussed below.

LONG-RUN PRISON POPULATIONS
DEPEND MOSTLY ON CRIME AND POLICY

The prison population model described in this article only holds if a long-term equilibrium relationship exists between PRISON and some combination of the independent variables.

Some variables have a significant impact on PRISON in the short run but not in the long run. Previous capital spending (our proxy for increased prison capacity) and current state spending (net of spending on mandatory functions) clearly affect annual changes in prison populations in the expected (positive) direction. However, they do not seem to have long-term effects. Thus, capacity and funding affect the timing of prison population increases: Populations only increase when the beds and the money are available. But sooner or later, they will be available.

Other variables affect prison populations in both the short run and the long run. Crime rates are a clear example. In the short run, prison populations seem to increase as drug arrests increase and property crimes decrease. This result is unexpected, but it can be explained by the countervailing effects of prison on crime rates. We can be sure that prisons reduce crime, at least to some extent (cf. Levitt, 1996; Western, 2006). If increases in crime also lead to increased prison populations, the apparent short-run effects of violent and property crime rates as well as (perhaps) drug arrests would be a mixture of these two effects. If the effects of prison on crime are mostly short run in nature, however, we can expect these countervailing effects to be much less apparent in the long-run estimates. Indeed they are: In the long run, prison populations increase as violent and property crime rates as well as drug arrests increase (although only the violent and drug effects are statistically significant). The net result of the short-run and long-run effects is positive.

Sentencing policies also seem to have both immediate and long-run effects in the expected directions. Presumptive sentencing and marijuana decriminalization reduce prison populations in both the short run and the long run. Truth-in-sentencing laws have little immediate effect but a substantial long-run effect. This analysis makes sense: Truth-in-sentencing laws increase time served and reduce the number of offenders released in future years; the full effect would only be observed after prisoners sentenced under the old regime are replaced by those sentenced under the new law. Habitual offender laws seem to have little effect at all, perhaps because they only affect the sentences of a small number of offenders (Zimring, Hawkins, and Kamin, 2001).

The most important results here may be the dogs that do not bark. A conservative electorate and a Republican legislature are more likely to increase capital spending and subsequent availability of prison space, but they do not seem to have any direct effect once capital spending has been taken into account. Crowding behaves much the same way: It affects populations only through capital spending. Prison populations, like capital spending, do not seem to respond at all to economic threats, underclass threats, or institutional threats.

CRIME AND STATE SPENDING ARE THE BEST PREDICTORS OF PRISON POPULATION

Judging from the coefficients alone, the story looks fairly complicated. Many variables—which represent a wide variety of social, political, and economic explanations—seem to be related to prison capital spending or populations. It is difficult to tell which are most important.

For prison capital spending, economic threat, the electoral cycle, and crowding are all statistically significant, but 67% of the variance is explained by politics and current spending. For prison populations, sentencing policy and current spending are statistically significant, but crime and previous capital spending—more or less, current prison capacity—seem to explain more than the others. In no case did removal of a category appreciably affect the remaining coefficients, so we can be fairly certain that these estimates are untainted by colinearity across categories.

Capital spending is an intervening variable in this analysis. It does not itself cause prison populations to increase, but it makes future increases possible. Thus, the other variables affect prison populations in two ways: directly (in the prison equation) and indirectly (by affecting capital spending, which affects future prison populations). When direct and indirect effects are combined, eliminating current capacity as an explanation, the critical categories are crime and state spending, followed by sentencing policy, politics, and crowding. That is, the principal drivers of prison populations are the apparent need for more prisons and the ability to pay for them. Politics matters, too, but not as much. Other social threats do not matter at all.

Crowding, politics, state resources, and prison capacity all affect the timing of prison population increases. New prison capacity is most likely to be made available when prisons are crowded, the electorate and the legislature are politically conservative, and money is available to pay for prison construction. In the long run, however, the critical factors are increased crime rates and state policies that increase time served.

DISCUSSION

Some of these findings are expected. It comes as no surprise to find that prison populations increase with prison capacity or crime rates, or in response to more or less punitive sentencing policies. However, the importance of state financial resources—explaining nearly 30% of the total variation in prison populations—may be surprising. How can money be a cause of our problem? Wouldn't this affect everything else that states do, too? Of course it would. It did. As Figure 3 shows, spending increased for all state functions between 1977 and 2005. The prison increase was higher than for most other functions: Spending on prison operations quadrupled (as did prison populations); operational spending on primary and secondary education, higher education, and health only doubled. Nonetheless, all boats rose with the tide of cash.

The capital spending pattern suggests why prison operational spending increased faster than the others. Figure 4 shows cumulative capital spending by function. Higher education tops the list, with $259 billion in real spending, nationwide, across the period. States spent $77 billion on parks and natural resources, $61 billion on health and hospitals, and another $30 billion on primary and secondary education. Viewed in this context, the $55 billion we spent on the correctional system—most of it on new prisons—is hardly exceptional. We built a lot of new prisons, but we built a lot of roads, hospitals, and parks, too.

An important difference must be examined here. Some roads and parks are congested, but many are not; thus, the annual changes in lane miles and state parkland acreage are not very highly correlated with the changes in vehicle miles traveled and the numbers of park visitors. However, prison beds are typically filled to capacity soon after they come online. Since capacity estimates became available in 1984, nationwide custody populations have run at about 107% of nationwide capacity, with a range of 97% (in 2005) to 118% (in 1994). Prison populations quadrupled because capital spending

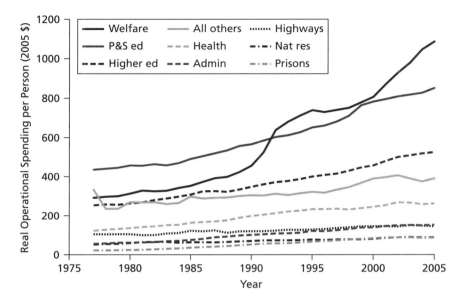

Figure 3 State operational spending, per capita, by function

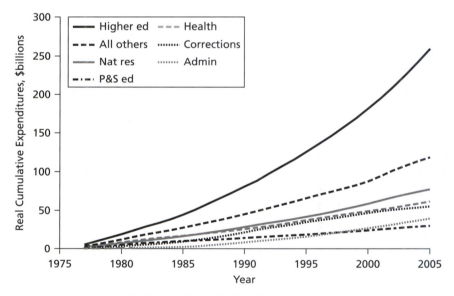

Figure 4 Cumulative capital expenditures by function

went into capacity increases, which were used almost immediately after they came online.

The apparent importance of prison capacity can be explained in two ways. The first is simple and direct: Prison populations are largely driven by available capacity; when the money was available to increase capacity, policy makers spent it; when the beds were available, criminal justice agencies filled them.

Thus, prison populations increased by more than the numbers of park visitors in large part because small changes in prison release decisions—entirely under centralized control and easy to change quickly—can keep prisons filled, even if police, prosecutors, and judges do not change their behavior at all (which they may). In contrast, demand for other state functions depends on the slowly changing habits of millions of actors. New highways may eventually persuade people to drive further, but new highways are rarely filled to capacity within a year or two of construction.

An alternative explanation is less consistent with the data presented here. When making decisions about prison capacity, state officials may attempt to meet future demands; in addition to posing an immediate problem, increases in crime, prison crowding, and the like send a signal that the demand for prison space is increasing. If the signal is accurate, then capacity increases may not be a cause of subsequent prison populations at all. They did not come because we built it; we built it, knowing they were on the way, and they came right on schedule. Under this explanation, capital spending is irrelevant, except to explain the timing of capacity increases that were eventually more or less inevitable. Capital spending would no longer be interpreted as a cause. The apparent indirect effects are not causes, either. Prison crowding and conservative politics are now merely signs of increasing demand.

Both of these explanations are probably valid to some extent. Whether it is possible at all to distinguish between the two, it will certainly be difficult to do so in the absence of some kind of experiment. Nevertheless, the second explanation suffers from some anomalies that the first explanation does not. If capital spending decisions were made largely with expected growth in mind, we could reasonably expect that sentencing policy variables would have similar effects on capital spending as they do on prison populations. They do not. When recent arrest rates and prison populations are included in the capital spending equation—the most obvious bases for prison population forecasts—they do not approach statistical significance. More generally, we would expect crime rates and prison crowding to be better predictors of capital spending than politics and state spending. These predictors are not even close. Perhaps most telling is the response to the crime reductions of the 1990s: The number of prison beds continued to increase, for a few years at least; the definition of "demand" was sufficiently elastic to ensure that they were more or less filled to capacity. Like nature, correctional systems nationwide abhorred a vacuum.

This analysis by no means proves that capital spending and resulting prison capacity are important drivers of prison populations, but it does make it seem more plausible.

Although we probably cannot obtain a definitive answer to the causation question, we can test its effects on the remaining findings. Specifically, suppose capital spending is entirely caused by expectations of future prison populations. In this case, none of the apparent capital spending effects and none of the indirect effects that work through capital spending would be causal. Alternatively, it may be that capital spending is completely independent of expectations, and all the apparent indirect effects are causal. The most likely case is somewhere in between; let us set bounds of 25% and 75% (that is, between 25% and 75% of the apparent effects are causal).

No matter how much of the relationship between capital spending and population is causal, current state spending explains 29% of the explainable variance. Crime explains 32% to 44%, sentencing policy explains 15% to 20%, and prison crowding explains 6% or 7%.

Prison populations may respond to social threats, but all of these effects combined explain no more than 4% of the explicable variance. Prison populations did not increase because society was worried about the economy, the underclass, or the family. We were worried about crime. Getting a handle on prison populations requires that we develop new responses to the crime problem.

Although it may be simple, this explanation accounts for two of the most puzzling aspects of the prison boom: why it started when it did and why it lasted so long. State revenues increased throughout the 1950s, but crime rates were largely flat. When the increase in crime became a serious issue in the 1960s, prisons filled and legislatures began spending money to construct more. Prison populations increased as new beds began to come online in the early 1970s. The lag between external conditions and public policy response continued on the back end, as well. Crime started to decrease in the 1990s; it took a while for legislators to conclude that this decrease was permanent and not just a temporary blip. Eventually, capital spending was reduced and—a few years later—prison capacity and populations flattened out.

These findings also suggest what may happen if crime rates begin to increase again: Prison officials will seek, and legislatures will authorize, yet more prisons to be constructed and filled. So long as incarceration remains our primary (state-level) response to crime, we will continue ratcheting up prison populations whenever crime rates increase, and the boom will start all over again.

EFFECTS OF THE 1994 CRIME BILL

The 1994 Crime Bill underscores the need to develop alternative responses. The Clinton administration touted the bill for funding 100,000 new police officers, and this objective seems to have been met (Koper, Moore, and Roth, 2002). But to get the bill passed, the White House and congressional Democrats had to accept another proviso: The federal government would provide $10 billion to states for prison construction between 1995 and 2000, but the money would only be available to those states that passed truth-in-sentencing laws that eliminated most "good time" provisions and required convicted offenders to serve 85% of their prison sentence.

The effect on state policy was almost immediate. The number of states with truth-in-sentencing statutes went from 4 in 1992, to 17 in 1995, to 27 in 1998. States with truth-in-sentencing statutes will eventually have prison populations about 13% larger than those without them, even after controlling for capital spending. Thus, the crime bill increased prison populations two ways: by making it cheaper for states to build new prisons and by making it more difficult to control populations downstream. This result, of course, was the intent.

Truth-in-sentencing was first adopted by Washington State in 1984, but diffusion was slow. By 1994, a new state was adopting it every 4 years or so, and it is reasonable to expect that this would have continued in the absence of the crime bill's capital funding provision. Let us also assume that all the capital funding provided to states as part of the crime bill simply offset funds that states would have spent anyway. That is, assume the crime bill did not increase prison capacity at all. Now suppose that, instead of using the promise of funding to promote truth-in-sentencing, the funds had been made available to all states on three alternative bases:

- No policy requirement—all states were invited to obtain funding on an equal basis, regardless of sentencing policy.
- Presumptive sentencing requirement—only states that had adopted presumptive sentencing would be eligible.
- Presumptive sentencing and marijuana decriminalization requirement—in addition to presumptive sentencing, states had to decriminalize possession of 1 ounce or less of marijuana.

The alternative bases are not at all far-fetched. Early versions of the crime bill included no sentencing policy requirements (Greene, 2002). Presumptive sentencing is intended to make sentencing policy fairer and more even across cases, courtrooms, and counties within a state; mandating such levels of fairness in exchange for federal funding is hardly unreasonable. Popular opinion on the merits of marijuana decriminalization was about evenly split in 1994 (Pastore and Maguire, 2008), but it would not have been unreasonable for the federal government to have insisted that its funds be reserved to reduce crimes with clear victims and social costs. In 1994, 12 states had adopted presumptive sentencing and 12 had decriminalized marijuana; let us assume that all states that adopted truth-in-sentencing between 1995 and 2000 would have adopted presumptive sentencing or decriminalized marijuana to obtain access to federal prison construction funding.

Figure 5 shows the results of this thought experiment. Between 1994 and 2005, the state prison population increased by 372,000. Had the crime bill not required truth-in-sentencing legislation, the population would still have increased, but only by 305,000. If presumptive sentencing had been required instead of truth-in-sentencing, the population increase would have been 238,000 and the incarceration rate per capita would have been essentially flat since 1999. If the crime bill had also required decriminalization of marijuana, the increase would have been only 155,000 and the incarceration rate would have peaked in 1999.

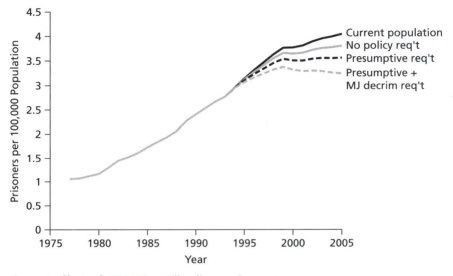

Figure 5 Effects of 1994 Crime Bill policy requirements

These figures are obviously back-of-the-envelope calculations, but the basic point is clear enough: The effect of sentencing policies on the prison population was large enough that changes in policy could have reversed the prison growth of the last few years. It is also not difficult to make the case that by focusing scarce prison resources on the most violent and dangerous criminals, presumptive sentencing, decriminalization, or similar policies would have improved the benefit-cost ratio of incarceration, regardless of the prison population.

VALUE OF FINANCIAL INCENTIVES

The findings described in this article provide no evidence that the deinstitutionalization of the mentally ill had any effect on prison construction or on prison populations. Nevertheless, the case is instructive because of what caused states to deinstitutionalize: the availability of alternatives and a substantial federal funding incentive.

In 1955, the state mental hospital population was 559,000—nearly as large on a per capita basis as the prison population is today. Beginning in the late 1950s, states began to let patients out of mental hospitals. As Figure 6 shows, the decrease was precipitous. By 1972, the number of patients had decreased by 50%, and by 2000, the number had decreased by 90%.

As usual, the reasons are complex, but most observers of the subject identify two critical explanations. First, the development of drugs such as reserprine and Thorazine relieved some patients of the symptoms of mental illness. This result reduced the need for physical restraints and, after a lengthy

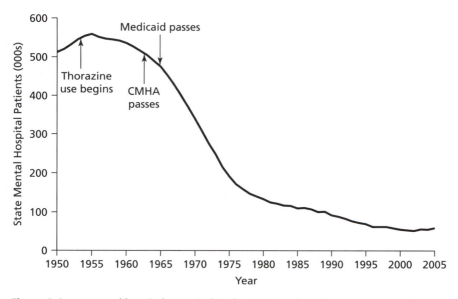

Figure 6 State mental hospitals emptied in the 1960s and 1970s

period of local experimentation, led to an increase in early discharge programs. Perhaps more importantly, it shifted public attitudes toward the problem, "promot[ing] psychiatrists to physicians in the eyes of some of their colleagues, and the insane to the status of patients in the eyes of many members of the public" (Roberts, 1967:25). Even if the mentally ill could not be cured, they could be made relatively harmless to themselves and others.

Although Thorazine and its kin made community treatment possible, treatment remained a state responsibility until the 1960s. This rule changed in 1963 with passage of the federal Community Mental Health Act. The act provided grants to local governments (but not to states) to create community alternatives to state hospital systems. By the mid-1970s, 650 community mental health centers were in operation, which served almost 2 million patients per year (Koyanagi, 2007).

The real financial impetus for deinstitutionalization came in 1965 with the passage of Medicaid. Through this program, the federal government paid for in-patient care of the mentally ill in local hospitals and nursing homes, but not in state mental hospitals. For the first time, states could offload financial responsibility for caring for the mentally ill. Some mental patients were simply shifted from one long-term institution to another. However, most patients were released into the community (Rochefort, 1984).

Of course, it is highly unlikely that prison deinstitutionalization could ever be so complete. Even if alternatives could be found for property, drug, and public order offenders, something like 40% of prison inmates nationwide were convicted of violent offenses, many for the second or third time. It is very likely that the public will insist on some measure of incapacitation for most of them. Nevertheless, most of the U.S. public supports alternative sanctions for nonviolent and first-time offenders (Farkas and Gutmann, 1992; Langer, 2002). Reducing the number of prisoners by 30% or 40%—roughly the amount needed to obtain a benefit-cost ratio close to 1.0—is not out of the question.

The mental hospital case suggests that the availability of publicly acceptable alternatives to incarceration may not by itself be sufficient to reduce prison populations. Like the mental hospitals of the 1950s, prisons are operated and supported by a large, well-entrenched, and politically adept bureaucracy. Alternatives, like community mental health until the mid 1960s, have no such political backing. Despite the periodic fiscal crises of the 1980s and 1990s, states have found the money to increase funding for all state functions. If this continues—and particularly if more states adopt laws that increase sentence lengths—more growth in prison populations is nearly certain.

That is, unless we can remove the financial incentives. A federal program of funding for alternatives to incarceration—but not prisons—would very likely have the same effects as Medicaid did on mental hospital populations, and for that matter as the 1994 Crime Bill had on prison populations. State legislatures are likely to respond to financial incentives by offloading the responsibility for drug users, property offenders, and first-time violent offenders. If the alternatives are available and well managed, the result could be a more cost-effective and sensible corrections system.

CONCLUSION

All of this discussion suggests that the prison boom may be largely over, as long as crime rates stay flat. If they begin to increase again, in the absence of persuasive alternatives, states will once again do the only thing they know how to do to solve the problem. This result also suggests what it might take to reverse the buildup: a dramatic improvement in the infrastructure for delivery of alternative sanctions, combined with substantial federal funding for these alternatives (but not for institutions). This formula succeeded in reducing the institutional population of the mentally ill in the 1970s and 1980s; appropriately retooled, it could reduce the institutional population of criminal offenders in the 2010s.

Regardless of what instrument we choose, the more basic finding is that nothing was inevitable about prison buildup in the United States. It was motivated by concern about crime and (to an extent) prison crowding—narrowly framed problems that can be dealt with through alternative means. Whatever symbolic value prisons may hold responded to the market for funding in the same way as all other state functions. It is fully under control of public policy makers. If it continues, it is because we have failed to heed Cassius' advice: "The fault, dear Brutus, is not in our stars, but in ourselves."

DISCUSSION QUESTIONS

1. What effects may a Republican-controlled legislature have on a state prison population?
2. How can the prison boom be explained?
3. In what two ways is the prison population affected?
4. How does overcrowding, politics, state resources, and prison capacity affect the timing of prison population increases?
5. What were the effects of the 1994 Crime Bill?

REFERENCES

Bane, Mary Jo and David T. Ellwood. 1986. Slipping into and out of poverty: The dynamics of spells. *Journal of Human Resources*, 21:1–23.

Beck, Allen J. and Darrell K. Gilliard. 1995. *Prisoners in 1994*. Bureau of Justice Statistics Bulletin. Washington, DC: U.S. Department of Justice, Bureau of Justice Statistics.

Beckett, Katherine. 1997. *Making crime pay: Law and order in contemporary American politics*. New York: Oxford University Press.

Beckett, Katherine and Bruce Western. 2001. Governing social marginality: Welfare, incarceration, and the transformation of state policy. In (David Garland, ed.), *Mass imprisonment: Social causes and consequences*. London: Sage.

Berry, William D., Evan J. Ringquist, Richard C. Fording, and Russell L. Hanson. 1998. Measuring citizen and government ideology in the *American states, 1960–1993. American Journal of Political Science*, 42:327–348.

Blumstein, Alfred and Allen J. Beck. 1999. Population growth in U.S. prisons, 1980–1996. *Crime and Justice*, 26:17–61.

Blumstein, Alfred and Jacqueline Cohen. 1973. A theory of the stability of

punishment. *Journal of Criminal Law and Criminology*, 64:198–207.

Blumstein, Alfred, Jacqueline Cohen, and William Gooding. 1983. The influence of capacity on prison population: A critical review of some recent evidence. *Crime and Delinquency*, 29:1–51.

Box, George E.P. and George C. Tiao. 1972. *Bayesian inference in statistical analysis*. Reading, MA: Addison-Wesley.

Burns, Leland S. and Leo Grebler. 1984. Is public construction countercyclical? *Land Economics*, 60:367–377.

Cagan, Phillip D. 1956. The monetary dynamics of hyperinflation. In (Milton Friedman, ed.), *Studies in the quantity theory of money*. Chicago, IL: University of Chicago Press.

Carlson, Kenneth. 1980. *American prisons and jails, vol. II: Population trends and projections*. Final Report to the National Institute of Justice. Cambridge, MA: Abt Associates.

Catalano, Shannon M. 2006. *Criminal victimization, 2005*. Bureau of Justice Statistics Bulletin. Washington, DC: U.S. Department of Justice, Bureau of Justice Statistics.

Cherry, Todd and Mitch Kunce. 2001. Do policymakers locate prisons for economic development? *Growth and Change*, 32:533–547.

Cohen, Lawrence E. and Marcus Felson. 1979. Social change and crime rate trends: A routine-activities approach. *American Sociological Review*, 44:588–608.

Donohue, John J., III. 2007. Economic models of crime and punishment. *Social Research*, 74:379–412.

Donohue, John J., III and Peter Siegelman. 1998. Allocating resources among prisons and social programs in the battle against crime. *Journal of Legal Studies*, 27:1–43.

Engle, Robert and Clive Granger. 1987. Co-integration and error correction: Representation, estimation, and testing. *Econometrica*, 55:251–276.

Farkas, Steve and Ethan Gutmann. 1992. *Punishing criminals: Pennsylvanians consider the options.* New York: Public Agenda.

Fording, Richard C. 2007. Most recently updated measures of citizen and government ideology. Retrieved January 15, 2008 from uky.edu/~rford/Home_files/page0005.htm.

Frase, Richard S. 2005. State sentencing guidelines: Diversity, consensus, and unresolved policy issues. *Columbia Law Review*, 105:1190–1232.

Gauger, Glenn E. and Curtiss Pulitzer. 1991. Capitalizing on lease-purchase initiative for prison construction. *Corrections Today*, 53:90–95.

Granger, Clive W.J. and Paul Newbold. 1974. Spurious regressions in econometrics. *Journal of Econometrics*, 2:111–120.

Greenberg, David F. and Valerie West. 2001. State prison populations and their growth, 1971–1991. *Criminology*, 39:615–653.

Greene, Judith. 2002. Getting tough on crime: The history and context of sentencing reform developments leading to the passage of the 1994 Crime Act. In (Cyrus Tata and Neil Hutton, eds.), *Sentencing and society: International perspectives.* Aldershot, England: Ashgate.

Haag, James J. 1999. *Discretionary and required spending in the state budget.* Legislative briefing. Lansing, MI: House Fiscal Agency.

Hindelang, Michael J., Michael R. Gottfredson, and James Garofalo. 1978. *Victims of personal crime: An empirical foundation for a theory of personal victimization.* Cambridge, MA: Ballinger.

Im, Kyung So, M. Hashem Pesaran, and Yongcheol Shin. 2003. Testing for unit roots in heterogeneous panels. *Journal of Econometrics*, 115:53–74.

Jacobs, David and Jason T. Carmichael. 2001. The politics of punishment across time and space: A pooled time-series analysis of imprisonment rates. *Social Forces*, 80:61–91.

Jacobs, David and Ronald E. Helms. 1996. Toward a political sociology of punishment: Politics and changes in the incarcerated population. *Social Science Research*, 30:171–194.

King, Ryan Scott, Marc Mauer, and Tracy Huling. 2004. An analysis of the economics of prison siting in rural communities. *Criminology & Public Policy*, 3:453–480.

Klarner, Carl. 2003. The measurement of the partisan balance of state government. *State Politics and Policy Quarterly*, 3:309–319.

Klarner, Carl. 2007. State partisan balance, 1959–2007. Retrieved January 15, 2008 from ipsr.ku.edu/SPPQ/journal_datasets/klarner.shtml.

Kleykamp, Meredith, Jake Rosenfeld, and Roseanne Scotti. 2008. Wasted money, wasted lives: *Calculating the hidden costs of incarceration in New Jersey.* Trenton, NJ: Drug Policy Alliance.

Koper, Christopher S., Gretchen E. Moore, and Jeffrey A. Roth. 2002. *Putting 100,000 officers on the street: A survey-*

based assessment of the federal COPS
Program. Research report. Washington,
DC: Urban Institute.

Koyanagi, Chris. 2007. *Learning from history:
Deinstitutionalization of people with
mental illness as precursor to long-term
care reform.* Washington, DC: Kaiser
Commission on Medicaid and the
Uninsured.

Langan, Patrick A. 1991. America's soaring
prison population. *Science*, 251:
1568–1573.

Langer, Gary. 2002. Poll: Give non-violent
crooks a 4th chance. Retrieved June
12, 2008 from abcnews.go.com/US/
Story?id=903738&page=1.

Leamer, Edward E. 1983. Let's take the
con out of econometrics. *American
Economic Review*, 73:31–43.

Levitt, Steven D. 1996. The effect of
prison population size on crime rates:
Evidence from prison overcrowding
litigation. *Quarterly Journal of Economics*,
111:319–351.

Little Hoover Commission. 1998. *Beyond
bars: Correctional reforms to lower prison
costs and reduce crime.* Sacramento,
CA: Commission on California
State Government Organization and
Economy.

MacCoun, Robert J. and Peter Reuter.
2001. *Drug war heresies: Learning from
other vices, times, and places.* New York:
Cambridge University Press.

Marvell, Thomas B. 1995. Sentencing
guidelines and prison population
growth. *Journal of Criminal Law and
Criminology*, 85:696–709.

Michaelowski, Raymond J. and Michael
A. Pearson. 1990. Punishment and
social structure at the state level: A
cross-sectional comparison of 1970 and
1980. *Journal of Research in Crime and
Delinquency*, 27:52–78.

Miller, Ted R., Mark A. Cohen, and Brian
Wiersema. 1996. *Victim costs and consequences: A new look.* Washington, DC:

U.S. Department of Justice, National
Institute of Justice.

Pastore, Ann L. and Kathleen Maguire.
2008. *Sourcebook of Criminal Justice
Statistics.* Retrieved June 11, 2008 from
albany.edu/sourcebook/index.html.

Pedroni, Peter. 2001. *Panel cointegration:
Asymptotic and finite sample properties of
pooled time series tests, with an application
to the PPP hypothesis.* Revised working
paper. Bloomington: Indiana University.

Pesaran, M. Hashem. 2005. A simple panel
unit root test in the presence of cross-
section dependence. *Journal of Applied
Econometrics*, 22:265–312.

Raphael, Steven. 2000. *The
deinstitutionalization of the mentally ill
and growth in the U.S. prison populations:
1971–1996.* Working paper. Berkeley,
CA: University of California, Goldman
School of Public Policy.

Ricketts, Erol R. and Isabel V. Sawhill.
1988. Defining and measuring the
underclass. *Journal of Policy Analysis and
Management*, 7:316–325.

Roberts, Nesta. 1967. *Mental health and
mental illness.* New York: Humanities
Press.

Rochefort, David A. 1984. Origins of the
"third psychiatric revolution": The
Community Mental Health Centers
Act of 1963. *Journal of Health Politics,
Policy, and Law*, 9:1–30.

Sabol, William J., Katherine Rosich, Kamala
Mallik Kane, David P. Kirk, and Glenn
Dubin. 2002. *The influences of truth-
in-sentencing reforms on changes in states'
sentencing practices and prison populations.*
Washington, DC: The Urban Institute.

Smith, Kevin B. 2004. The politics of
punishment: Evaluating political
explanations of incarceration rates.
Journal of Politics, 66:925–938.

Sparks, Richard F. 1981. Multiple
victimization: Evidence, theory, and
future research. *Journal of Criminal Law
and Criminology*, 72:762–778.

Spelman, William. 2005. Jobs or jails? The crime drop in Texas. *Journal of Policy Analysis and Management*, 24:133–165.

Spelman, William. 2008. Specifying the relationship between crime and prisons. *Journal of Quantitative Criminology*, 24:149–178.

Texas Criminal Justice Policy Council. 1992. Jail backlog projection for fiscal years 1992–1998: Update for Texas Attorney General. Austin: Author.

Turner, Susan, Peter W. Greenwood, Elsa Chen, and Terry Fain. 1999. The impact of truth-in-sentencing and three strikes legislation: Prison populations, state budgets, and crime rates. *Stanford Law & Policy Review*, 11:75–91.

Walmsley, Roy. 2007. *World prison population list*, 7th edition. London: International Centre for Prison Studies, King's College.

Waud, Roger N. 1966. Small sample bias due to misspecification in the "partial adjustment" and "adaptive expectations" models. *Journal of the American Statistical Association*, 12: 1130–1152.

Western, Bruce. 2006. *Punishment and inequality in America*. New York: Russell Sage Foundation.

Zimring, Franklin E., Gordon J. Hawkins, and Sam Kamin. 2001. *Punishment and democracy: Three strikes and you're out in California*. New York: Oxford University Press.

4

✪

Legitimacy: Promoting Support and Cooperation

Tom R. Tyler

This article makes three points. First, the police need public support and cooperation to be effective in their order-maintenance role, and they particularly benefit when they have the voluntary support and cooperation of most members of the public, most of the time. Second, such voluntary support and cooperation is linked to judgments about the legitimacy of the police. A central reason people cooperate with the police is that they view them as legitimate legal authorities, entitled to be obeyed. Third, a key antecedent of public judgments about the legitimacy of the police and of policing activities involves public assessments of the manner in which the police exercise their authority. Such procedural-justice judgments are central to public evaluations of the police and influence such evaluations separately from assessments of police effectiveness in fighting crime. These findings suggest the importance of enhancing public views about the legitimacy of the police and suggest process-based strategies for achieving that objective.

PUBLIC COOPERATION WITH THE POLICE

One way to approach the relationship between the police and the public is to consider how the public impacts on the effectiveness of the police in their efforts to combat crime and maintain social order. Traditional discussions of

Source: Tom R. Tyler, "Enhancing Police Legitimacy" The ANNALS of the American Academy of Political and Social Science, vol. 593 no. 1 84–99. Copyright © 2004 Sage Publications, Inc. Reprinted with permission.

the effective exercise of legal authority have focused on the ability of legal authorities to shape the behavior of the people within the communities they police. The ability of the police to secure compliance with their directives and with the law more generally—the ability to be authoritative-—is widely identified as one key indicator of their viability as authorities (Easton 1975; Fuller 1971). To be effective as maintainers of social order, in other words, the police must be widely obeyed (Tyler 1990). This obedience must occur both during personal encounters between police officers and members of the public (Tyler and Huo 2002) and in people's everyday law-related behavior (Tyler 1990).

While compliance is widespread, it can never be taken for granted. Studies of policing suggest that "although deference to legal authorities is the norm, disobedience occurs with sufficient frequency that skill in handling the rebellious, the disgruntled, and the hard to manage—or those potentially so—have become the street officer's performance litmus test" (Mastrofski, Snipes, and Supina 1996, 272; also see Sherman 1993). Studies of police encounters with members of the public suggest overall noncompliance rates of around 20 percent (Mastrofski, Snipes, and Supina 1996; McCluskey, Mastrofski, and Parks 1999).

Furthermore, it is difficult to gain compliance solely via the threat of use of force (Tyler 1990, 1997b, 1997c). The police need for people to both accept their decisions and follow the law at least in part because they choose to do so (Easton 1975; Parsons 1967; Sarat 1977; Tyler 1990). Why is such voluntary compliance important? Although the police represent the threat of force and carry guns and clubs with them, it is impractical for the police to be everywhere all of the time. The police must rely upon widespread, voluntary law-abiding behavior to allow them to concentrate their resources on those people and situations in which compliance is difficult to obtain. This is first true in personal encounters. When people comply in the immediate presence of the police but later return to noncompliance (since "citizens who acquiesce at the scene can renege"; Mastrofski, Snipes, and Supina 1996, 283), the police have difficulty maintaining order in the long term. In addition, the people in the community need to defer to the law in their everyday behavior. When people widely ignore the law, the resources of the police quickly become inadequate to the maintenance of order. In both situations, the police benefit from widespread, voluntary deference.

In addition to the importance of gaining compliance with the law, more recent discussions of crime and social disorder emphasize the important role of public cooperation to the success of police efforts to fight crime by preventing crime and disorder and bringing offenders to account for wrongdoing (Sampson, Raudenbush, and Earls 1997). The public supports the police by helping to identify criminals and by reporting crimes. In addition, members of the public help the police by joining together in informal efforts to combat crime and address community problems, whether it is by working in "neighborhood watch" organizations or by attending community-police meetings. As was the case with compliance, these cooperative efforts are largely voluntary in character, and the police are not generally in a position to reward members of the public for their aid. Instead, the police rely on willing public cooperation with police efforts to control crime and community disorder.

LEGITIMACY

The value of voluntary cooperation and support from the public raises the question of how such cooperation and support can be created and maintained (Tyler and Blader 2000). Traditionally, the focus in policing has been on instrumental models of policing. For example, compliance with the law has been viewed as being motivated through the creation of a credible risk that people will be caught and punished for wrongdoing, that is, "by manipulating an individual's calculus regarding whether crime pays in the particular instance" (Meares 2000, 396). Similarly, public cooperation in fighting crime is motivated by evidence that the police are performing effectively in their efforts to control crime and urban disorder.

Evidence suggests that these instrumental perspectives are inadequate models with which to explain public cooperation. In the case of sanction threat and compliance, the findings of research support the argument that sanction risks do shape compliance behavior (Nagin 1998), but the magnitude of their influence is typically small. For example, based on a review of research on the influence of deterrence on drug use, MacCoun (1993) estimates that variations in the certainty and severity of punishment account for only approximately 5 percent in the variance in drug-related behavior, a finding consistent with the suggestion of Paternoster (1987) that "perceived certainty [of punishment] plays virtually no role in explaining deviant criminal conduct (191)" (also see Paternoster et al.1983). The low level of this relationship may be due to the difficulties that the police have bringing the risk of being caught and punished for wrongdoing to high-enough levels to effectively influence public behavior (Ross 1982; Robinson and Darley 1995, 1997). This evidence suggests that deterrence is an inadequate basis for securing compliance with the law.

In the case of police effectiveness in fighting crime, evidence suggests that police innovations in the management of police services may have contributed to the widespread declines in crime reported in major American cities during recent decades (Kelling and Coles 1996; Silverman 1999). Furthermore, indicators show increasing professionalism in policing, including declining rates of complaints against the police and lower levels of excessive police use of force against community residents. However, studies of the public and public views about and cooperation with the police suggest that the public's reactions to the police are again only loosely linked to police effectiveness in fighting crime, suggesting that police performance is an insufficient basis for gaining the cooperation of the public.

How can the police encourage public cooperation and support? To have an effective strategy for encouraging cooperation, people need to have additional reasons for cooperating beyond instrumental assessments of police performance. One alternative perspective is linked to the recognition that people have internalized values upon which the police might draw to secure compliance and to gain cooperation (Sherman 1993; Tyler 1990). A key value that people hold is their widespread support for the legitimacy of the police—the belief that the police are entitled to call upon the public to follow the law and help combat crime and that members of the public have an obligation to engage in cooperative behaviors. When people feel that an authority is legitimate, they authorize that authority to determine what their behavior will be within a given set of situations. Such an authorization of an authority "seem[s] to carry automatic justification. . . . Behaviorally, authorization obviates the necessity of making judgments or choices. Not only do normal moral principles become inoperative, but—particularly when the actions are explicitly ordered—a different type of morality, linked to duty to obey superior orders, tends to take over" (Kelman and Hamilton 1989, 16). People, in other words, feel responsible for following the directives of legitimate authorities (French and Raven 1959; Merelman 1966).

The roots of the modem use of legitimacy are usually traced to the writings of Weber (1968).Weber argued that the ability to issue commands that will be obeyed did not rest solely on the possession or ability to deploy power. In addition, there were rules and authorities that people would voluntarily obey. These rules and authorities possessed the quality of legitimacy, the belief by others that they ought to be obeyed. Weber's framing of the issue of legitimacy is important because his articulation of the question of why people obey authorities defines the modern focus of social science perspectives on legitimacy. In addition, he distinguished this issue from the philosophical question of why people ought to obey, which is central to discussions within law and political philosophy (Beetham 1991).

The argument that people's feelings about their internal obligation to obey social norms and rules also shape their behavior is equally central to the writings of Freud (Hoffman 1977) and Durkheim (1947, 1986), although these authors focused on people's moral values. This legitimacy argument is not particular to the police. On the contrary, legitimacy is suggested to be central to the exercise of all forms of authority. For example, Selznick's classic examination of authority in industrial settings argues that "there is a demand that rules be legitimate, not only in emanating from established authority, but also in the manner of their formulation, in the way they are applied, and in their fidelity to agreed-upon institutional purposes. . . . [The] obligation to obey has some relation to the quality of the rules and the integrity of their administration" (Selznick 1969, 29).

A legitimacy-based strategy of policing increases cooperation with the law by drawing on people's feelings of responsibility and obligation. The advantage of such a strategy lies in its ability to facilitate voluntary cooperation. To the degree that cooperation is motivated by personal values, it is self-regulatory and does not depend upon the ability of the authorities to effectively deploy incentives or sanctions to secure desired public behavior. In such a society, only minimal levels of societal resources are needed to maintain social order, and those resources can be redirected toward meeting other needs (Tyler 2001a; Tyler and Darley 2000). Furthermore, such voluntary deference is more reliable than instrumentally motivated compliance because it does not vary as a function of the circumstances or situation involved. Driving up to a stop sign on a deserted road at night, internal values motivate a person to stop, even when the possibility of punishment for law-breaking behavior is minimal.

The key empirical issue underlying a legitimacy-based strategy of policing is whether people's views about the legitimacy of the law and the police actually shape their cooperative behavior. The importance of legitimacy has been examined on two distinct levels: first, in studies of everyday interactions with police officers; and second, on the community level, with people evaluating the characteristics of their community police force—irrespective of whether they have had personal experience with police officers.

Studies of the influence of legitimacy typically assess people's views about the legitimacy of the police in three ways. First, people are asked about their sense of obligation to obey the police and the law, for example, whether they feel that "people should obey the law even if it goes against what they think is right" and that "disobeying the law is seldom justified." When asked questions of this type, Americans are generally found to express a strong sense of obligation to defer to law and to legal authorities. Second, legitimacy has been assessed by asking about institutional trust and confidence. People are asked, for example, which statements they agree with: "The police are generally honest"; "I respect the police"; and "I feel proud of the police." Finally, legitimacy is sometimes measured by assessing feelings about the police.

When they have personal experiences with the police, people sometimes have to decide whether to accept outcomes that they do not regard as desirable, or even as fair. The key question is whether their views about the legitimacy of the police in general, and/or of the particular officers with whom they are dealing, shape this willingness. Tyler and Huo (2002) studied this question using a sample of 1,656 residents of Los Angeles and Oakland. They found that two factors shaped the willingness to accept decisions: the degree to which the decisions were regarded as favorable and fair and the degree to which the police were generally regarded as legitimate authorities. These two factors were of approximately equal importance.

Tyler and Huo (2002, and reviewed in this volume) further found that the degree to which people generally viewed the police as legitimate influenced the basis upon which they decided whether to accept decisions. People could potentially accept decisions because those decisions were favorable or fair. They could also accept them because they believed that the police had acted appropriately when dealing with them—that is, due to procedural justice. Procedural justice will be discussed in more detail in the next section. Process-based reactions benefit the police, however, because they cannot always provide desirable outcomes, but it is almost always possible to behave in ways that people experience as being fair. The key finding of this study of personal experiences was that when people generally viewed the police as legitimate authorities, people's decisions about whether to accept police decisions were more strongly based upon evaluations of the procedural justice of police actions. Hence, having prior legitimacy facilitated the task of the police by leading people to assess police actions in more heavily procedural terms.

These studies do not examine the impact of legitimacy on whether people help the police. We might anticipate, for example, that people who viewed the police as more legitimate would be more willing to help them during personal encounters by, for example, volunteering information about conditions in the neighborhood or the identity or location of wrongdoers. Similarly, they might be more willing to volunteer to attend police-community meetings.

Legitimacy might also have an important influence on everyday compliance with the law. Much of peoples' law-related behavior occurs outside the immediate presence of legal authorities, although some possibility of sanctions always exists. Theories of legitimacy predict that in such settings, people's feelings of obligation will shape their behavior, leading to deference to the law. Tyler (1990) tested this argument in a study of the attitudes and behaviors of the residents of Chicago. He found that legitimacy has a significant influence on the degree to which people obeyed the law. Furthermore, that influence was distinct from and greater in magnitude than the influence of estimates of the likelihood of being caught and punished for wrongdoing. These findings suggest that as predicted by theories of legitimacy, people's views about the legitimacy of authorities influence the degree to which people obey the law in their everyday lives.

More recently, Sunshine and Tyler (2003) replicated this test of the influence of legitimacy on compliance within two samples of the residents of New York City. In both studies, they also found that the legitimacy of the police significantly influenced compliance with the law. Their study also extended consideration of the influence of legitimacy to a second area of concern: cooperation with the police. They found that those residents who viewed the police as more legitimate were more willing to cooperate with them both by reporting crimes or identifying criminals and by engaging in community activities to combat the problems of crime.

These findings support the basic premise of legitimacy theories. People are more willing to cooperate with legal authorities when they believe that those authorities are legitimate. This includes both deferring to their decisions during personal encounters and generally obeying legal rules in their everyday lives. Furthermore, people are more cooperative in helping the police to deal with crime in their communities when they view the police as legitimate. Hence, as anticipated in the work of Weber, legitimacy does represent a basis upon which authorities can act that is distinct from the possession or use of power and resources.

Legitimacy-based policing has clear advantages for the police and the community. When people act based upon their feelings of obligation and responsibility, they are engaging in self-regulatory behavior. Society and social authorities benefit from the occurrence of such behavior because it does not depend upon the maintenance of a credible system of deterrence or upon the quality of police performance. Studies suggest that the maintenance of such a system is always costly and inefficient, and in times of financial difficulty or crisis, when public cooperation is most clearly needed, it poses special difficulties for authorities.

One reason for focusing on issues of legitimacy at this time is that recent evidence shows public mistrust and lack of confidence in the law and the legal authorities (Tyler 1997a, 1998). For example, in 2002, the National Institute of Justice (NIJ) found that only 27 percent of Americans expressed "a great deal" of confidence in the criminal justice system. Within this broad category, the police have traditionally received high ratings. For example, in this same study, 59 percent expressed "a great deal" of confidence in the police. This is consistent with the suggestion that it is the courts that are the particular target of public dissatisfaction. In 1998, the General Social Survey found that only 22 percent of Americans expressed "a great deal" of confidence in the courts. While the higher levels of confidence expressed in the police are encouraging from the perspective of a legitimacy-based approach to policing, a second troubling aspect of public views is the finding that there is a striking racial gap in views about legal authorities. For example, in a 2001 study conducted by the NIJ, 63 percent of whites expressed a great deal of confidence in the police, as compared with 31 percent of African Americans. In the case of the overall criminal justice system, 27 percent of whites expressed a great deal of confidence, as compared with 22 percent of African Americans.

The argument that legitimacy is a key antecedent to public cooperation with the police highlights the importance of being able to create and maintain a climate of public opinion in which community residents generally view the police as legitimate authorities. Given that perspective on policing, it is important to take seriously the evidence of public dissatisfaction and mistrust and to ask how legitimacy can be enhanced.

ENHANCING POLICE LEGITIMACY: THE INFLUENCE OF PROCEDURAL JUSTICE

Given the important role that legitimacy can play in determining the level of public cooperation with the police, it is important to try to understand how the police shape public views about their legitimacy. Public views about the legitimacy of the police might, for example, be the result of public assessments of police performance, in terms of either the ability of the police to create a credible sanction risk for wrongdoers or the effectiveness of the police in fighting crime and urban disorder. To the extent that this is true, the already-outlined importance of legitimacy would not have new or novel implications for polic-ing. To enhance their legitimacy, the police would need to effectively combat crime and apprehend wrongdoers.

An alternative perspective on legitimacy is provided by the literature on procedural justice. That literature argues that the legitimacy of authorities and institutions is rooted in public views about the appropriateness of the man-ner in which the police exercise their authority. In other words, people are viewed as evaluating authorities by assessing whether they use fair procedures when engaging in policing activities. These procedural judgments are distinct from judgments about the effectiveness, valence, or fairness of the outcomes of those activities.

As in the case of legitimacy, the key empirical issue is whether people consider procedural-justice issues when making inferences about the legiti-macy of the police. Studies of people's evaluations of all types of authorities—police officers, judges, political leaders, managers, and teachers—have all provided strong support for the basic procedural-justice argument. When people are dealing with authorities or institutions, their evaluations of legiti-macy are primarily linked to assessments of the fairness of the authority's or the institution's procedures. Such procedural-justice assessments are consis-tently found to be more strongly linked to legitimacy judgments than are the evaluations of their effectiveness or the valence or fairness of the outcomes they deliver (Lind and Tyler 1988; Tyler 1990, 2000a; Tyler et al. 1997; Tyler and Smith 1997).

In the case of personal experiences, studies find that when authorities act in ways that people experience as being fair, people are more willing to vol-untarily accept the authorities' decisions (Kitzman and Emery 1993; Lind et al. 1993; MacCoun et al. 1988; Wissler 1995). These field studies confirm the findings of the earlier experimental findings of social psychological research (Thibaut and Walker 1975). Procedural-justice judgments are found to have an especially important role in shaping adherence to agreements over time. Pruitt et al. (1993) studied the factors leading those involved in disputes to adhere to mediation agreements over time and found that the procedural fair-ness of the initial mediation setting was a central determinant of adherence six months later. A second study suggested that procedural justice encourages long-term obedience to the law. Paternoster et al. (1997) found that spouse abusers were less likely to commit future abuses when they experienced pro-cedural justice with the police during an initial encounter.

These findings also receive support in the context of encounters between police and members of the public. Tyler and Huo (2002) found that procedural-justice judgments shaped people's willingness to accept the deci-sions made by police officers and are more important than are judgments about the favorability or fairness of the outcomes of the encounter. Similarly, Mastrofski, Snipes, and Supina (1996) and McCluskey, Mastrofski, and Parks (1999) found that the experience of disrespect from the police reduces compli-ance. This is consistent with the finding by Casper, Tyler, and Fisher (1988) that the satisfaction of felony defendants with their experiences with the police and courts was strongly linked to their assessments of the fairness of the process by which their cases were handled.

In a recent study of police encounters with community residents in two American cities that involved both interviews and observational analysis, McCluskey (2003) used a wide variety of indicators of procedural justice and found that five aspects of procedural justice influenced the willingness to comply with police requests for self-control. In particular, he found that, holding all else constant, citizens who receive respectful treatment from authorities are almost twice as likely to comply, and those receiving disrespectful treatment are nearly twice as likely to rebel. If the citizen's voice is terminated by the police they are more than twice as likely to rebel against the police request for self-control. If the police demonstrate their commitment to making an informed decision by seeking information about the presenting situation, citizens are more than twice as likely to comply with the phase 1 request for self-control (p. 91). The impact of procedural justice is greatest early in the encounter, and at that time, "the likelihood of citizen compliance is strongly affected by procedurally just tactics" (p. 114).

These findings suggest that procedural justice has a broad impact upon people's reactions to their experiences with the police. In particular, people's willingness to buy into and voluntarily accept decisions that may require them to accept outcomes that they do not want, or to engage in self-control over their actions, is enhanced by the judgment that one has been treated fairly by the police. Furthermore, evidence shows that this deference continues over time and shapes people's law-related behavior in the future. These findings suggest that the procedural justice that members of the public experience during their personal encounters with the police has both immediate and long-term behavior effects. It is also important to note, however, that procedural justice is not always found to be important. For example, McClusky (2003) did not find that procedural justice mattered when people were stopped by the police on the street and asked for identification, and Hickman and Simpson (2003) found that receiving procedurally fair treatment from the police did not encourage the victims of domestic violence to report future violent incidents to the police. Hence, procedural justice often, but not always, facilitates favorable reactions to policing activities.

Research further suggests that procedural justice during a personal encounter with the police influences views about the legitimacy of the police. Tyler (1990) demonstrated that the procedural justice of a personal experience with the police shaped general views about the legitimacy of the law, a finding replicated by Tyler and Huo (2002). Similarly, Tyler, Casper, and Fisher (1989) found that the procedural justice of their case disposition process shaped the views of felony defendants about the legitimacy of the criminal justice system and of the law.

More recently, Barnes (1999) has examined the influence of procedural justice in a Reintegrative Shaming Experiments (RISE)–based study of 900 Australians arrested for intoxicated driving. In a field experiment, these drivers had their cases referred to traditional courts or diversionary conferences. These

conferences, designed using restorative-justice ideals, were viewed by participants as procedurally fairer. As procedural-justice models would predict, those
who attended such conferences expressed more positive views about the legitimacy of the legal system than did those who went to court. They also expressed
stronger intentions to obey the law in the future. Whether these differences
lead to differences in actual behavior over time is unclear (Sherman 2003).

Of course, not all members of the community have personal contact with
the police. It is also important to consider people's general views about the
police and policing activities in their communities. Based upon a secondary
analysis of prior surveys, Tyler (2001b) argued that procedural-justice judgments play a central role in shaping people's views about the legitimacy of
the police and the courts. The findings of the four surveys reviewed by Tyler
(2001b) suggest that people consider both performance in controlling crime
and procedural fairness when evaluating the police and the courts. The major
factor, however, is consistently found to be the fairness of the manner in
which the police and the courts are believed to treat citizens. For example, in
a study of Oakland residents living in high-crime areas, it was found that the
primary factor shaping overall evaluations of the police was the quality of their
treatment of community residents (which explained 26 percent of the unique
variance in evaluations), with a secondary influence of performance evaluations (which explained 5 percent of the unique variance).

Sunshine and Tyler (2003) find support for this argument in two surveys
of the residents of New York City. In both studies, the key antecedent of
legitimacy was procedural justice. Those community residents who thought
that the police exercised their authority in fair ways were also more willing to
comply with the law and to cooperate with the police. Even in more coercive
settings, like prisons, cooperation is found to be linked to procedural justice
(Sparks, Bottoms, and Hay 1996).

WHAT IS PROCEDURAL JUSTICE?

Studies have identified a wide variety of issues that influence the degree to
which people evaluate a procedure's fairness. Furthermore, it has been found
that the importance of procedural criteria varies depending upon the setting
(Tyler 1988). However, studies consistently point to several elements as key
to people's procedural-justice judgments.

Participation is one key element. People are more satisfied with procedures that allow them to participate by explaining their situations and com-
municating their views about situations to authorities. This participation effect
explains, for example, why mediation procedures are popular (Adler, Hensler,
and Nelson 1983; McEwen and Maiman 1981) and settlement conferences are
not (Lind et al. 1990). It suggests to police officers the importance of allowing
people to have input before they make decisions about how to handle a problem. Interestingly, being able to control the outcome is not central to feeling

that one is participating (Heinz and Kerstetter 1979). What people want is to feel that their input has been solicited and considered by decision makers, who can then frame their concerns into an appropriate resolution (Conley and O'Barr 1990).

A second key element is neutrality. People think that decisions are being more fairly made when authorities are unbiased and make their decisions using objective indicators, not personal views. As a consequence, evidence of even-handedness and objectivity enhances perceived fairness. Basically, people are seeking a level playing field in which no one is unfairly advantaged. Because people are seldom in a position to know what the correct or reasonable outcome is, they focus on evidence that the decision-making procedures by which outcomes are arrived at show evidence of fairness. Transparency provides an opportunity to make that judgment, while evidence of factuality and lack of bias suggest that those procedures are fair.

Third, people value being treated with dignity and respect by legal authorities. The quality of interpersonal treatment is consistently found to be a distinct element of fairness, separate from the quality of the decision-making process. Above and beyond the resolution of their problems, people value being treated with politeness and having their rights acknowledged. The importance of interpersonal treatment is emphasized in studies of alternative dispute resolution procedures, which suggest that people value evidence that authorities "took the litigants and the dispute seriously," "after all, the trial was in all likelihood one of the most meticulous, most individualized interactions that the litigant had ever experienced in the course of his or her contacts with government agencies" (Lind et al. 1990). Their treatment during this experience carries for them important messages concerning their social status, their self-worth, and their self-respect. In other words, reaffirming one's sense of his or her standing in the community, especially in the wake of events that demean status, such as crime victimization or being publicly stopped and questioned by the police, can be a key issue to people dealing with legal authorities.

Finally, people feel that procedures are fairer when they trust the motives of decision makers. If, for example, people believe that authorities care about their well-being and are considering their needs and concerns, they view procedures as fairer. People are seldom able to judge the actions of authorities with specialized expertise (doctors, judges, police officers, etc.) since people lack the training and experience to know if the actions taken were reasonable and sufficient. Hence, they depend heavily upon their inferences about the intentions of the authority. If the authorities are viewed as having acted out of a sincere and benevolent concern for those involved, people infer that the authorities' actions were fair. Authorities can encourage people to view them as trustworthy by explaining their decisions and justifying and accounting for their conduct in ways that make clear their concern about giving attention to people's needs.

Why is trust such a key issue? Tyler (1990) found that the people he interviewed acknowledged that unfair treatment was widespread when people dealt with the police and courts. Nonetheless, over 90 percent predicted that if they had contact with the police or courts in the future, they would receive fair treatment. People, in other words, have a strong desire to view the authorities as benevolent and caring. This view is directly tested during a personal encounter with those authorities, and people's views are powerfully shaped by whether they do, in fact, receive the behavior they expect from the police or courts.

ETHNIC GROUP DIFFERENCES

These findings suggest that the roots of public trust and confidence in the police lie in public views about how the police exercise their authority. Given the already-noted ethnic group differences in trust and confidence, it is important to consider whether the argument outlined applies equally to the members of all ethnic groups.

Tyler and Huo (2002) address this issue directly in their study of the acceptance of decisions made by the police. Their findings suggest that procedural justice is an equally important issue to the members of three major ethnic groups: whites, African Americans, and Hispanics. Tyler (1994, 2000b) suggests that this finding is broader in scope. His analysis suggests that the importance of procedural justice is maintained across ethnicity, gender, income, education, age, ideology, and political party. As a result, a process-based approach to policing is an ideal way to bridge ethnic and other social divisions in society.

THE IDEA OF A LAW-ABIDING SOCIETY

The distinction between risk/gain estimates, performance evaluations, and legitimacy as antecedents of behavior highlights the possibility of two types of legal culture. The first is a culture that builds public compliance on the basis of people's judgments about police performance. Such a society depends upon the ability of legal authorities to create and maintain a credible presence by combating crime and punishing wrongdoers. The studies outlined demonstrate that while instrumental issues are important, it is difficult for legal authorities to sustain a viable legal system simply based upon performance.

The important role played by legitimacy in shaping people's law-related behavior indicates the possibility of creating a law-abiding society in which citizens have the internal values that lead to voluntary deference to the law and to the decisions of legal authorities such as the police. Such a society is based upon the willing consent and cooperation of citizens. That cooperation develops from people's own feelings about appropriate social behavior and is not linked to the risks of apprehension and punishment or to the estimates of the nature and magnitude of the crime problem that people estimate to exist in their social environment. Tyler (2001a) refers to such a society as a law-abiding society. The studies outlined make clear that such a society is possible in the sense that if people think authorities are legitimate, they are more likely to obey and to cooperate with authorities (Tyler 2003; Tyler and Blader 2000).

A law-abiding society cannot be created overnight through changes in the allocation of resources within government agencies, changes that would alter the expected gains and/or risks associated with cooperation. It depends upon the socialization of appropriate social and moral values among children and the enhancement of those values among adults. Evidence suggests that a core element to the creation and enhancement of such social values is the judgment that legal authorities exercise their authority following fair procedures. This is true both during personal experiences with the police and the courts, where people are found to be more willing to accept decisions that are fairly made, and in general evaluations of the police and courts, where people are found to comply with the law and support the police and courts as institutions when they think that these same institutions generally exercise authority fairly.

DISCUSSION QUESTIONS

1. What is the importance of public compliance to law enforcement?
2. What are the benefits of voluntary support and how is it linked to police legitimacy?
3. Why are procedural justice judgments central to public evaluations?
4. How does public view affect the legitimacy of the police?

REFERENCES

Adler, Patricia, Deborah Hensler, and Charles E. Nelson. 1983. *Simple justice: How litigants fare in the Pittsburgh Court arbitration program*. Santa Monica, CA: RAND.

Barnes, Geoffrey C. 1999. *Procedural justice in two contexts: Testing the fairness of diversionary conferences for intoxicated drivers*. Ph.D. diss., University of Maryland.

Beetham, David. 1991. *The legitimation of power*. Atlantic Highlands, NJ: Humanities Press.

Casper, Jonathan D., Tom R. Tyler, and Bonnie Fisher. 1988. Procedural justice in felony cases. *Law and Society Review* 22:483-507.

Conley, John M., and William M. O'Barr. 1990. *Rules versus relationships*. Chicago: University of Chicago Press.

Durkheim, Emile. 1947. *The division of labor*. Translated by George Simpson. New York: Free Press.

———. 1986. *Moral education*. Translated by Paul Fauconnet and Herman Schnurer. New York: Free Press.

Easton, David. 1975. A reassessment of the concept of political support. *British Journal of Political Science* 5: 435-57.

French, John R. P., and Bertrand Raven. 1959. The bases of social power. In *Studies in social power,* edited by Dorwin Cartwright. Ann Arbor: University of Michigan Press.

Fuller, Lon. 1971. Human interaction and the law. In *The rule of law,* edited by Robert P. Wolff. New York: Simon and Schuster.

Heinz, Anne M., and Wayne A. Kerstetter. 1979. Pretrial settlement conference: Evaluation of a reform in plea bargaining. *Law and Society Review* 13:349-66.

Hickman, Laura J., and Sally S. Simpson. 2003. Fair treatment or preferred outcome? The impact of police behavior on victim reports of domestic violence incidents. *Law and Society Review* 37:607-34.

Hoffman, Martin. 1977. Moral internalization: Current theory and research. *Advances in Experimental Social Psychology* 10:85-133.

Kelling, George L., and Catherine M. Coles. 1996. *Fixing broken windows.* New York: Touchstone.

Kelman, Herbert C., and V. Lee Hamilton. 1989. *Crimes of obedience.* New Haven, CT: Yale University Press.

Kitzman, Katherine M., and Robert E. Emery. 1993. Procedural justice and parents' satisfaction in a field study of child custody dispute resolution. *Law and Human Behavior* 17:553-67.

Lind, E. Allan, Carol T. Kulik, Maureen Ambrose, and Maria de Vera Park. 1993. Individual and corporate dispute resolution. *Administrative Science Quarterly* 38:224-51.

Lind, E. Allan, Robert J. MacCoun, Patricia A. Ebener, William L. F. Felstiner, Deborah R. Hensler, Judith Resnik, and Tom R. Tyler. 1990. In the eye of the beholder: Tort litigants' evaluations of their experiences in the civil justice system. *Law and Society Review* 24:953-96.

Lind, E. Allan, and Tom R. Tyler. 1988. *The social psychology of procedural justice.* New York: Plenum.

MacCoun, Robert J. 1993. Drugs and the law: A psychological analysis of drug prohibition. *Psychological Bulletin* 113:497-512.

MacCoun, Robert J., E. Allan Lind, Deborah R. Hensler, D. L. Bryant, and Patricia A. Ebener. 1988. *Alternative adjudication: An evaluation of the New Jersey automobile arbitration program.* Santa Monica, CA: RAND.

Mastrofski, Stephen D., Jeffrey B. Snipes, and Anne E. Supina. 1996. Compliance on demand: The public's responses to specific police requests. *Journal of Crime and Delinquency* 33:269-305.

McCluskey, John D. 2003. *Police requests for compliance: Coercive and procedurally just tactics.* New York: LFB Scholarly Publishing.

McCluskey, John D., Stephen D. Mastrofski, and Roger B. Parks. 1999. To acquiesce or rebel: Predicting citizen compliance with police requests. *Police Quarterly* 2:389-416.

McEwen, Craig A., and Richard J. Maiman. 1981. Small claims mediation in Maine. *Maine Law Review* 33:237-68.

Meares, Tracey L. 2000. Norms, legitimacy, and law enforcement. *Oregon Law Review* 79:391-415.

Merelman, Richard J. 1966. Learning and legitimacy. *American Political Science Review* 60:548-61.

Nagin, Daniel S. 1998. Criminal deterrence research at the outset of the twenty-first century. In vol. 23 of *Crime and justice: A review of research,* edited by Michael Tonry, 1-42. Chicago: Chicago University Press.

Parsons, Talcott. 1967. Some reflections on the place of force in social process. In *Sociological theory and modem society,* edited by Talcott Parsons. New York: Free Press.

Paternoster, Raymond. 1987. The deterrent effect of the perceived certainty and severity of punishment. *Justice Quarterly* 4:173-217.

Paternoster, Raymond, Ronet Brame, Robert Bachman, and Lawrence W. Sherman. 1997. Do fair procedures matter? *Law and Society Review* 31: 163-204.

Paternoster, Raymond, Linda E. Saltzman, Gordon P. Waldo, and Theodore G. Chiricos. 1983. Perceived risk and social control: Do sanctions really deter? *Law and Society Review* 17:457-79.

Pruitt, Dean G., Robert S. Peirce, Neil B. McGillicuddy. Gary L. Welton, and Lynn M. Castrianno. 1993. Long-term success in mediation. *Law and Human Behavior* 17:313-30.

Robinson, Paul H., and John M. Darley. 1995. *Justice, liability, and blame: Community views and the criminal law.* Boulder, CO: Westview.

———. 1997. The utility of desert. *Northwestern University Law Review* 91:453-99.

Ross, H. Lawrence. 1982. *Deterring the drinking driver: Legal policy and social control.* Lexington, MA: Heath.

Sampson, Robert J., Stephen Raudenbush, and Felton Earls. 1997 Neighborhoods and violent crime. *Science* 277:918-24.

Sarat, Austin. 1977. Studying American legal culture. *Law and Society Review* 11:427-88.

Selznick, Philip. 1969. *Law, society, and industrial justice.* New York: Russell Sage.

Sherman, Lawrence W. 1993. Defiance, deterrence, irrelevance: A theory of the criminal sanction. *Journal of Research in Crime and Delinquency* 30:445-73.

———. 2003. Reason with emotion: Reinventing justice with theories, innovations, and research. *Criminology* 41:1-37.

Silverman, Eli B. (1999). *NYPD battles crime: Innovative strategies in policing.* Evanston, IL: Northwestern University Press.

Sparks, Richard, Anthony Bottoms, and Will Hay. 1996. *Prisons and the problem of order.* Oxford, UK: Clarendon.

Sunshine, Jason, and Tom R. Tyler. 2003. The role of procedural justice and legitimacy in shaping public support for policing. *Law and Society Review* 37:513-48.

Thibaut, John W., and Laurens Walker. 1975. *Procedural justice: A psychological analysis.* Hillsdale, NJ: Lawrence Erlbaum.

Tyler, Tom R. 1988. What is procedural justice? Criteria used by citizens to assess the fairness of legal procedures. *Law and Society Review* 22:103-35.

———. 1990. *Why people obey the law.* New Haven, CT: Yale University Press.

———. 1994. Governing amid diversity: Can fair decision-making procedures bridge competing public interests and values? *Law and Society Review* 28: 701-22.

———. 1997a. Citizen discontent with legal procedures. *American Journal of Comparative Law* 45:869-902.

———. 1997b. Compliance with intellectual property laws: A psychological perspective. *Journal of International Law and Politics* 28:101-15.

———. 1997c. Procedural fairness and compliance with the law. *Swiss Journal of Economics and Statistics* 133:219-40.

———. 1998. Public mistrust of the law: A political perspective. *University of Cincinnati Law Review* 66:847-76.

———. 2000a. Social justice: Outcome and procedure. *International Journal of Psychology 35:111-25.*

———. 2000b. Multiculturalism and the willingness of citizens to defer to law and to legal authorities. *Law and Social Inquiry* 25 (3): 983-1019.

———. 2001a. Trust and law abidingness: A proactive model of social regulation. *Boston University Law Review* 81:361-406.

————. 2001b. Public trust and confidence in legal authorities: What do majority and minority group members want from legal authorities? *Behavioral Sciences and the Law* 19: 215-35.

————. 2003. Procedural justice, legitimacy, and the effective rule of law. In vol. 30 of *Crime and justice—A review of research,* edited by M. Tonry, 431-505. Chicago: University of Chicago Press.

Tyler, Tom R., and Steve Blader. 2000. *Cooperation in groups.* Philadelphia: Psychology Press.

Tyler, Tom R., Robert J. Boeckmann, Heather J. Smith, and Yuen J. Huo. 1997. *Social justice in a diverse society.* Boulder, CO: Westview.

Tyler, Tom R., Jonathan D. Casper, and Bonnie Fisher. 1989. Maintaining allegiance toward political authorities. *American Journal of Political Science* 33:629-52.

Tyler, Tom R., and John Darley. 2000. Building a law abiding society: Taking public views about morality and the legitimacy of legal authorities into account when formulating substantive law. *Hofstra Law Review* 28:707-39.

Tyler, Tom R., and Yuen J. Huo. 2002. *Trust in the law.* New York: Russell Sage.

Tyler, Tom R., and Heather J. Smith. 1997. Social justice and social movements. In vol. 2 of *Handbook of social psychology,* 4th ed., edited by Daniel Gilbert, Susan Fiske, and Gardiner Lindzey, 595-629. New York: Addison-Wesley.

Weber, Max. 1968. *Economy and society.* Edited by G. Roth and C. Wittich. New York: Bedminster.

Wissler, Roselle L. 1995. Mediation and adjudication in small claims court. *Law and Society Review* 29:323-58.

5

✦

Criminal Justice Policy without Theory or Research

Daniel Mears

Daniel Mears argues throughout the chapter that some of our nation's policies are not created with empirical support. He suggests that there are many reasons for the creation of policies not grounded in theory or empirical research, among which are politicization of crime, false dichotomies, extreme shifts, anecdotal evidence, symbolic gestures, misunderstandings, easy fixes to complicated problems, and limited policy research. Mears discusses that policies based on anything but research often fail to meet their goals and lead to very high expenditures. With all of this in mind, he suggests that a more systematic approach to creating, monitoring, and assessing criminal justice policies is needed.

THE POLICY CONTEXT AND THE STAKES INVOLVED

A central aim of this chapter is to argue, through the use of the evaluation hierarchy, that many of the nation's most prominent criminal justice policies lack a solid theoretical and empirical foundation and that the necessary ingredients for holding the criminal justice system accountable and making it effective do not yet exist. Here I want to turn to the national criminal justice policy context to highlight some of the stakes involved in allowing criminal justice policy to be irrational.

Source: Mears, Daniel P., "Criminal Justice Policy Without Theory or Research," American Criminal Justice Policy: An Evaluation Approach To Increasing Accountability and Effectiveness (pp. 12–34). Copyright © Cambridge University Press. Reprinted with the permission of Cambridge University Press.

CRIME RATES

To begin, let us first focus on crime rates. Many different sources of data can be used to examine crime. For example, arrests and calls to the police frequently serve as the basis for establishing whether crime has increased, decreased, or remained stable. Many news accounts focus on such data. If the number of robbery arrests increases from, for example, 100 to 110, a news account may well report that crime is up 10 percent. That would be incorrect. Law enforcement data reflect two factors: crime and law enforcement behavior. Observe, for example, that a community's true crime rate could decrease, but if the number of police officers doubled you likely would see a dramatic increase in arrests and possibly reported crime. So, a more accurate news account would say that arrests have gone up 10 percent and that the increase reflects increased crime, increased law enforcement activity, or both. If we want to determine what the true rates of crime are, it would be far better to conduct offender and victimization surveys. The first would allow us to determine how many offenders exist and how much crime they commit, while the latter would allow us to identify the total number of victims of crime. No large-scale, nationally representative offender surveys exist in the United States, though a number of small-scale studies exist. By contrast, the U.S. federal government has invested a considerable amount of money and effort into conducting a large, nationally representative victimization survey, titled, appropriately enough, the National Crime Victimization Survey (NCVS). The first data collection for the study began in 1973 and today includes more than 60,000 households and the victimization experiences of persons ages twelve or older.

When we examine the trends in violent crime (rape or sexual assault, robbery, and aggravated and simple assault), which typically seem to garner the most concern among the public and policy makers, we see that such crime remained relatively stable throughout the 1970s and declined in the early 1980s, as shown in Figure 1. Then, around 1986, it began to rise steadily, peaking in 1994 before beginning a steady decline during the next decade. The victimization survey entails the interviewing of individuals and so does not capture homicides. However, for that offense, law enforcement data tend to be relatively accurate; analyses of such data reveal that the trend in homicides during the same time period largely mirrored the trend for violent crime generally. When we turn to property crime (burglary, motor vehicle theft, and theft)—as depicted in Figure 2 and as measured by the NCVS—we see a steady decline over three decades. In short, except for the rise in violent crime from 1986 to 1994, crime has been stable or declining since 1973.

CORRECTIONAL SYSTEM GROWTH

On the basis of analysis of these trends, we might reasonably hypothesize that the criminal justice system would have increased modestly in the 1980s to early 1990s to address the rise in violent crime but that it otherwise would have remained stable and perhaps even decreased in size. Such a prediction would be wrong. Juxtaposed against the overall decline in violent and property crime has been

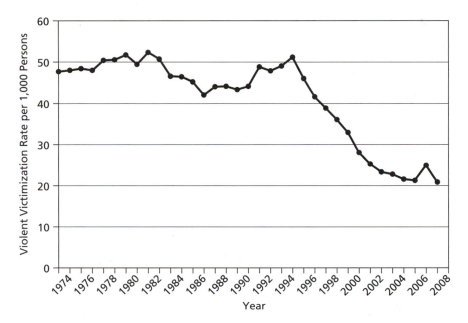

FIGURE 1 Violent Victimization, 1973–2008. The increase from 2005 to 2006 is not likely a reflection of a true increase in victimization, but rather reflects a change in the methodology used with the National Crime Victimization Survey, the source for the victimization estimates (Rand 2008:2).

Sources: Rand, Michael R. 2009. *Criminal Victimization*, 2008. Washington, D.C.: Bureau of Justice Statistics. Rand, Michael R. 2008. *Criminal Victimization*, 2007. Washington, D.C.: Bureau of Justice Statistics. Rand, Michael R., and Shannan Catalano, 2007. *Criminal Victimization*, 2006. Washington, D.C.: Bureau of Justice Statistics.

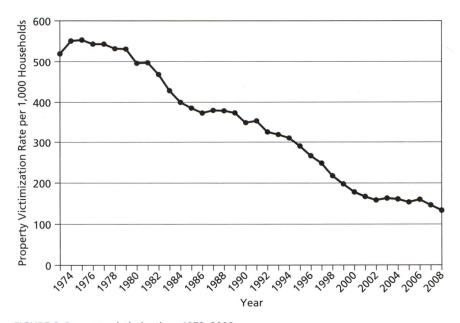

FIGURE 2 Property victimization, 1973–2008.

Sources: Rand, Michael R. 2009. *Criminal Victimization*, 2008. Washington, D.C.: Bureau of Justice Statistics. Rand, Michael R. 2008. *Criminal Victimization*, 2007. Washington, D.C.: Bureau of Justice Statistics. Rand, Michael R., and Shannan Catalano, 2007. *Criminal Victimization*, 2006. Washington, D.C.: Bureau of Justice Statistics.

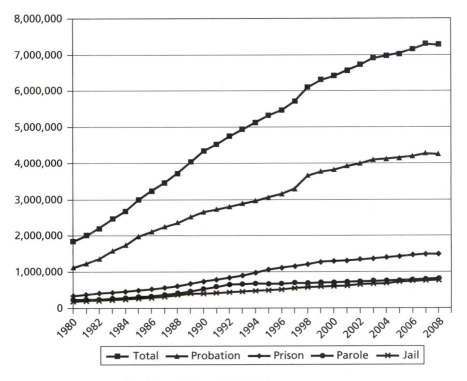

FIGURE 3 U.S. Correctional Populations, 1980–2008.

Source: Bureau of Justice Statistics. 2009. *Correctional Populations in the United States,* Washington, D.C.: U.S. Department of Justice. Available online: http://www.ojp.usdoj-gov/bjs/glance/tables/corr2tab.htm (accessed December 15, 2009).

unprecedented growth in the criminal justice system. The growth in corrections alone is striking, as can be seen in Figure 3. In 1980, there were 1.8 million individuals under some form of state or federal supervision or incarcerated in jail or prison. By 2008, that number more than quadrupled, rising to 7.3 million.

By far, the biggest driver of that growth has been the increase in the probation population, which has risen from 1.1 million to 4.3 million. Even so, the jail and prison populations increased at higher rates. For example, the number of individuals in jail grew from 183,988 to 785,556, an increase of 327 percent. Prison populations grew even more, increasing from 319,598 inmates to more than 1.5 million, or 375 percent. That growth is striking given that jails and prisons typically cost considerably more to build and operate compared with the costs of probation and parole or various types of community supervision and intermediate sanctions. They also, for all intents and purposes, constitute permanent investments. For example, once a prison is built, it generally will remain in use for decades. So, any expansion in prison capacity essentially represents an indefinite commitment to increased prison costs. Why? When states decide to expand prison capacity, they cannot easily undo that decision if, at a later point, they determine that less capacity is needed.

PRISONER REENTRY

The large-scale increase in the number of individuals incarcerated in jails and prisons translates into a new social problem—namely, the return of large numbers of ex-prisoners back into communities, what has been termed "prisoner reentry." Annually, more than 735,000 inmates leave state or federal prisons and undergo the process of transitioning from institutional life to a context in which they have few opportunities for employment and frequently suffer from a number of problems, including mental and physical health problems, substance abuse, family dysfunction, histories of physical and sexual abuse, and spotty educational and employment histories. Of particular concern is the high likelihood that these individuals will recidivate. Figure 4 shows the rates of recidivism from one of the largest national studies ever conducted. It reveals that, in 1994, more than two-thirds (68 percent) of released prisoners were rearrested within three years.

Remarkably, after the large-scale increases in the correctional system and the spate of "get tough" crime policies in the 1980s and 1990s, this level of recidivism was higher than it was a decade earlier. (In 1983, "only" 63 percent of released prisoners were rearrested within three years.) It remains unclear why

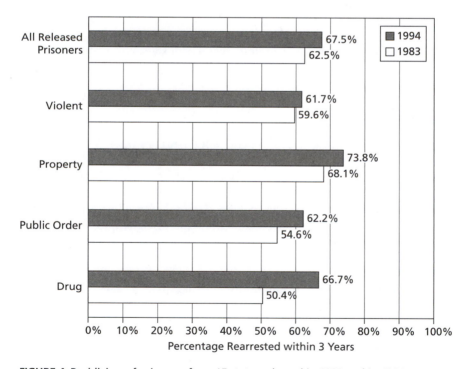

FIGURE 4 Recidivism of prisoners from 15 states released in 1983 and in 1994.

Source: Langan, Patrick A., and David J. Levin. 2002. *Recidivism of Prisoners Released in 1994.* Washington, D.C.: Bureau of Justice Statistics.

the increase occurred, although it may have stemmed in part from a decline in educational, vocational, and treatment programming in prisons during this time period. It also may have reflected more vigorous law enforcement activity. For example, numerous efforts were taken to target drug crimes, which would have increased drug arrests. Indirect support for that explanation can be seen at the bottom of the figure—the percentage of drug offenders rearrested increased from 50 percent to 67 percent between 1983 and 1994. Observe that recidivism in the study was measured using rearrest. That means that the study included only those crimes for which a released prisoner was arrested. If measured using self-reported offending data, the recidivism rate assuredly would have been higher.

In short, America now faces a situation in which ever-greater numbers of individuals are returning to communities and almost all of these individuals continue to commit crime. The "glass half full" view of the situation is that considerable room for improvement exists, especially given the ubiquity of reoffending among people released from prison. The "glass half empty" view, however, is that we may not be able to make much of a dent in recidivism rates given the commitment to increased incarceration. Of course, it can be argued that incarceration helps society by reducing crime through incapacitation or general deterrent effects. So, even if recidivism rates remain high or increase, perhaps that negative is offset by the positive of overall decreased rates of crime. There is some evidence—although far from compelling—to suggest warrant for such optimism, as will be discussed in later chapters. Regardless, recidivism stands as a concern in its own right—few of us want someone who may reoffend moving next door to where we live.

CRIMINAL JUSTICE EXPENDITURES

Putting aside such concerns, the stakes involved in criminal justice policy can be highlighted by turning to economic considerations. Given the growth in the criminal justice system, it perhaps should come as no surprise that criminal justice expenditures have dramatically increased as well, as is evident from Figure 5. From 1982 to 2006, the United States increased its investment in police more than fivefold, from $19 billion to more than $99 billion. It increased its investment in corrections almost eightfold during the same time span, from $9 billion to $69 billion. And it increased its investment in the judiciary—which is required to process the large influx of new cases—from almost $8 billion to $47 billion. Adding all functions together, from 1982 to 2006, criminal justice expenditures rose by 500 percent, from $36 billion to $215 billion. Inflation accounts only for $30 billion or so of that increase. The burden of these new costs has largely fallen to local jurisdictions and to states, not the federal government. Figure 6 depicts the trends in criminal justice expenditures by level of government. The most dramatic increase, in absolute

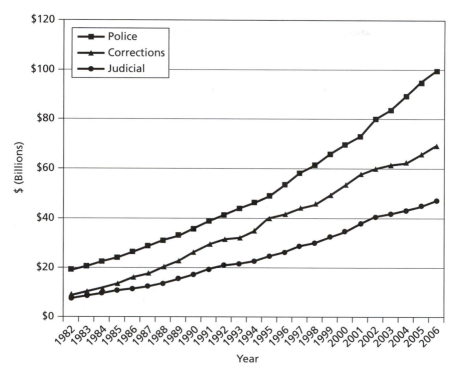

FIGURE 5 Criminal justice expenditures by function, 1982–2006.

Source: Bureau of Justice Statistics. 2009. *Justice Expenditure and Employment Extracts.* Washington, D.C.: U.S. Department of Justice. Available online: http://www.ojp.usdoj.gov/bjs/glance/tables/exptyptab.htm (accessed October 1, 2009).

amounts, clearly lies with local jurisdictions. In 1982, localities had $21 billion in criminal justice expenditures. By 2006, their expenditures increased to $109 billion. States' investments in criminal justice rose almost as dramatically during this same time period, from $11 billion to $69 billion. And federal expenditures rose from $4 billion to $36 billion. As of 2006, roughly 51 percent of all criminal justice expenditures were borne by local jurisdictions, 32 percent by states, and 17 percent by the federal government.

EVIDENCE FOR CURRENT CRIMINAL JUSTICE POLICIES

Set against a backdrop of dramatic increases in criminal justice funding and in federal funding for a wide range of crime prevention and crime control policies is the pressing concern that too little research exists to support the selection and continued support of many of these policies. Several criminal justice policy reviews that have emerged in recent years suggest, in fact, that

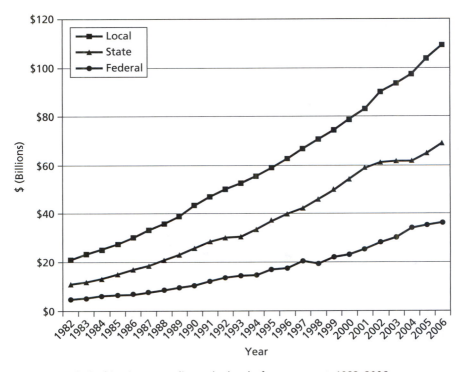

FIGURE 6 Criminal justice expenditures by level of government, 1982–2006.

Source: Bureau of Justice Statistics. 2009. *Justice Expenditure and Employment Extracts.* Washington, D.C.:
U.S. Department of Justice. Available online: http://www.ojp.usdoj.gov/bjs/glance/tables/expgov.htm
(accessed October 1, 2009).

most criminal justice policies lack a strong empirical foundation. A National
Academy of Sciences review found, for example, that "scientifically strong
impact evaluations of [crime prevention and crime control] programs, while
improving, are still uncommon in the context of the overall number of programs that have received funding." Similar critiques have been leveled against
many different parts of the criminal justice system.

In various ways, this book will tackle the question of whether the criminal
justice policy investments of the past several decades have been wise choices.
What I will argue is that, by and large, local and state governments, and the
country as a whole, lack an institutionalized foundation for conducting the
types of research necessary to produce wise choices, much less to show that
existing choices are sensible. The result? Too little evidence exists to support
many if not most of the policies and practices that constitute the nation's
criminal justice system.

Ultimately, the failure to use research to inform criminal justice policy
constitutes a profound mistake with real-world consequences. Society spends a
great deal of resources on catching and punishing as well as treating offenders.

It has spent even more in recent decades. Even so, a limited supply of funds exists. We cannot, for example, build enough prisons to house every person who commits a crime. As with our individual financial decisions, mistakes about the allocation of large amounts of time and money can have dramatic effects. They can, for example, contribute to a lack of accountability; to a failure to identify or implement evidence-based policies; and, more generally, to ineffective and inefficient criminal justice policies.

INFLUENCES ON CRIMINAL JUSTICE POLICY

Given the pronounced increase in calls for greater government accountability and evidence-based practice, why does so much of the criminal justice system and the laws, practices, programs, rules, and protocols that constitute it remain unexamined and largely hidden in the equivalent of a "black box"? Why, more generally, is there a seemingly large disjuncture between calls for accountability and evidence-based policy and the realization of these calls through the research base necessary to have accountability or to identify evidence-based policies that are effective and cost efficient?

Many scholars have tackled these questions, including the broader one of why any criminal justice policy is adopted. In the following discussion, I describe several possible explanations. In so doing, I recognize that any adequate account about the emergence of specific policies or policy trends typically must reference a multitude of social and economic conditions and their interactions with one another over time. Nonetheless, this discussion serves to highlight the many and varied forces that can conspire against rational, evidence-based policy. In turn, it underscores the need for systematic integration of evaluation research into policy development, implementation, and assessment to help address this situation.

POLITICIZATION OF CRIME

One prominent explanation for why many criminal justice policies emerge can be summarized in one word—politicization. From this perspective, policy makers focus on crime to advance their interests. That is, they are motivated more by the thought of political gain than by a sincere belief that crime will be affected. Of course, many policy makers sincerely believe that crime merits attention not because of any political gain that may accrue to them but because, in their view, it constitutes a substantial problem.

Nonetheless, the politicization of crime has featured prominently in many compelling accounts of crime policies. What benefits, though, does this strategy—what some scholars characterize as "symbolic politics"— confer upon policy makers? Among other things, it may enhance their electability and divert attention from other, more divisive social problems.

It also, as scholars have argued, may enhance state power and the interests of an elite social class at the expense of the socially disadvantaged. For example, David Garland, who has written at great length about the crime policies of the 1980s and 1990s in the United States and in Great Britain, has noted: "Crime—together with associated 'underclass' behaviors such as drug abuse, teenage pregnancy, single parenthood, and welfare dependency—came to function as a rhetorical legitimation for social and economic policies that effectively punished the poor and as a justification for the development of a strong disciplinary state."

Why would crime serve as a convenient target for generating political capital among policy makers and, more generally, for increasing state power? Garland's work highlights that the ideological rhetoric employed in policy discussions in the 1980s and 1990s viewed individual behavior as resulting largely; if not exclusively, from self-discipline and moral character, not from the social contexts and conditions in which individuals reside. Such a view, which represents a philosophical orientation more than a scientific one, dovetails with the more general political ideologies of the conservative governments that prevailed in both the United States and the United Kingdom during these decades. Garland and others have argued that support for a broad array of conservative policies at this time was facilitated by focusing on crime and, in particular, by framing crime policy decisions using the language of conservative political ideologies.

Crime served as a useful target for additional reasons. One is that violent crime worsened during the 1980s. Another is that little political fallout occurs when policy makers focus on criminals. In fact, a failure to establish a record of being tough on criminals can substantially limit a policy maker's career, as occurred when George H. W. Bush ran the now-famous Willy Horton advertisement in his campaign against Massachusetts Governor Michael Dukakis for the presidency. Horton, incarcerated in a Massachusetts prison for murder, was released on furlough during Dukakis's time as governor; while on furlough, he raped a woman. The advertisement was widely viewed as contributing to Dukakis's defeat. Another prominent example rose in Texas in the early 1990s. Ann Richards, a Democrat, ran against George W. Bush for governor in 1994 and, unlike Dukakis, attempted to compete in part on the basis of her ability to be tougher on crime than her opponent. Ultimately, she, too, lost out to a conservative candidate who more strongly emphasized a tough-on-crime platform.

Arguments about the politicization of crime have emerged in an era in which conservatives arguably have had a greater role in dictating the tenor of criminal justice policy. Concomitantly, "get tough" approaches to crime and punishment have predominated. It would be reasonable, therefore, to assume that conservatives politicize crime and liberals do not. The assumption would, however, be incorrect. Crime has been and can be politicized by conservatives and liberals alike, as the Ann Richards example illustrates and as research attests.

FALSE DICHOTOMIES

Whether one accepts arguments about the politicization of crime, politics may influence criminal justice policy in other ways. For example, the nature of political debates, especially in contexts where two political parties predominate, tends to create false either-or dichotomies. In any democracy, policy makers must strive to gauge the public will and determine which social problems merit attention and what should be done about them. Necessarily, then, policy makers must reduce a great deal of complexity to simplified descriptions of the problems and the options for addressing them. Such an approach unfortunately lends itself to creating overly simplified distillations, and, indeed, to two-scenario options—there is X way of doing things or Y way of doing things. That approach neatly accords with a conservative-liberal dichotomy. Even so, it frames discussions and debates in terms that frequently misrepresent reality.

One prominent example consists of the rehabilitation versus punishment divide in American politics. Media accounts present anyone who promotes rehabilitation as a liberal and anyone who promotes punishment as conservative. The problem lies in the fact that few policy makers hew exclusively to one or the other dimension but instead differ in the extent to which they support both approaches to managing and sanctioning offenders. In a class I teach on juvenile justice, students frequently express surprise that the public strongly supports punishment of violent offenders and that the public also strongly supports providing rehabilitative services to such offenders. On the face of it, the students seem justified in their surprise. How could the public support both punishment and rehabilitation? Observe, however, that nothing about one view precludes the other. Consider, for example, that parents typically employ many different strategies—including a diverse array of "carrots" and "sticks"—for managing children who break rules and, more generally, for socializing them into the ways of the world. Few of us would level the critique that doing so is necessarily inconsistent or odd. By extension, there should appear nothing especially notable or contradictory about the public supporting diverse approaches to addressing juvenile or adult crime.

Such nuances frequently get lost in the policy-making arena, which all too often glosses over nuance and substitutes in its place dichotomies that not only simplify but also distort public views. To illustrate, a policy maker who holds the view that punishment and rehabilitation should be weighted equally may nonetheless feel compelled to emphasize one more than the other. The tenor of a political debate may require such a packaging of one's views. Recent news accounts about, say, a felon who committed a violent crime while on probation, may force policy makers to articulate more extreme versions of their viewpoints. As the Willy Horton example illustrates, such possibilities are far from hypothetical. During the 1980s and 1990s, it would have been difficult for many policy makers to be elected or reelected if they argued for policies that equally balanced rehabilitation and punishment.

Long ago, Benjamin Franklin held up as a virtue the notion that we should do everything in moderation. Following that dictum may not always lead to good outcomes, but in some cases it would appear to be the better part of wisdom. In the case of criminal justice policies, extreme policies constitute the equivalent of stock-market speculation, where you sink all your eggs into one company's stock in the hopes that it will produce fabulous returns. That may happen. However, it may not, and on the face of it, such returns seem highly unlikely. Criminology offers little by way of research that establishes whether punishment or rehabilitation produces the most or greatest impact. Clearly, punishment seems like the hands-down winner if the goal is retribution. Not everyone weights retribution in the same manner, however. More relevant is the fact that if our goal is reduced recidivism, the research evidence to date would suggest that either can be effective, depending on how they are implemented. That is, punishment can reduce recidivism, but it also may increase it, and rehabilitation may reduce recidivism, but it also may have no impact. Much rests on the precise type of punishment or rehabilitation and how exactly it is implemented. In short, when policy makers create or are pushed into accepting false dichotomies, the likelihood increases that ineffective and inefficient criminal justice policies will emerge.

SWINGS FROM ONE EXTREME TO ANOTHER

The false dichotomy problem is compounded by a similar yet slightly different political dynamic. Specifically, the nature of many political systems, and certainly of America's political system, leads to dramatic swings in policy. In the United States, for example, the country's crime policy approaches have changed dramatically from one era to the next, most recently transitioning away from the rehabilitation-oriented, crime prevention approaches that prevailed in the 1960s and 1970s and toward the more punishment-oriented approaches that have prevailed since. Thomas Bernard has illustrated this problem in his account of the juvenile justice system, noting that, regardless of juvenile crime trends, policy makers and the public become increasingly disenchanted with the current set of policies in place and substitute in their place policies that lie at the other end of the philosophical spectrum. As a result, juvenile justice tends to cycle back and forth between lenient policies and harsh, punitive policies. Such transitions frequently occur with little to no assessment of the precise problems, the effectiveness of the current set of policies, or the best mix of strategies for addressing crime and improving criminal justice operations. The end result is a costly transitioning from one set of approaches to another and the whole-cloth adoption of many new strategies that have been unevaluated and that, after implementation, remain so.

As the preceding discussions have indicated, the latest swing in American criminal justice policy has been toward "get tough" punishment-oriented philosophies. The effect of this swing arguably has been and will be greater than earlier ones given the dramatic growth in America's prison population and the attendant fixed commitment of resources for incarceration. It is relatively easy to dismantle a particular law or program. Politically, however, it is not easy to generate support for dismantling prisons, and indeed, one rarely reads accounts where a given state's prison capacity declines. In the past decade, many policy makers have derided the growth in prison populations, noting that it cannot be sustained and calling for "get smart" rather than "get tough" options. Even so, prison populations have steadily continued to grow. One benefit of the situation may be that it reduces the likelihood of a dramatic swing toward a different set of policies. Yet it also reduces the ability to achieve what might constitute a more balanced and ultimately more effective portfolio of strategies for managing, reducing, and preventing crime and for achieving justice.

BAD CASES MAKE FOR BAD POLICIES

Another influence on policy is a political dynamic in which cases that are not representative of most others serve as the basis for new laws and policies. The expression "bad cases make for bad laws" captures this idea. In any given year, atrocious examples—such as the Willy Horton case—exist of the criminal justice system having failed. The problem arises from the fact that virtually any policy, no matter how effective, will include failures. Consider that, on average, and as shown in Figure 4, roughly two-thirds of individuals released from prison will be rearrested within three years. Suppose a program in a particular state could reduce that rate of recidivism to 50 percent. Such a reduction would be greater than many of the best programs. Still, a large number of released inmates would still go on to commit more crime, providing endless fodder for complaints that somehow the criminal justice system is "broke" and requires fundamentally new responses. Of course, if one is going to complain, it helps to focus on the most extreme cases. The problem lies in the fact that such cases not only always occur but also are just that: extreme and not representative of the overwhelming majority of offenders or cases that enter the juvenile or criminal justice systems.

This situation is complicated by the fact that policy makers attempt to respond to the public and, at the same time, frequently must respond to issues as they are depicted in media accounts. So, if the media, as much research attests, is biased toward publicizing the most sensational crimes, policy makers feel compelled to respond. The public's lack of understanding of many aspects of the criminal justice system, including the amount of crime and the levels and quality of punishment and rehabilitative services, further compounds this problem. A dynamic thus ensues in which sensational cases, not the everyday ones, drive criminal justice policy. Indeed, one might argue that a "perfect storm" of distortion emerges because many public opinion polls ask only a few questions, focusing on sensational cases, and then the media publicizes these responses. Policy makers proceed to interpret such results as representative of public opinion about crime and its solutions, although the findings speak only to public views about a very particular type of crime.

In reality, public views about crime and justice are complicated, nuanced, and highly variable depending on such factors as the issue involved and the nature of the question wording and the response options. For example, support for the death penalty drops roughly 20 percentage points when respondents are asked to express their level of support in a context where life in prison without the option of parole is included as part of the set of options for sanctioning murderers.

SYMBOLIC GESTURES

Paralleling and contributing to these problems is a situation in which policy makers frequently feel pushed into doing something—anything, in fact—that demonstrates their responsiveness to crime as a problem. The result can be a penchant for responding to the latest crisis with some type of new, and typically extreme, response rather than to deliberate assessment of the problem and what can and should be done about it. In recent decades, for example, many new penalties have been imposed on convicted felons, creating a penumbra of "invisible" or hidden punishments, such as restrictions on employment, housing, welfare, and voting, all of which go well beyond the traditional notion of having inmates serve their time and then reenter society as citizens with the full set of rights they had prior to incarceration. Perhaps such restrictions were needed to create a more powerful general deterrent effect to would-be offenders, and perhaps they help to reduce the recidivism of the released prisoners. There is, however, little theoretical or empirical research to support such a claim.

These additional invisible punishments arguably emerged not from a considered assessment of the need for them or their effectiveness, but rather from policy makers' desire to provide symbolic gestures of their responsiveness to public concern about crime. Here, again, it is important to recognize that such arguments assume a level of political calculation that does not necessarily accord with reality. For example, many policy makers clearly want to serve the public interest and do so with a sincere commitment to pursuing policies that they feel are needed and will be effective.

PUBLIC OPINION AND POLICY MAKERS' MISUNDERSTANDING OF IT

Reviews of public opinion research consistently reveal that public views about crime are, as discussed earlier, complicated and nuanced. Studies typically show that the public supports a range of strategies, some rehabilitative in nature and some punishment oriented, for reducing crime and that the level of support varies over time. They show that the majority of the public views prison as a breeding ground for crime but that they also, while supportive of rehabilitation, have doubts about the effectiveness of rehabilitation as it occurs in practice. As Julian Roberts and Mike Hough found in their review of public opinion research on views toward rehabilitation in the prison system, "People around the world support the principle that prisons should rehabilitate offenders, however, they do not believe that in practice it succeeds in doing so."

The public also tends to know very little about the criminal justice system as it operates in practice. With respect to prisons, for example, "the public around the world underestimates the severity of life inside prison." Indeed, many view prisoners as having an "easy ride" that amounts to a vacation with no work responsibilities and innumerable opportunities to play and watch television in well-heated or air-conditioned housing. Not surprisingly, then, studies frequently show that the public supports lengthier and tougher prison sentences. The unfamiliarity with criminal justice extends to more than just prison, however. As Francis Cullen and his colleagues have noted, for many areas of criminal justice, "including knowledge of trends in crime rates, of the prevalence of violent crimes, of recidivism rates, of specific criminal laws, of legal reforms, of legal rights in the criminal justice process, and of the extent to which the insanity plea is used successfully—the lack of knowledge [among the public] is widespread." This lack of knowledge "allows cynical use of simplistic slogans and policies that respond to the public's emotional needs but do not address the substantive challenge," as Alfred Blumstein has noted.

Given this lack of knowledge and the complexity of public opinion, it should not be surprising that the views of the public do not readily translate into simple either-or (e.g., rehabilitate or punish) options. As a case in point, studies find that even when the public believes prison time is too lenient and filled with too many amenities, they do not "necessarily want to make it more aversive," but rather want to do away with idleness and replace it with work.

Policy makers appear to operate within a political context in which the complexity of public views sometimes must be downplayed or ignored. As but one example, many of the "get tough" reforms of the 1990s emerged from policy makers' assumption that the public called for such reforms and not for any other approaches. However, studies have shown that policy makers overestimated how much the public wanted punitive sanctions and underestimated how much they wanted such things as vocational training; conjugal visits for inmates; counseling and therapy; and, more generally, rehabilitation. One striking example of this phenomenon can be seen in a study of Michigan policy makers, which found that "while only 12 percent of policy makers believed the public would support rehabilitation as a criminal justice objective, in reality two-thirds of the public took this view."

In a democracy, we expect that the public should at least inform policy discussions and debates. It should not necessarily dictate policy. Even so, public views are foundational to democracy. For that reason, one of the more striking findings from public opinion research is the fact that policy makers frequently misestimate or distort, whether consciously or not, public views about crime and its causes and solutions. Given the way in which political decision making occurs, such misunderstanding helps contribute to policies that not only reflect extreme and unrepresentative cases but also fail to reflect public sentiment.

BELIEF IN "SILVER BULLET" CAUSES AND SOLUTIONS TO CRIME

Another factor that contributes to ineffective policy is the seemingly wide-spread belief among policy makers that there exist "silver bullet" causes of criminal justice problems and "silver bullet" solutions to them A silver bullet approach is effective when, among other things, the following conditions hold: the targeted cause is truly a cause of the outcome of interest (e.g., criminal behavior), the cause is widespread, and the cause is easily amenable to modification. These conditions rarely if ever hold true in criminal justice, and yet many—although certainly not all—policies take a largely single-minded focus toward reducing crime.

To illustrate, a plethora of laws and programs have emerged that focus on illegal drug use and selling. Many of these efforts create enhanced penalties for such crimes, or for committing other crimes while using illegal drugs, and are widely viewed as contributing to the dramatic growth in the correctional system in recent decades. At the same time, drug courts, which specialize in handling drug offenders and drug-using offenders, have proliferated since the early 1990s.

In part, the focus on drugs appears to be fueled by a belief that illegal drug use causes crime and that it does so in a dramatic way. Notably, however, it remains unclear how strong the relationship between individual drug use and offending is and whether the relationship is causal. In asserting a causal relationship, one might point to the fact that many people in prison have or had drug problems or were using drugs at the time of their offense. If that were the only problem that prisoners exhibited, the causal claim would be easier to accept. Yet the reality is that the profile of the typical prisoner leads to a host of factors—such as mental illness, homelessness, unemployment, abuse—that could be the cause of their behavior, including their drug use. Complicating matters is the fact that, while various sanctions and treatments can reduce drug problems, resolution of these problems is not simple; relapse is common, and many interventions are costly, especially if implemented as intended. In short, two of the conditions for an effective silver bullet solution do not appear to be present when it comes to drug-related offending. At the same time, a large body of research points to many other factors that cause crime and to the likelihood that the most effective approaches to crime prevention involve a focus on multiple causes of offending.

To be clear, there seems little doubt that drugs play some role in crime and offending. It remains unclear, however, whether a largely exclusive focus on drug-related crime would substantially reduce overall crime or recidivism rates. Certainly, a balanced approach to reducing crime might involve a focus on illegal drugs. The silver bullet approach, however, places a primary emphasis on drugs. For example, when a criminal justice system gives priority to drug treatment, it typically must reduce its emphasis on other approaches to resolving crime, if only because most systems operate within a zero-sum environment in which a limited pool of resources exist. So, if jurisdiction decides to create a drug court, it necessarily will have fewer resources to devote specialized attention to other populations.

It may be argued that many jurisdictions and many correctional systems embrace a diversified portfolio of approaches, not a silver bullet approach, to fighting crime. In reality, however, priority is frequently given to a select few approaches. Consider, for example, that while drug courts have proliferated nationally, few other such specialized (e.g., mental health, drug, community) courts have enjoyed such popularity. Consider, too, at a national level, the dramatic increase in prison systems, which is tantamount to a belief that increased incarceration, more than a range of other approaches, can substantially reduce crime. Here, again, the point is not that such approaches are ineffective. Rather, it is that much criminal justice policy making is aimed at finding silver bullet solutions rather than at creating comprehensive, research-based approaches to crime reduction.

LIMITED PRODUCTION OF POLICY RESEARCH

To this point, many of the factors that have been described as influencing criminal justice policy and that serve as barriers to research-based criminal justice policy making have centered on political factors. What about research itself, or, perhaps more precisely, the lack of research, as a barrier to better policies? As a general matter, most accounts—including American Society of Criminology presidential addresses—wax pessimistic about the influence of research on policy. They point to innumerable instances in which policies get adopted with little to no attention to prim research and in which poorly conceived policies continue unabated and unevaluated. Even so, a number of scholars have pointed to evidence that, at least on occasion, research influences policy. If we were to average the two views, the situation might be aptly described as one where, by and large, research provides little by way of a positive influence on policy but where many exceptions exist. Assuming that this assessment is correct, the question emerges as to why research had relatively little influence on policy. Here, I will briefly touch on some of the major factors scholars have identified.

The first and perhaps most important problem is the lack of an institutionalized foundation for systematically integrating evaluation research into decisions about criminal justice policies and for monitoring and assessing the criminal justice system as a whole. For example, federal funding for crime and justice research is minimal relative to investments in other policy areas. At the state, county, city, and municipal levels, few agencies allot much funding for research, and what funding exists typically is provided for compiling highly descriptive annual reports that say little about the need for or the design, implementation, effectiveness, or efficiency of a range of policies.

This situation is compounded by a second problem: specifically, policy evaluation research—what sometimes gets referred to as "applied research" because of the focus on applying research to policy—traditionally gets short shrift within universities. Many factors have contributed to this dynamic. By historical standards, criminology is a newcomer in the academic world. As Joan Petersilia has noted, criminology was not offered as a major in universities until the early 1930s, and it was not until 1950 that the first criminology program formally emerged. As a newcomer, considerable pressure existed to elevate the status of the discipline to a "science," which meant focusing on questions about the causes of crime and not necessarily the solutions to it.

Not surprisingly, such circumstances can lead to a bias away from policy research and toward so-called basic research. In turn, not only do university scholars tend to shy away from policy research, but they also tend not to train graduate students in the art and science of evaluation research. In addition, the orientation toward basic research diminishes the likelihood of developing strong institutional ties between university researchers and local, state, and federal criminal justice system agencies. Notably, when criminology programs first emerged, practitioners held more sway in the classroom, "but since the academic has largely replaced the practitioner in the classroom and in research, the link has grown weaker and, with it, that kind of immediate influence."

Even when scholars undertake policy-related research, they typically do not translate their findings in a way that is accessible to policy makers and practitioners. Other researchers have the training and time to sift through myriad statistical analyses; policy makers and practitioners typically do not. Even so, translating sophisticated analyses so that nonresearchers can easily digest them can be challenging, especially if, as is frequently the case, many caveats and limitations bear emphasis. To illustrate, a study may show that a given program reduces recidivism, but that finding may apply only to similar programs, such as those that serve similar clients. It may be that the effect was not particularly large. It may be that only drug recidivism was reduced but not violent or property recidivism. It also may be that the effect only emerged when participants fully completed all aspects of the program. Scholars are trained to give considerable weight to such nuances and to stick closely to the limits of what the type and quality of data and analyses allow. Consequently, it can be a struggle to try to discuss the results in a way that runs counter to their training. That struggle can turn into resistance if they feel that policy makers or the media purposely or unwittingly distort such results.

A third problem is the limited funding for criminal justice and crime policy research. Petersilia has remarked that "the federal government is, by orders of magnitude, the largest funder of research on criminal justice policy." However, federal funding for criminal justice research has been nominal and remains so. Consider the funding of the National Institute of Justice (NIJ), which serves as the main federal agency focused on criminal justice evaluation and policy researches. Writing in 1995, Blumstein and Petersilia observed that NIJ's budget "has been essentially flat (with slight declines in real terms) since 1981 and has stayed in the range of about $20 million to $30 million since then—well short of a priority." By 2008, more than a decade after that observation, funding for the agency had increased to $37 million, a modest increase but still well short of constituting a priority, especially in a context where federal and state criminal justice expenditures, well into the billions of dollars, escalated dramatically and where baseline levels of funding were minimal compared to federal investments in other social policy arenas. The point was made bluntly by Petersilia, who, in 1991, commented that "for every U.S. citizen, federal funders spend $32 on health research, but only 13 cents on criminal justice research." That situation remains largely the same today despite the dramatic increases in violent crime and in criminal justice system expenditures that occurred during the decades after Petersilia made this observation.

A fourth problem has been the relative lack of investment in high-quality impact evaluations that rely on experimental designs. The gold standard for impact evaluations is the experiment, precisely because, if well conducted, the results can be interpreted in a straightforward manner as indicating that a program "works" or does not. Most criminal justice policies go unevaluated, and the few that are evaluated typically get examined using nonexperimental research designs. The use of the latter type of designs can be problematic because they tend to find positive impacts of programs in cases where the impacts are not real. Consequently, the results of many studies rest on shaky foundations and so lead to a situation in which researchers must be highly cautious in reporting results. A typical example, created for illustrative purposes here, would be a study in which the hypothetical conclusion reads as follows:

> The results here suggest that program X may reduce the recidivism of moderate-risk male offenders but not necessarily affect the recidivism of high-risk or low-risk offenders or of female offenders. In addition, the results should be interpreted with caution given that the study sample consisted of a highly select group, including inmates who volunteered to participate in the study, and given that many acts of recidivism may have gone unreported to law enforcement. Indeed, because the study could not fully address important potential selection effects, the estimated effects of the program may be biased. Put differently, were the selection effects better addressed, the study may have found no difference between the treatment and comparison groups in their rates of recidivism.

A policy maker would understandably view such an account as not especially helpful in making a decision about whether to close down, continue, or expand the program.

The problem lies not just with a lack of experiments in criminal justice policy research but also with a lack of high-quality quasi-experimental research (i.e., studies that attempt to approximate an experimental design). All too often, the design of such research is weak, and the result tends to be a situation in which the positive impacts of a program are overstated. Frequently, too, experimental and quasi-experimental research designs rely on sample sizes that are too small to allow one to detect anything other than an extremely large impact. Many policies and programs that may be effective thus are reported not to be.

A fifth problem is that researchers frequently focus their attention on the problems and policies that policy makers emphasize or that constitute the "hot topics" of the day. In so doing, they ignore a wide range of important policies and policy emphases. Francis Cullen and Paul Gendreau have drawn attention, for example, to the fact that in the 1970s, a period when rehabilitation increasingly was viewed as ineffective, "the study of corrections became largely the study of social problems," and so "criminologists paid scant attention to 'what works' to change offenders." Indeed, this bias was institutionalized through publishing biases: "[scholars] were praised and rewarded with opportunities to publish their research when they could show that an acclaimed program did not live up to its billing." Criminologists thus tended to emphasize the negative over the positive and did so in part because of a political climate in which rehabilitation came into disrepute.

Other barriers related to the production of research exist as well. For example, evaluations sometimes take years to complete, but policy makers frequently need and want results sooner. This problem is amplified by the lack of institutionalized linkages among universities, research organizations, and the agencies that constitute the criminal justice system, in part because the absence of such linkages delays access to data.

All is not bleak, however. As Petersilia has emphasized, research can and does exert a positive effect on policy. It has "helped shape the way police are deployed," "demonstrated the effectiveness of career criminal programs in prosecutors' offices," "improved the ability to classify offenders and to predict recidivism," "provided information about the relationship between drug abuse and crime" and "participation in rehabilitation programs [does not] necessarily [reduce] recidivism." That said, substantial improvements could be made for potentially little cost.

CONCLUSION

America stands at a unique juncture in the history of its criminal justice system. Unprecedented growth in this system and in criminal justice expenditures, along with an ever-growing panoply of policies, create substantial concerns about whether the growth, expenditures, and policies make sense. The evaluation hierarchy highlights some of the critical concerns. Have the growth and the investments been needed? Do the policies rest on sound theoretical grounds? Have they been well implemented? Do they achieve expected outcomes? And have the investments been allocated to the problems and policies where the greatest gain will accrue? By and large, and as subsequent chapters will argue, research is silent about such questions as they relate to the criminal justice system's many policies, practices, protocols and rules. In those cases where research exists, it sometimes waxes positive. However, it all too frequently suffers from critical problems or provides pessimistic or equivocal assessments.

This situation is cause for particular concern, especially given the unprecedented growth in the size and costs of the American criminal justice system and the more than 735,000 prisoners released back into society annually, more than two-thirds of whom will recidivate. The very real possibility exists that this growth and the many policies enacted in recent decades have done little to make the public safer or as safe as might be possible with investments in other approaches to crime control and prevention.

Juxtaposed against this situation is a context in which myriad forces—such as the politicization of crime and the belief in silver bullet solutions to crime—lead to continued creation of and investment in criminal justice policies that may not be the most effective or efficient. Policies will always result from a constellation of factors. Nonetheless, efforts to make criminal justice more accountable or to place it on a more evidence-based foundation will not likely succeed without more and better research. What is needed is a systematic approach to developing, monitoring, and assessing criminal justice policy.

DISCUSSION QUESTIONS

1. What is the value of measuring victimization?
2. Why are recidivism rates increasing and what does the "glass half empty" mean?
3. Is it incorrect to support both punishment of violent offenders and the rehabilitation of them?
4. Why is public view on crime complicated?
5. What makes criminal justice research important to implementing public policy?

PART II

✪

Police

Contemporary democratic societies debate whether police exist for protection or prevention. History doesn't resolve this debate, because police agencies have played many different and contradictory roles. Are the police to be concerned primarily with crime fighting or peace keeping? Should they be social workers with guns or gun-toters in social work? Should they be instruments of social change or defenders of the faith?

THREE ERAS OF AMERICAN POLICING

American policing is often described in terms of three historical periods: the political era (1840–1920), the professional era (1920–1970), and the community era (1970–Present). These eras are useful as a framework through which we can note differences in the organization of the policies, the primary tasks they are charged with, and the specific policies and strategies that they are instructed to follow.

The first era was the political era, which ran from 1840 through 1920. It was referred to as the political era because of the close ties that existed between the police and urban political leaders. Urban police often appeared to work for the mayor or the political party in power rather than for the citizens in general. Some jurisdictions issued guns and badges to white males who supported the mayor or those in political power. During this era the police focused on crime prevention and order maintenance by foot patrol. The officer on the beat dealt with crime, disorder, and other problems as they arose. In addition, the police in urban areas carried out service functions such as caring for derelicts, operating soup kitchens, regulating public health, and handling medical and social emergencies. Through their closeness to the communities they served, the police often enjoyed citizen support. As urbanization increased during the twentieth century, so did criticism of the influence of politics on the police in these urban enclaves. Efforts to reform the nature and organization of the police began, and reformers sought to make police into law enforcement professionals, reducing their connection to local politics.

The collapse of the political era gave rise to the professional era, which began in 1920 and lasted until 1970. The Progressive reform movement of the early twentieth century had a significant influence on policing. These typically educated, upper-middle class Progressives were interested in two primary goals: efficient government and the provision of government services to improve the conditions of the less fortunate. One of the goals was the removal of political influences, such as party politics and patronage, on government. When the Progressives applied these goals to the police, they envisioned professional law enforcement officials who would use modern technology to benefit the entire society, not just the local politicians. Reformers argued that the police should be a professional force, a nonpartisan agency of government committed to the highest ideals of public service. With the switch to professional policing came an emphasis on crime fighting as the prominent role of the police. Reemphasizing crime control instead of maintaining order probably did more than anything else to change the nature of American policing. This narrow focus on crime fighting severed many of the ties that the police had developed with communities they served. The 1960s were a time of social awakenings, with the civil rights and antiwar movements, urban riots, and rising crime rates. These cultural markers challenged many assumptions of the professional model. Although the police continued to portray their public identity as that of a crime fighting force, citizens recognized that the police were often ineffective in this role. Crime rates rose for many offenses, and the police were unable to change the perception that the quality of urban life was diminishing.

The 1970s revealed calls for a movement away from the overriding crime-fighting focus and toward greater emphasis on maintaining order and providing services to the community, which brought about the community-policing era that is still currently used. During this time, the complexities of police work were increasingly illustrated in academic and policy research. In their chapter "The Preventative Effects of Arrest on Intimate Partner Violence," Maxwell and his colleagues expand on the complexities of police work by discussing the inconsistent results of research on how police should handle intimate partner violence. They explain that originally research illustrated that arrest had a deterrent effect on intimate partner violence; however, once more studies were conducted, it appeared that other factors could be more important.

Critics argued that the professional style isolated the police from the communities and reduced their knowledge about and accountability to the neighborhoods they served. Motorized patrols sealed officers inside their patrol cars so that they had few personal contacts with citizens. Advocates of the community policing approach urged greater use of foot patrols so that officers would become known to citizens, which has the potential to maximize cooperation with the police. They believe that through attention to little problems, the police may not only reduce disorder and fear, but also improve public attitudes toward policing. Wilson and Keeling expand on this idea in their chapter, "Broken Windows: The Police and Neighborhood Safety." Their research illustrates that the residents of neighborhoods that have foot patrols feel safer than the residents of neighborhoods that do not have foot patrols. Through a problem-oriented approach to policing, officers should identify the underlying causes of problems such as rowdy teenagers, spouse batterers, and abandoned buildings used as drug houses. By addressing various problems, small or large, within neighborhoods, the police can reduce disorder and the fear of crime; however, in his chapter, "Militarizing the Police," Kraska claims that law enforcement agencies are becoming more aggressive, even though they claim to have a community oriented approach. Kraska bases his claim on data that show a rise in the number and normalization of police paramilitary units.

NEW CHALLENGES FOR COMMUNITY-ORIENTED POLICING

Since the 1970s, the police have been more focused on the community and maintaining order; however, recently the police have encountered new challenges in community policing. In the past few decades, issues such as immigration, terrorism, and protest movements, such as the Occupy movements, have presented new trials for the police.

Terrorism

Following the 9/11 attacks terrorism has become a highly salient aspect of law enforcement. It is now clear that police play an important role in investigating local terrorist threats and protecting vulnerable targets. These duties add a number of new dimensions to policing that extend beyond the normal functions of community protection and crime prevention. Clarke and Newman expand on these issues in their chapter, "Terrorism and Local Police." They examine the new roles and functions the police have to take on, and how these new roles are changing policing.

The police now have new responsibilities to help protect the community against local terrorist threats. For example, it is becoming more common to give police officers fixed geographic responsibilities as a means of preventing local terrorism. An officer who works in a specific community for an extended period of time is better able to gather intelligence on the residents of that community and their activities. It is now the responsibility of police officers to examine their jurisdiction and determine what major areas could be targets for terrorist attacks. They are encouraged to conduct complex analysis on the likelihood of terrorist attacks occurring at these locations. Along with this is their responsibility to develop crisis strategies in the event of a terrorist attack in their assigned location.

Not only are police involved in protecting citizens from crime, but they are also necessary for reducing the fear of crime among citizens. Now, the police's role in reducing citizens' fear of crime has been extended to reducing their fear of terrorism as well. After September 11, 2001, citizens' fear of another terrorist attack rose substantially. More than 10 years later, fear of terrorism is not quite as high, but it is still a concern to citizens. Police could help ease the fears of citizens by increasing their use of community policing, which research has shown can make citizens feel safer.

Along with the new responsibilities given to the police to help prevent terrorism, come new practices and procedures. Between 2003 and 2007, fusion centers were created as a way for law enforcement departments to share information and analyze possibilities of domestic terrorist threats. These centers bring together all of the scattered information on crime and terrorist activities. With fusion centers, government agencies and state and local law enforcement can share intelligence. The police can also use Graphing Information Systems (GIS) mapping technology to plot crime data on a digitized geographic map of an area. This crime data can be analyzed and compared with other outside data sources to prevent local attacks. Crime prevention through Environmental Design (CPTED) can also be used to help protect against terrorism. This strategy emphasizes that future terrorism and crime can be prevented by designing physical environments in ways that minimize the incidence and fear of crime. This can be done by increasing surveillance and controlling access to buildings and neighborhoods, as well as increasing a sense of security for citizens.

Immigration

Policing immigration has become the enforcement of a national legal issue at the local level. Local governments are now asking their police departments to act more aggressively in their enforcement of immigration laws. Like policing terrorism, local police are forced to add another role that goes beyond their normal everyday duties. Decker and colleagues examine the enforcement of federal immigration laws at the local level in greater detail, in their chapter, "Policing Immigration: Federal Laws and Local Police." They find that police departments approach the enforcement of illegal immigration differently, and they argue that the reason is a lack of clear policy guidance.

Arizona has been at the forefront of the immigration debate since its creation of one of the strictest anti–illegal immigration laws. This law makes it a misdemeanor for an alien to be in the state of Arizona without carrying his or her required documentation at all times. According to this law, during "lawful stops, detention, or arrests," the police must determine the immigration status of the individual, if they have reasonable suspicion that the individual is an illegal immigrant. This law brings the police's new role in the controversial fight against illegal immigration to light. Now the police have the responsibility to determine the immigration status of individuals, mostly based on appearance. This law has been heavily debated, and has been accused of promoting racial profiling. Recently, the constitutionality of this law has come under review, and the United States Supreme Court stated that it would decide on the constitutionality of certain provisions of Arizona's immigration laws. The Supreme Court's ruling on this issue could have serious impacts on similar immigration laws adopted by other states, as well as future immigration laws.

The sheriff of Maricopa County in Arizona, Joe Arpaio, has been making headlines with his radical views on immigration, and his support for strict anti-illegal immigration laws. He is known for his crackdowns on illegal immigration and large scale "sweeps" of Hispanic neighborhoods. Recently, the Department of Justice conducted an investigation on the Arizona sheriff, and declared that Joe Arpaio was engaged in "unconstitutional policing," due to his unreasonable targeting of Latinos. The Department of Justice is questioning Arpaio's methods of reasonable suspicion. Their investigation finds that the sheriff encourages his officers to approach Latinos that are gathered in front of stores and ask for their documentation. This brings up questions on how to define probable cause, and how police use their discretion. In their chapter, "Suspicion and Discretion: Decision Making During Citizen Stops," Alpert and his colleagues expand on the issue of how minority status affects a police officer's decision to stop and question suspicious persons. Generally, courts tend to give police officers the benefit of the doubt when dealing with questions of discretion in street arrests.

Protest Movements

The Occupy movement is one of several non-violent movements that have presented police with new challenges and tools. This movement is characterized by protests toward economic and social inequalities, and is known for its slogan "we are the 99 percent." Protesters would like to see bank reforms, more equal distribution of income, more jobs, and less influence of corporations on politics. Occupy movements have been seen all over the United States, but some of the largest and most well-known have appeared in New York and California. Although the movement is characterized by non-violent protests, the members of the movement are still involved in civil disobedience. Also, it has been reported that crime has been taking place within the movement. These issues provide new challenges for police officers.

New York's Occupy movement, Occupy Wall Street, is one of the most well-known Occupy movements. These protesters were camping out and occupying Zucotti Park, which is located in New York's financial district. It was reported that crime was occurring in the park during the protest. Multiple incidents of dealing drugs, assault, and sexual assault were reported.

The police have had a difficult time arresting individuals for crimes within the Occupy movement though, because the protesters are reluctant to report the crimes; however, the police have arrested hundreds of protesters for crimes of civil disobedience. During one of the Occupy Wall Street protests, protesters flooded the streets near the New York Stock Exchange, blocking off intersections. The police arrested 177 of the protesters. Later, the police arrested 99 more protesters for attempting to block off the Brooklyn Bridge. Officials reported that seven police officers were injured during the struggle. This brings to light the potential risk of being a police officer. Waters and Ussery discuss the stressors involved in having a job that has potential risks, in their chapter, "Enforcing the Law: The Stress of Being a Police Officer." They also discuss the physical and psychological symptoms that can arise from these stressors.

Police use of force during protests has been highly controversial. Due to its controversial nature, the police have been using less lethal weapons against individuals. Weapons such as impact projectile weapons, irritant sprays, and conductive energy devices provide police with an intermediate level of force to control individuals. In their chapter "Less Than Lethal Use of Force," Vilke and Chan explore the lethality of these devices and examine the physiological and medical effects of each. Although some believe that weapons that use nonlethal force are a good tool for police officers, others believe that these weapons constitute excessive force. This issue was brought to light in the media in 2007, following a speech by Senator John Kerry at the University of Florida. During the question and answer session following the senator's speech, a student became belligerent and started cursing. Subsequently, the police removed the student, and during the struggle, a police officer stunned the student with a taser. This incident was best known for the phrase "don't tase me bro," which the student screamed while he was being tased. This example of use of nonlethal force by police caused a huge controversy, which lead to protest movements on the University of Florida campus.

WRITING ASSIGNMENTS

1. What are the pros and cons of each of the three eras of policing? Is our current era of policing the most appropriate?

2. Describe the discretion a police officer has. How does police discretion affect the criminal justice system?

3. What effect might policing terrorism and immigration have on local law enforcement?

4. Discuss the use of nonlethal weapons by police. Are these tools helpful or hurtful?

6

✦

Broken Windows:

The Police and

Neighborhood Safety

James Q. Wilson
George Kelling

The role of the police in the United States today is being reexamined. After almost a half-century of emphasis on professionalism, crime control, and efficiency, James Q. Wilson and George L. Kelling argue that there should be a shift in patrol strategy toward a focus on order maintenance and community accountability.

In the mid-1970s, the state of New Jersey announced a "Safe and Clean Neighborhoods Program," designed to improve the quality of community life in twenty-eight cities. As part of that program, the state provided money to help cities take police officers out of their patrol cars and assign them to walking beats. The governor and other state officials were enthusiastic about using foot patrol as a way of cutting crime, but many police chiefs were skeptical. Foot patrol, in their eyes, had been pretty much discredited. It reduced the mobility of the police, who thus had difficulty responding to citizen calls for service, and it weakened headquarters control over patrol officers.

Many police officers also disliked foot patrol, but for different reasons: it was hard work, it kept them outside on cold, rainy nights, and it reduced their chances for making a "good pinch." In some departments, assigning officers to foot patrol had been used as a form of punishment. And academic experts on policing doubted that foot patrol would have any impact on crime rates; it was,

Source: Wilson, James Q. & Kellings, G., "Broken Windows: The Police and Neighborhood Safety." Atlantic Monthly 249 (March 1982): 29–38. Reprinted with permission.

in the opinion of most, little more than a sop to public opinion. But since the state was paying for it, the local authorities were willing to go along.

Five years after the program started, the Police Foundation, in Washington, D.C., published an evaluation of the foot-patrol project. Based on its analysis of a carefully controlled experiment carried out chiefly in Newark, the foundation concluded, to the surprise of hardly anyone, that foot patrol had not reduced crime rates. But residents of the foot-patrolled neighborhoods seemed to feel more secure than persons in other areas, tended to believe that crime had been reduced, and seemed to take fewer steps to protect themselves from crime (staying at home with the doors locked, for example). Moreover, citizens in the foot-patrol areas had a more favorable opinion of the police than did those living elsewhere. And officers walking beats had higher morale, greater job satisfaction, and a more favorable attitude toward citizens in their neighborhoods than did officers assigned to patrol cars.

These findings may be taken as evidence that the skeptics were right—foot patrol has no effect on crime; it merely fools the citizens into thinking that they are safer. But in our view, and in the view of the authors of the Police Foundation study (of whom Kelling was one), the citizens of Newark were not fooled at all. They knew what the foot-patrol officers were doing, they knew it was different from what motorized officers do, and they knew that having officers walk beats did in fact make their neighborhoods safer.

But how can a neighborhood be "safer" when the crime rate has not gone down—in fact, may have gone up? Finding the answer requires first that we understand what most often frightens people in public places. Many citizens, of course, are primarily frightened by crime, especially crime involving a sudden, violent attack by a stranger. This risk is very real, in Newark as in many large cities. But we tend to overlook or forget another source of fear: the fear of being bothered by disorderly people—not violent people, nor, necessarily, criminals, but disreputable or obstreperous or unpredictable people: panhandlers, drunks, addicts, rowdy teenagers, prostitutes, loiterers, the mentally disturbed.

What foot-patrol officers did was to elevate, to the extent they could, the level of public order in these neighborhoods. Though the neighborhoods were predominantly black and the foot patrolmen were mostly white, this "order-maintenance" function of the police was performed to the general satisfaction of both parties.

One of us (Kelling) spent many hours walking with Newark foot-patrol officers to see how they defined "order" and what they did to maintain it. One beat was typical: a busy but dilapidated area in the heart of Newark, with many abandoned buildings, marginal shops (several of which prominently displayed knives and straight-edged razors in their windows), one large department store, and, most important, a train station and several major bus stops. Though the area was run-down, its streets were filled with people, because it was a major transportation center. The good order of this area was important not only to those who lived and worked there but also to many others who had to move through it on their way home, to supermarkets, or to factories.

The people on the street were primarily black; the officers who walked the street were white. The people made up of "regulars" and "strangers." Regulars included both "decent folk" and some drunks and derelicts who were always there but who "knew their place." Strangers were, well, strangers, and viewed suspiciously, sometimes apprehensively. The officer—call him Kelly—knew who the regulars were, and they knew him. As he saw his job, he was to keep an eye on strangers, and make certain that the disreputable regulars observed some informal but widely understood rules. Drunks and addicts could sit on the stoops, but could not lie down. People could drink on the side streets, but not on the main intersection. Bottles had to be in paper bags. Talking to, bothering, or begging from people waiting at the bus stop was strictly forbidden. If a dispute erupted between a businessman and a customer, the businessman was assumed to be right, especially if the customer was a stranger. If a stranger loitered, Kelly would ask him if he had any means of support and what his business was; if he gave unsatisfactory answers, he was sent on his way. Persons who broke the informal rules, especially those who bothered people waiting at bus stops, were arrested for vagrancy. Noisy teenagers were told to keep quiet.

These rules were defined and enforced in collaboration with the "regulars" on the street. Another neighborhood might have different rules, but these, everybody understood, were the rules for *this* neighborhood. If someone violated them, the regulars not only turned to Kelly for help but also ridiculed the violator. Sometimes what Kelly did could be described as "enforcing the law," but just as often it involved taking informal or extralegal steps to help protect what the neighborhood had decided was the appropriate level of public order. Some of the things he did probably would not withstand a legal challenge.

A determined skeptic might acknowledge that a skilled foot-patrol officer can maintain order but still insist that this sort of "order" has little to do with the real sources of community fear—that is, with violent crime. To a degree, that is true. But two things must be borne in mind. First, outside observers should not assume that they know how much of the anxiety now endemic in many big-city neighborhoods stems from a fear of "real" crime and how much from a sense that the street is disorderly, a source of distasteful, worrisome encounters. The people of Newark, to judge from their behavior and their remarks to interviewers, apparently assign a high value to public order, and feel relieved and reassured when the police help them maintain that order.

Second, at the community level, disorder and crime are usually inextricably linked, in a kind of developmental sequence. Social psychologists and police officers tend to agree that if a window in a building is broken *and is left unrepaired*, all the rest of the windows will soon be broken. This is as true in nice neighborhoods as in run-down ones. Window breaking does not necessarily occur on a large scale because some areas are inhabited by determined window breakers whereas others are populated by window lovers; rather, one unrepaired broken window is a signal that no one cares, and so breaking more windows costs nothing. (It has always been fun.)

Philip Zimbardo, a Stanford psychologist, reported in 1969 on some experiments testing the broken-window theory. He arranged to have an automobile without license plates parked with its hood up on a street in the Bronx and a comparable automobile on a street in Palo Alto, California. The car in the Bronx was attacked by "vandals" within ten minutes of its "abandonment." The first to arrive were a family—father, mother, and young son—who removed the radiator and battery. Within twenty-four hours, virtually everything of value had been removed. Then random destruction began—windows were smashed, parts torn off, upholstery ripped. Children began to use the car as a playground. Most of the adult "vandals" were well-dressed, apparently clean-cut whites. The car in Palo Alto sat untouched for more than a week. Then Zimbardo smashed part of it with a sledgehammer. Soon, passersby were joining in. Within a few hours, the car had been turned upside down and utterly destroyed. Again, the "vandals" appeared to be primarily respectable whites.

Untended property becomes fair game for people out for fun or plunder, and even for people who ordinarily would not dream of doing such things and who probably consider themselves law-abiding. Because of the nature of community life in the Bronx—its anonymity, the frequency with which cars are abandoned and things are stolen or broken, the past experience of "no one caring"—vandalism begins much more quickly than it does in staid Palo Alto, where people have come to believe that private possessions are cared for, and that mischievous behavior is costly. But vandalism can occur anywhere once communal barriers—the sense of mutual regard and the obligations of civility—are lowered by actions that seem to signal that "no one cares."

We suggest that "untended" behavior also leads to the breakdown of community controls. A stable neighborhood of families who care for their homes, mind each other's children, and confidently frown on unwanted intruders can change, in a few years or even a few months, to an inhospitable and frightening jungle. A piece of property is abandoned, weeds grow up, a window is smashed. Adults stop scolding rowdy children; the children, emboldened, become more rowdy. Families move out, unattached adults move in. Teenagers gather in front of the corner store. The merchant asks them to move; they refuse. Fights occur. Litter accumulates. People start drinking in front of the grocery; in time, an inebriate slumps to the sidewalk and is allowed to sleep it off. Pedestrians are approached by panhandlers.

At this point it is not inevitable that serious crime will flourish or violent attacks on strangers will occur. But many residents will think that crime, especially violent crime is on the rise, and they will modify their behavior accordingly. They will use the streets less often, and when on the streets will stay apart from their fellows, moving with averted eyes, silent lips, and hurried steps.

"Don't get involved." For some residents, this growing atomization will matter little, because the neighborhood is not their "home" but "the place where they live." Their interests are elsewhere; they are cosmopolitans. But it will matter greatly to other people, whose lives derive meaning and satisfaction from local attachments rather than worldly involvement; for them, the neighborhood will cease to exist except for a few reliable friends whom they arrange to meet.

Such an area is vulnerable to criminal invasion. Though it is not inevitable, it is more likely that here, rather than in places where people are confident they can regulate public behavior by informal controls, drugs will change hands, prostitutes will solicit, and cars will be stripped. That the drunks will be robbed by boys who do it as a lark, and the prostitutes' customers will be robbed by men who do it purposefully and perhaps violently. That muggings will occur.

Among those who often find it difficult to move away from this are the elderly. Surveys of citizens suggest that the elderly are much less likely to be the victims of crime than younger persons, and some have inferred from this that the well-known fear of crime voiced by the elderly is an exaggeration: perhaps we ought not to design special programs to protect older persons; perhaps we should even try to talk them out of their mistaken fears. This argument misses the point. The prospect of a confrontation with an obstreperous teenager or a drunken panhandler can be as fear-inducing for defenseless persons as the prospect of meeting an actual robber; indeed, to a defenseless person, the two kinds of confrontation are often indistinguishable. Moreover, the lower rate at which the elderly are victimized is a measure of the steps they have already taken—chiefly, staying behind locked doors—to minimize the risks they face. Young men are more frequently attacked than older women, not because they are easier or more lucrative targets but because they are on the streets more.

Nor is the connection between disorderliness and fear made only by the elderly. Susan Estrich, of the Harvard Law School, has recently gathered together a number of surveys on the sources of public fear. One, done in Portland, Oregon, indicates that three-fourths of the adults interviewed cross to the other side of a street when they see a gang of teenagers; another survey, in Baltimore, discovered that nearly half would cross the street to avoid even a single strange youth. When an interviewer asked people in a housing project where the most dangerous spot was, they mentioned a place where young persons gathered to drink and play music, despite the fact that not a single crime had occurred there. In Boston public housing projects, the greatest fear was expressed by persons living in the buildings where disorderliness and incivility, not crime, were the greatest. Knowing this helps one understand the significance of such otherwise harmless displays as subway graffiti. As Nathan Glazer has written, the proliferation of graffiti, even when not obscene, confronts the subway rider with the "inescapable knowledge that the environment he must endure for an hour or more a day is uncontrolled and uncontrollable, and that anyone can invade it to do whatever damage and mischief the mind suggests."

In response to fear, people avoid one another, weakening controls. Sometimes they call the police. Patrol cars arrive, an occasional arrest occurs, but crime continues and disorder is not abated. Citizens complain to the police chief, but he explains that his department is low on personnel and that the courts do not punish petty or first-time offenders. To the residents, the police who arrive in squad cars are either ineffective or uncaring; to the police, the residents are animals who deserve each other. The citizens may soon stop calling the police, because "they can't do anything."

The process we call urban decay has occurred for centuries in every city. But what is happening today is different in at least two important respects. First, in the period before, say, World War II, city dwellers—because of money costs, transportation difficulties, familial and church connections—could rarely move away from neighborhood problems. When movement did occur, it tended to be along public-transit routes. Now mobility has become exceptionally easy for all but the poorest or those who are blocked by racial prejudice. Earlier crime waves had a kind of built-in self-correcting mechanism: the determination of a neighborhood or community to reassert control over its turf. Areas in Chicago, New York, and Boston would experience crime and gang wars, and then normalcy would return, as the families for whom no alternative residences were possible reclaimed their authority over the streets.

Second, the police in this earlier period assisted in that reassertion of authority by acting, sometimes violently, on behalf of the community. Young toughs were roughed up, people were arrested "on suspicion" or for vagrancy, and prostitutes and petty thieves were routed. "Rights" were something enjoyed by decent folk, and perhaps also by the serious professional criminal, who avoided violence and could afford a lawyer.

This pattern of policing was not an aberration or the result of occasional excess. From the earliest days of the nation, the police function was seen primarily as that of a night watchman: to maintain order against the chief threats to order—fire, wild animals, and disreputable behavior. Solving crimes was viewed not as a police responsibility but as a private one. In the March 1969 *Atlantic*, one of us (Wilson) wrote a brief account of how the police role had slowly changed from maintaining order to fighting crimes. The change began with the creation of private detectives (often ex-criminals), who worked on a contingency-fee basis for individuals who had suffered losses. In time, the detectives were absorbed into municipal police agencies and paid a regular salary; simultaneously, the responsibility for prosecuting thieves was shifted from the aggrieved private citizen to the professional prosecutor. The process was not complete in most places until the twentieth century.

In the 1960s, when urban riots were a major problem, social scientists began to explore carefully the order-maintenance function of the police, and to suggest ways of improving it—not to make streets safer (its original function) but to reduce the incidence of mass violence. Order maintenance became, to a degree, co-terminous with "community relations." But, as the crime wave that began in the early 1960s continued without abatement throughout the decade and into the 1970s, attention shifted to the role of the police as crime fighters. Studies of police behavior ceased, by and large, to be accounts of the order-maintenance function and became, instead, efforts to propose and test ways whereby the police could solve more crimes, make more arrests, and gather better evidence. If these things could be done, social scientists assumed, citizens would be less fearful.

A great deal was accomplished during this transition, as both police chiefs and outside experts emphasized the crime-fighting function in their plans, in the allocation of resources, and in deployment of personnel. The police may well have become better crime fighters as a result. And doubtless they remained aware of their responsibility for order. But the link between order maintenance and crime prevention, so obvious to earlier generations, was forgotten.

That link is similar to the process whereby one broken window becomes many. The citizen who fears the ill-smelling drunk, the rowdy teenager, or the importuning beggar is not merely expressing his distaste for unseemly behavior, he is also giving voice to a bit of folk wisdom that happens to be a correct generalization—namely, that serious street crime flourishes in areas in which disorderly behavior goes unchecked. The unchecked panhandler is, in effect, the first broken window. Muggers and robbers, whether opportunistic or professional, believe they reduce their chances of being caught or even identified if they operate on streets where potential victims are already intimidated by prevailing conditions. If the neighborhood cannot keep a bothersome panhandler from annoying passersby, the thief may reason, it is even less likely to call the police to identify a potential mugger or to interfere if the mugging actually takes place.

Some police administrators concede that this process occurs, but argue that motorized patrol officers can deal with it as effectively as foot patrol officers. We are not so sure. In theory, an officer in a squad car can observe as much as an officer on foot; in theory, the former can talk to as many people as the latter. But the reality of police–citizen encounters is powerfully altered by the automobile. An officer on foot cannot separate himself from the street people; if he is approached, only his uniform and his personality can help him manage whatever is about to happen. And he can never be certain what that will be—a request for directions, a plea for help, an angry denunciation, a teasing remark, a confused babble, a threatening gesture.

In a car, an officer is more likely to deal with street people by rolling down the window and looking at them. The door and the window exclude the approaching citizen; they are a barrier. Some officers take advantage of this barrier, perhaps unconsciously, by acting differently if in the car than they would on foot. We have seen this countless times. The police car pulls up to a corner where teenagers are gathered. The window is rolled down. The officer stares at the youths. They stare back. The officer says to one,"C'mere." He saunters over, conveying to his friends by his elaborate casual style the idea that he is not intimidated by authority. "What's your name?" "Chuck." "Chuck who?" "Chuck Jones." "What'ya doing, Chuck?" "Nothin'." "Got a P.O. [parole officer]?" "Nah." "Sure?" "Yeah." "Stay out of trouble, Chuckie." Meanwhile, the other boys laugh and exchange comments among themselves, probably at the officer's expense. The officer stares harder. He cannot be certain what is being said, nor can he join in and, by displaying his own skill at street banter, prove that he cannot be "put down." In the process, the officer has learned almost nothing, and the boys have decided the officer is an alien force who can safely be disregarded, even mocked.

Our experience is that most citizens like to talk to a police officer. Such exchanges give them a sense of importance, provide them with the basis for gossip, and allow them to explain to the authorities what is worrying them (whereby they gain a modest but significant sense of having "done something" about the problem). You approach a person on foot more easily, and talk to him more readily, than you do a person in a car. Moreover, you can more easily retain some anonymity if you draw an officer aside for a private chat. Suppose you want to pass on a tip about who is stealing handbags, or who offered to sell you a stolen TV. In the inner city, the culprit, in all likelihood, lives nearby. To walk up to a marked patrol car and lean in the window is to convey a visible signal that you are a "fink."

The essence of the police role in maintaining order is to reinforce the informal control mechanisms of the community itself. The police cannot, without committing extraordinary resources, provide a substitute for that informal control. On the other hand, to reinforce those natural forces the police must accommodate them. And therein lies the problem.

Should police activity on the street be shaped, in important ways, by the standards of the neighborhood rather than by the rules of the state? Over the past two decades, the shift of police from order maintenance to law enforce-ment has brought them increasingly under the influence of legal restrictions, provoked by media complaints and enforced by court decisions and depart-mental orders. As a consequence, the order-maintenance functions of the police are now governed by rules developed to control police relations with suspected criminals. This is, we think, an entirely new development. For cen-turies, the role of the police as watchmen was judged primarily not in terms of its compliance with appropriate procedures but rather in terms of its attaining a desired objective. The objective was order, an inherently ambiguous term but a condition that people in a given community recognized when they saw it. The means were the same as those the community itself would employ, if its members were sufficiently determined, courageous, and authoritative. Detecting and apprehending criminals, by contrast, was a means to an end, not an end in itself; a judicial determination of guilt or innocence was the hoped-for result of the law-enforcement mode. From the first, the police were expected to follow rules defining that process, though states differed in how stringent the rules should be. The criminal-apprehension process was always understood to involve individual rights, the violation of which was unaccept-able because it meant that the violating officer would be acting as a judge and jury—and that was not his job. Guilt or innocence was to be determined by universal standards under special procedures.

Ordinarily, no judge or jury ever sees the persons caught up in a dispute over the appropriate level of neighborhood order. That is true not only because most cases are handled informally on the street but also because no universal standards are available to settle arguments over disorder, and thus a judge may not be any wiser or more effective than a police officer. Until quite recently in many states, and even today in some places, the police make arrests on such charges as "suspicious person" or "vagrancy" or "public drunkenness"—charges with scarcely any legal meaning. These charges exist not because society wants judges to punish vagrants or drunks but because it wants an officer to have the legal tools to remove undesirable persons from a neighborhood when informal efforts to preserve order in the streets have failed.

Once we begin to think of all aspects of police work as involving the application of universal rules under special procedures, we inevitably ask what constitutes an "undesirable person" and why we should "criminalize" vagrancy or drunkenness. A strong and commendable desire to see that people are treated fairly makes us worry about allowing the police to rout persons who are undesirable by some vague or parochial standard. A growing and not-so-commendable utilitarianism leads us to doubt that any behavior that does not "hurt" another person should be made illegal. And thus many of us who watch over the police are reluctant to allow them to perform, in the only way they can, a function that every neighborhood desperately wants them to perform.

This wish to "decriminalize" disreputable behavior that "harms no one"— and thus remove the ultimate sanction the police can employ to maintain neighborhood order—is, we think, a mistake. Arresting a single drunk or a single vagrant who has harmed no identifiable person seems unjust, and in a sense it is. But failing to do anything about a score of drunks or a hundred vagrants may destroy an entire community. A particular rule that seems to make sense in the individual case makes no sense when it is made a universal rule and applied to all cases. It makes no sense because it fails to take into account the connection between one broken window left untended and a thousand broken windows. Of course, agencies other than the police could attend to the problems posed by drunks or the mentally ill, but in most communities—especially where the "deinstitutionalization" movement has been strong—they do not.

The concern about equity is more serious. We might agree that certain behavior makes one person more undesirable than another, but how do we ensure that age or skin color or natural origin or harmless mannerisms will not also become the basis for distinguishing the undesirable from the desirable? How do we ensure, in short, that the police do not become the agents of neighborhood bigotry?

We can offer no wholly satisfactory answer to this important question. We are not confident that there *is* a satisfactory answer, except to hope that by their selection, training, and supervision the police will be inculcated with a clear sense of the outer limit of their discretionary authority. That limit, roughly, is this—the police exist to help regulate behavior, not to maintain the racial or ethnic purity of a neighborhood.

Consider the case of the Robert Taylor Homes in Chicago, one of the largest public housing projects in the country. It is home for nearly 20,000 people, all black, and extends over ninety-two acres along South State Street.

It was named after a distinguished black who had been, during the 1940s, chairman of the Chicago Housing Authority. Not long after it opened, in 1962, relations between project residents and the police deteriorated badly. The citizens felt that the police were insensitive or brutal; the police, in turn, complained of unprovoked attacks on them. Some Chicago officers tell of times when they were afraid to enter the Homes. Crime rates soared.

Today, the atmosphere has changed. Police-citizen relations have improved—apparently, both sides learned something from the earlier experience. Recently, a boy stole a purse and ran off. Several young persons who saw the theft voluntarily passed along to the police information on the identity and residence of the thief, and they did this publicly, with friends and neighbors looking on. But problems persist, chief among them the presence of youth gangs that terrorize residents and recruit members in the project. The people expect the police to "do something" about this, and the police are determined to do just that.

But do what? Though the police can obviously make arrests whenever a gang member breaks the law, a gang can form, recruit, and congregate without breaking the law. And only a tiny fraction of gang-related crimes can be solved by an arrest; thus, if an arrest is the only recourse for the police, the residents' fears will go unassuaged. The police will soon feel helpless, and the residents will again believe that the police "do nothing." What the police in fact do is to chase known gang members out of the project. In the words of one officer, "We kick ass." Project residents both know and approve of this. The tacit police-citizen alliance in the project is reinforced by the police view that the cops and the gangs are the two rival sources of power in the area, and that the gangs are not going to win.

None of this is easily reconciled with any conception of due process or fair treatment. Since both residents and gang members are black, race is not a factor. But it could be. Suppose a white project gang confronted a black gang, or vice versa. We would be apprehensive about the police taking sides. But the substantive problem remains the same: How can the police strengthen the informal social-control mechanisms of natural communities in order to minimize fear in public places? Law enforcement, per se, is no answer. A gang can weaken or destroy a community by standing about in a menacing fashion and speaking rudely to passersby without breaking the law.

We have difficulty thinking about such matters, not simply because the ethical and legal issues are so complex but because we have become accustomed to thinking of the law in essentially individualistic terms. The law defines *my* rights, punishes *his* behavior, and is applied by *that* officer because of *this* harm. We assume, in thinking this way, that what is good for the individual will be good for the community, and what doesn't matter when it happens to one person won't matter when it happens to many. Ordinarily, those are plausible assumptions. But in cases where behavior that is tolerable to one person is intolerable to many others, the reactions of the others—fear, withdrawal, flight—may ultimately make matters worse for everyone, including the individual who first professed his indifference.

It may be their greater sensitivity to communal as opposed to individual needs that helps explain why the residents of small communities are more satisfied with their police than are the residents of similar neighborhoods in big cities. Elinor Ostrom and her co-workers at Indiana University compared the perception of police services in two poor, all-black Illinois towns—Phoenix and East Chicago Heights—with those of three comparable all-black neighborhoods in Chicago. The level of criminal victimization and the quality of police-community relations appeared to be about the same in the towns and the Chicago neighborhoods. But the citizens living in their own villages were much more likely than those living in the Chicago neighborhoods to say that they do not stay at home for fear of crime, to agree that the local police have "the right to take any action necessary" to deal with problems, and to agree that the police "look out for the needs of the average citizen." It is possible that the residents and the police of the small towns saw themselves as engaged in a collaborative effort to maintain a certain standard of communal life, whereas those of the big city felt themselves to be simply requesting and supplying particular services on an individual basis.

If this is true, how should a wise police chief deploy his meager forces? The first answer is that nobody knows for certain, and the most prudent course of action would be to try further variations on the Newark experiment, to see more precisely what works in what kinds of neighborhoods. The second answer is also a hedge—many aspects of order maintenance in neighborhoods can probably best be handled in ways that involve the police minimally, if at all. A busy, bustling shopping center and a quiet, well-tended suburb may need almost no visible police presence. In both cases, the ratio of respectable to disreputable people is ordinarily so high as to make informal social control effective.

Even in areas that are in jeopardy from disorderly elements, citizen action without substantial police involvement may be sufficient. Meetings between teenagers who like to hang out on a particular corner and adults who want to use that corner might well lead to an amicable agreement on a set of rules about how many people can be allowed to congregate, where, and when.

Where no understanding is possible—or, if possible, not observed—citizen patrols may be a sufficient response. There are two traditions of communal involvement in maintaining order. One, that of the "community watchmen," is as old as the first settlement of the New World. Until well into the nineteenth century, volunteer watchmen, not policemen, patrolled their communities to keep order. They did so, by and large, without taking the law into their own hands—without, that is, punishing persons or using force. Their presence deterred disorder or alerted the community to disorder that could not be deterred. There are hundreds of such efforts today in communities all across the nation. Perhaps the best known is that of the Guardian Angels, a group of unarmed young persons in distinctive berets and T-shirts, who first came to public attention when they began patrolling the New York City subways but who claim now to have chapters in more than thirty American cities. Unfortunately, we have little information about the effect of these groups on crime. It is possible, however, that whatever their effect on crime, citizens find their presence reassuring, and that they thus contribute to maintaining a sense of order and civility.

The second tradition is that of the "vigilante." Rarely a feature of the settled communities of the East, it was primarily to be found in those frontier towns that grew up in advance of the reach of government. More than 350 vigilante groups are known to have existed; their distinctive feature was that their members did take the law into their own hands, by acting as judge, jury, and often executioner as well as policeman. Today, the vigilante movement is conspicuous by its rarity, despite the great fear expressed by citizens that the older cities are becoming "urban frontiers." But some community watchmen groups have skirted the line, and others may cross it in the future. An ambiguous case, reported in the *Wall Street Journal*, involved a citizens' patrol in the Silver Lake area of Belleville, New Jersey. A leader told the reporter, "We look for outsiders." If a few teenagers from outside the neighborhood enter it, "we ask them their business," he said. "If they say they're going down the street to see Mrs. Jones, fine, we let them pass. But then we follow them down the block to make sure they're really going to see Mrs. Jones."

Though citizens can do a great deal, the police are plainly the key to order maintenance. For one thing, many communities, such as the Robert Taylor Homes, cannot do the job by themselves. For another, no citizen in a neighborhood, even an organized one, is likely to feel the sense of responsibility that wearing a badge confers. Psychologists have done many studies on why people fail to go to the aid of persons being attacked or seeking help, and they have learned that the cause is not "apathy" or "selfishness" but the absence of some plausible grounds for feeling that one must personally accept responsibility. Ironically, avoiding responsibility is easier when a lot of people are standing about. On streets and in public places, where order is so important, many people are likely to be "around," a fact that reduces the chance of any one person acting as the agent of the community. The police officer's uniform singles him out as a person who must accept responsibility if asked. In addition, officers, more easily than their fellow citizens, can be expected to distinguish between what is necessary to protect the safety of the street and what merely protects its ethnic purity.

But the police forces of America are losing, not gaining, members. Some cities have suffered substantial cuts in the number of officers available for duty. These cuts are not likely to be reversed in the near future. Therefore, each department must assign its existing officers with great care. Some neighborhoods are so demoralized and crime-ridden as to make foot patrol useless; the best the police can do with limited resources is respond to the enormous number of calls for service. Other neighborhoods are so stable and serene as to make foot patrol unnecessary. The key is to identify neighborhoods at the tipping point—where the public order is deteriorating but not unreclaimable, where the streets are used frequently but by apprehensive people, where a window is likely to be broken at any time, and must quickly be fixed if all are not to be shattered.

Most police departments do not have ways of systematically identifying such areas and assigning officers to them. Officers are assigned on the basis of crime rates (meaning that marginally threatened areas are often stripped so that police can investigate crimes in areas where the situation is hopeless) or on the basis of calls for service (despite the fact that most citizens do not call the police when they are merely frightened or annoyed). To allocate patrol wisely, the department must look at the neighborhoods and decide, from first-hand evidence, where an additional officer will make the greatest difference in promoting a sense of safety.

One way to stretch limited police resources is being tried in some public housing projects. Tenant organizations hire off-duty police officers for patrol work in their buildings. The costs are not high (at least not per resident), the officer likes the additional income, and the residents feel safer. Such arrangements are probably more successful than hiring private watchmen, and the Newark experiment helps us understand why. A private security guard may deter crime or misconduct by his presence, and he may go to the aid of persons needing help, but he may well not intervene—that is, control or drive away—someone challenging community standards. Being a sworn officer—a "real cop"—seems to give one the confidence, the sense of duty, and the aura of authority necessary to perform this difficult task.

Patrol officers might be encouraged to go to and from duty stations on public transportation and, while on the bus or subway car, enforce rules about smoking, drinking, disorderly conduct, and the like. The enforcement need involve nothing more than ejecting the offender (the offense, after all, is not one with which a booking officer or a judge wishes to be bothered). Perhaps the random but relentless maintenance of standards on buses would lead to conditions on buses that approximate the level of civility we now take for granted on airplanes.

But the most important requirement is to think that to maintain order in precarious situations is a vital job. The police know this is one of their functions, and they also believe, correctly, that it cannot be done to the exclusion of criminal investigation and responding to calls. We may have encouraged them to suppose, however, on the basis of our oft-repeated concerns about serious, violent crime, that they will be judged exclusively on their capacity as crime fighters. To the extent that this is the case, police administrators will continue to concentrate police personnel in the highest-crime areas (though not necessarily in the areas most vulnerable to criminal invasion), emphasize their training in the law and criminal apprehension (and not their training in managing street life), and join too quickly in campaigns to decriminalize "harmless" behavior (though public drunkenness, street prostitution, and pornographic displays can destroy a community more quickly than any team of professional burglars).

Above all, we must return to our long-abandoned view that the police ought to protect communities as well as individuals. Our crime statistics and victimization surveys measure individual losses, but they do not measure communal losses. Just as physicians now recognize the importance of fostering health rather than simply treating illness, so the police—and the rest of us—ought to recognize the importance of maintaining, intact, communities without broken windows.

DISCUSSION QUESTIONS

1. Wilson and Kelling argue that there has been a shift in the role of policing. How has the role of the police changed and is it a positive change?

2. Discuss why one broken window will lead to more broken windows. How can we prevent this from happening?

3. Although the Safe and Clean Neighborhoods Program had no effect on crime, the citizens felt safer and believed that crime was down. Is it beneficial to keep programs such as these, or should they be replaced with programs that show an effect on the crime rate?

4. According to Wilson and Kelling, what is the advantage of having officers on foot patrol instead of officers in cars?

7

❖

The Preventative Effects of Arrest on Intimate Partner Violence

Christopher D. Maxwell
Joel H. Garner
Jeffrey A. Fagan

There is a large literature measuring varied police responses to calls for assistance. In incidents of domestic violence, jurisdictions have experimented with whether police tactical response—in this case, an arrest—may deter future acts of domestic violence. Mandatory removal or arrest does not increase the future risk for violence against women. Maxwell, Garner, and Fagan argue that arresting the offending partner for intimate violence does produce a reduction in subsequent violent offenses.

In the past quarter-century, many alternatives for the appropriate law enforcement response to intimate partner violence have been proposed, studied, recommended, adopted as policy, and enacted in federal and state laws. These alternatives have varied from doing nothing to on-scene counseling, temporary separation, and more formal criminal justice sanctions such as arrest, restraining orders, and coerced treatment (Fagan, 1996). The rationales for these policies were based on theories about deterrence rehabilitation, incapacitation, victim empowerment, officer safety, and a general concern for

Source: Christopher D. Maxwell, Joel H. Garner, and Jeffrey A. Fagan. "The Preventive Effects of Arrest on Intimate Partner Violence," in Criminology and Public Policy, vol. 2, no.1 (2002) pp. 51–80. Reprinted by permission of The American Society of Criminology.

the efficacy of criminal law regarding intimate private relationships (Pagan and Browne, 1994:3; Zimring, 1989:11). Until the 1980s, the empirical base for assessing the extent to which the alternative policies fulfilled the promises of their theoretical rationales was thin. In the foreword to a domestic violence research report that showed domestic violence was repetitive and highly visible to police, James Q. Wilson asserted that the criminal justice field lacks "reliable information as to the consequences of following different approaches" when responding to intimate partner violence. He argued that "gathering such information in a systematic and objective manner ought to be a high-priority concern for local police and prosecutors" (Wilson, 1977:v).

For the past 25 years, the law enforcement and research community has addressed Wilson's challenge by gathering systematic and objective information about alternative police responses to intimate partner violence. However, gathering information alone has not led to a clear understanding of the consequences of alternative policies or to the strength of the theories underlying those policies (Davis and Smith, 1995; Fagan, 1996). To alleviate this shortcoming, we use common data and consistent measures from 4,032 incidents of misdemeanor assault compiled in five jurisdictions to test the preventive effects of arrest on intimate partner violence. We begin by reviewing the published results from six field experiments that tested for the deterrent effects of arrest on intimate partner violence. Then we describe our methods for pooling data and conducting our analyses of the five coordinated field experiments known collectively as the Spouse Abuse Replication Program (SARP). Next, we present the results of analyses using multiple data sources, methods, and measures. We conclude with a discussion of the policy implications of our re-analysis.

BACKGROUND

In 1980, the Minneapolis Police Department and the Police Foundation accepted Wilson's challenge and proposed to compare three alternative police responses to partner violence: arrest, on-scene counseling, and separation (Sherman, 1980). This proposal was innovative in using arrest as the tested sanction rather than conviction or prison time. However, it took a more traditional approach to confirm specific deterrence theory by testing for a negative relationship between the use of a formal sanction against an individual and that person's subsequent illegal behavior. In this study, volunteer Minneapolis officers carried out one of the three alternative responses based on an experimental design. Sherman and Berk (1984b) reported that when police did not arrest the suspect during a misdemeanor spouse assault incident, 21% re-offended within six months according to official records, a rate 50% higher than the 14% re-offending rate of arrested suspects. Results were similar when re-offending was measured by victim interviews. Thus, the experiment designed to test a specific deterrence theory found consistent, statistically significant, and supportive findings for what was by 1984 becoming the preferred policy option among domestic violence reform advocates—arresting the suspect.

Policy Impact of the Minneapolis Experiment

Although the results of this experiment received extensive coverage on national television and in newspapers, the actual impact of this research is difficult to gauge. The policy debate about police response to domestic violence shifted quickly during the 1980s from one in which many jurisdictions did not authorize police officers to make arrests in misdemeanor assault unless they occurred in the officer's presence, to laws and policies that encouraged the use of arrest, to laws and policies that mandated arrest in at least some circumstances (Hirschel and Hutchison, 1991:3). Sherman and Berk (1984a) interpreted the Minneapolis findings as support for using arrest but not necessarily for the mandated use of arrest. Nevertheless, several indications show that the Minneapolis experiment influenced the policy debate about the appropriate police response to domestic violence (Boffey, 1983; Lempert, 1984; Sherman and Cohn, 1989; U.S. Attorney General's Task Force on Family Violence, 1984). What is less clear is whether this experiment's impact stems from its grounding in theory, experimental design, consistent findings, visibility of the research results, or compatibility of its pro-arrest findings with growing public support for more formal sanctions for domestic violence.

The Spouse Assault Replication Program

Support for replication of the Minneapolis experiment was widespread among researchers and policy makers. Sherman and Berk (1984b) urged replication, and some academics' early praise for the study also was tempered by others' preference for replication (Boffey, 1983; Lempert, 1984).The U.S. Attorney General's Task Force on Family Violence also encouraged replicating the Minneapolis experiment (1984). By 1986, six new experiments were initiated in Atlanta, Charlotte, Colorado Springs, Dade County, Milwaukee, and Omaha. Each new study involved experimental comparisons of arrest with alternative police responses to misdemeanor spouse assault incidents and measured victim safety using official police records and victim interviews (Gamer and Maxwell, 2000).

> These new experiments became known as the Spouse Assault Replication Program (SARP), but that name is a misnomer because the designers of the new experiments changed several crucial aspects of the Minneapolis design. For instance, in each new experiment, police officers determined case eligibility before the researchers assigned an alternative treatment to carry out. This method of determining eligibility without knowing the randomized treatment is preferred for experimental studies. The Minneapolis experiment, however, permitted officers to know the treatment before they decided case eligibility (Sherman and Berk, 1984b). In addition, the Minneapolis experiment attempted to interview victims by phone every two weeks. In the design of the SARP experiments, victim interviews were to occur twice, once within a month of the experimental incident and once at six months after the experimental

incident.[1] The SARP experiments also developed a series of common measures about suspects, victims, treatments, and outcomes. Overall, the SARP experiments built on the Minneapolis design, increasing the number of sites and experimental incidents, enhancing the rigor of the random assignment, archiving the research data, and promoting commonality among the new experiments at the expense of commonality with the original Minneapolis experiment (Garner and Maxwell, 2000; National Institute of Justice, 1985).

Synthesizing SARP Findings

The published findings from the SARP experiments generated a complex mixture of deterrence, null, and escalation effects. Where there once had been one experiment with two statistically significant and consistent results, there now were six experiments with their own set of internally and externally inconsistent findings. Seven prior efforts have tried synthesizing the substantive findings from these experiments. These efforts found deterrent effects where the original authors did not (Zorza and Woods, 1994), identified the inconsistent and incomplete nature of the published findings (Garner et al., 1995), produced deterrent effects from a meta-analysis of prevalence findings (Sugarman and Boney-McCoy, 2000), reported mixed effects by site in a review of each experiment including Minneapolis (Sherman, 1992b), asserted that the effects of arrest vary by the marital and employment status of suspects (Berk et al., 1992; Schmidt and Sherman, 1992), and made an expert assessment that "arrest in all misdemeanor cases will not, on average, produce a discernable effect on recidivism" (Chalk and King, 1998:176). Thus, prior efforts at synthesis vary almost as much as do the published reports from the individual sites.

Although alternative approaches to synthesizing a large body of research, such as qualitative literature reviews and meta-analysis of published findings, have contributed to our understanding of this and other bodies of research, the secondary analysis of case-level data provide the most rigorous method for combining information across a variety of studies (Cooper and Hedges, 1994). Although efforts at secondary analysis of the archived data from the SARP experiments (see Berk et al., 1992; Sherman et al., 1992) have provided insights into the conditions under which arrest may or may not improve women's safety, they still are incomplete for several reasons. First, they use only the official records as a measure of repeat offending and do not consider information generated by thousands of victim interviews. Second, Sherman et al. (1992a) considered only the frequency of re-offending and Berk et al. (1992) considered only the prevalence of re-offending. Finally, Sherman et al. (1992a) reported two single site analyses (Milwaukee and Omaha) and Berk et al. (1992) did not use information from the Charlotte experiment. For these and other reasons, the published syntheses of the SARP experiments cannot be the definitive assessments of the average effect of arrest on subsequent offending.

SARP's Policy Impact

The inconsistencies in the site-specific and the multisite analyses reported in the various SARP reviews generated some ambivalence among researchers (Berk, 1993; Fagan, 1996; Sherman, 1992b) and policy makers (Clark, 1993; Frisch, 1992; Lerman, 1992; Mitchell, 1992) about the efficacy of arrest as the primary mechanism to control intimate partner violence. However, this ambivalence does not appear to have influenced police practices. We know of no jurisdiction that revised its policy to reflect the concerns these scholars raised. Furthermore, under the authority of the 1994 Violence Against Women Act, the U.S. Department of Justice initiated the Grants to Encourage Arrest Policies Program. To support this program, Congress appropriated nearly $120 million between 1994 and 1996 for the Violence Against Women Office to help local jurisdictions "implement mandatory arrest or proarrest programs and policies in police departments, including mandatory arrest programs and policies for protection order violations" (Violence Against Women Grants Office, 1996:5). Thus, presently, the findings (and the interpretation of findings) from the SARP experiments are not as closely connected to current policies and practices as the findings from the Minneapolis experiment were in the 1980s and 1990s.

METHODS

This study builds on a body of research that addresses the specific deterrent effect of arrest on the subsequent aggressive behavior by intimate partners. We synthesize the original data generated by the SARP experiments and conduct analyses that differ from the site-specific analyses in several ways. First, in contrast to prior secondary analyses (see Berk et al., 1992; Sherman et al., 1992a), our design conforms to the program's original plans for a multisite analysis of the case-level data.[2] Second, we use information about subsequent offenses from all victim interviews and from all official police records. Third, we use common measures about suspects, victims, incidents, and treatments to apply consistent case eligibility standards across the five experiments in which arrest was one possible treatment. Finally, we address (1) the complexities of combining data from five independent studies with systematic design differences; (2) the variability in the existence, number, and timing of victim interviews; and (3) the differences in the collection of the official data. The SARP experiments, by design, drew cases from different populations. They varied in size from 330 to 1,600 cases. They randomly assigned arrest to two-thirds (Milwaukee), one-half (Dade), one-third (Omaha and Charlotte), and one-fourth (Colorado Springs) of the eligible cases. In Dade County, the experiment was initially limited to married couples; in Milwaukee, the experiment included assaults between siblings and gathered cases only from selected neighborhoods. Although there were other differences in incident eligibility rules between sites, this is the first effort to synthesize the SARP experiments that addresses these issues (see Maxwell, 1998 for a detailed listing of differences among sites).

Selection of Cases from the Pooled Data

We used common measures about suspects and experimental incidents (e.g., the incident at which the treatment was assigned and delivered) to select a research sample that best represents the archetypical male-on-female assaults that drive much of the policy debate about controlling intimate partner violence. The five sites collected data about 4,792 experimental incidents; we use information from the 4,032 incidents involving adult male suspects who assaulted their female intimate partner. To arrive at 4,032 cases, we excluded 306 incidents that involved a female suspect and 314 incidents that involved a male victim. Other experimental incidents excluded in our study involved victims and offenders whose relationships were not spouse-like, such as brothers and sisters ($n = 85$), and experimental incidents that did not involve an assault or victim injury ($n = 34$) (see Maxwell et al., 2001 for additional details about sample selection).

Treatments Assigned and Compared

One of the SARP requirements was that arrest be one of the alternative police treatments tested. The nature of the alternatives to arrest and the proportion of cases assigned to arrest and nonarrest treatments were left to the implementing teams of researchers and police agencies. Of the 4,032 suspects in the research sample, 43.4% were assigned to the arrest treatment and the remaining 56.6% were assigned to a variety of nonarrest treatments (see Table 1). In our analyses, we compare the arrest treatment with all of the nonarrest treatments. Binder and Meeker (1988) suggested this comparison of the formal sanction of arrest with the informal alternatives in their critique of the original Minneapolis analysis. This method also was used in subsequent analysis of the Minneapolis experiment (see Berk and Sherman, 1988), and in some original SARP analyses (see Pate and Hamilton, 1992; Sherman et al., 1992a).

The designs in each of the SARP sites allowed officers to avoid using the randomly assigned treatment and apply an alternative treatment under certain conditions, such as an assault on the victim in the officers' presence or an assault on the officers. Consequently, the treatments delivered differed from the treatment assigned in 6.7% of the incidents.[3] We chose to compare suspects based on the treatment randomly assigned. This is the only comparison for which we have a statistical basis for assuming uncorrelated error terms for both measured and unmeasured characteristics of suspects (Armitage, 1996:13; Heckman and Robb, 1986). This choice also was consistent with the method used in the original Minneapolis experiment, the SARP design, each of the original SARP analyses, and clinical trials in medical research.[4]

Sample characteristics vary by site and by treatment assigned. For instance, Colorado Springs contributes 30.7% of the research sample and Milwaukee provides 23.7% (see Table 1). The Omaha experiment contributed only 7.3% of the total sample. Thus, the larger sites contributed three or four times as many experimental incidents as did the smallest site. Approximately 19% of subjects in the research sample were less than 24 years of age, and almost 45% were older than 31. At the time of the experimental incident, either the police determined or the victim reported that the suspect was using an intoxicant—either alcohol or illegal drugs—in 45% of the incidents. In 37.5% of the research sample, the suspect's race was white. At the time of the experimental incident, most suspects were married to the victim (58.8%), most were employed (71.5%), and 40% had at least one prior arrest. As displayed in Table 2, the proportion of cases assigned to the arrest treatment varied significantly by site as well as by suspect's race, marital status, arrest record, employment condition, and use of intoxicants at the time of the experimental incident. All of these differences are statistically significant ($p < 0.05$). Suspect age was the only characteristic with similar distributions between the arrest and the nonarrest cases.

Characteristics of the Pooled Sample

Thus, Table 2 established that the research sample has unequal proportions in the characteristics of suspects assigned to arrest and nonarrest treatments. Unequal proportions in the treatment and control groups are unlikely in a single site experiment, but when we merged the data from the five experiments, three differences emerged: (1) Both criminal histories and social characteristics of suspects vary by site, (2) the sites have different numbers and types of incidents, and (3) the sites assigned different proportions of suspects to the arrest treatment. Accordingly, the unequal proportions of cases, the uneven distribution of victim and suspect characteristics, and the uneven allocation of cases to treatment groups are factors we must address in our multisite analyses that test for the effects of arrest on subsequent criminal behavior.

Victim Interviews

The SARP design called for initial victim interviews within a month of the experimental incident and a second interview six months after the experimental incident. However, the SARP researchers were not able to interview all of the victims; those victims interviewed were rarely interviewed according to the plan, and several sites added additional interviews or deviated from the basic design for some of their cases.[5] Initial victim interviews were completed in more than 70% of the research sample (see Table 1), but the rate varied from 60% in Milwaukee (where, by design, initial interviews were not attempted in 25% of the cases) to almost 80% in Omaha. In just less than 63% of the research sample, a final interview was obtained. Milwaukee had the highest proportion of final interviews, with more than 79%, and Charlotte, at 50%, had the lowest.

In more than 78% of the research sample ($n = 3,147$), at least one interview took place with the victim. Besides site differences in the proportion interviewed, the timing of the initial interviews varied from 1 to 776 days after the

Table 1 Sample Characteristics, Treatments Assigned, Victim Interview Rates by Site

	CHARLOTTE		COLORADO SPRINGS		DADE COUNTY		MILWAUKEE		OMAHA		ALL SITES	
Research Sample	Row %	N	Row %	N	Row %	N	Row %	N	Row %	N	Row %	N
	15.8	638	30.7	1,238	22.5	906	23.7	954	7.3	296	100.0	4,032
	Col. %	N	Col. %	N	Col. %	N	Col. %	N	Col. %	N	Col. %	N
	100.0	638	100.0	1,238	100.0	906	100.0	954	100.0	296	100.0	4,032
Treatment assigned												
Arrest	33.2	212	26.3	325	51.1	463	67.9	648	33.8	100	43.4	1,748
Non-arrest	66.8	426	73.7	913	48.9	443	32.1	306	66.2	196	56.6	2,284
Suspect characteristics												
Mean age	32.8		30.8		35.1		31.0		31.4		32.2	
Use of intoxicant	54.2	346	59.3	734	30.6	277	29.4	280	59.121	175	44.9	1,812
Race/Ethnicity												
African-American	69.9	446	30.2	374	41.8	379	75.4	719	41.9	124	50.6	2,042
White	27.7	177	54.2	671	36.1	327	19.9	190	50.3	149	37.5	1,514
Hispanic	0.3	2	14.5	180	22.1	200	4.2	40	4.7	14	10.8	436
Asian/Other	2.0	13	1.1	13	0.0	0	0.5	5	3.0	9	1.0	40
Relationship with victim												
Married	48.4	309	66.7	826	78.7	713	30.9	295	46.3	137	56.5	2,280
Separated	1.6	10	4.3	53	2.9	26	0.3	3	0.0	0	2.3	92
Divorced	0.3	2	0.6	8	2.0	18	0.7	7	1.4	4	1.0	39
Current/Past intimate	49.7	317	28.4	351	16.4	149	68.0	649	52.4	155	40.2	1,621
Prior arrest	30.7	196	42.8	530	12.1	110	61.8	590	64.9	192	40.1	1,618
Employed	77.1	492	86.7	1,073	70.5	639	47.2	450	78.0	231	71.6	2,885
Extent of victim interviews completion												
Initial	64.4	411	82.9	1,026	65.5	593	60.2	574	79.4	235	70.4	2,839
Final	50.2	320	70.4	872	42.4	384	77.9	743	73.0	216	62.9	2,535
Any victim interview	64.4	411	87.9	1,088	65.7	595	85.7	818	79.4	235	78.1	3,147

Table 2 Site, Suspect and Incident Characteristics by Treatment Assigned (*N* = 4.032)

| | TREATMENT ASSIGNMENT | | | | | |
| | NON-ARREST | | ARREST | | TOTAL | |
	Row %	N	Row %	N	Row %	N
Selected incidents	56.6	2,284	43.3	1,748	100	4,032
	Col. %	N	Col. %	N	Col. %	N
Selected incidents	100	2,284	100	1,748	100	4,032
Site						
Charlotte	18.7	426	12.1	212	15.8	638
Colorado Springs	40.0	913	18.6	325	30.7	1,238
Dade Co.	19.4	443	26.5	463	22.5	906
Milwaukee	13.4	306	37.1	648	23.7	954
Omaha	8.6	196	5.7	100	7.3	296
Age						
18 to 24	19.7	449	17.3	303	18.7	752
25 to 28	21.1	481	20.7	361	20.9	842
29 to 31	15.6	356	16.1	281	15.8	637
32 to 37	22.3	510	22.9	400	22.6	910
38 to 82	21.4	488	23.1	403	22.1	891
Use of intoxicant	49.5	1,130	39.0	682	44.9	1,812
Race						
Non-White	59.1	1350	66.8	1168	62.5	2,518
White	40.9	934	33.2	580	37.5	1514
Marital status						
Non-married	38.4	877	44.9	784	41.2	1,661
Married	61.6	1,407	55.1	964	58.8	2,371
Prior arrest	36.9	843	44.3	774	40.1	1,617
Employed	74.3	1,697	67.9	1,187	71.5	2,884

experimental incident; the mean number of days was 39.2. The actual time to the final interviews varied from 12 to 674 days, and the mean number of days was 280. Thus, the actual exposure time covered by the final interviews was, on average, 97 days longer than the planned 183 days.

We addressed the methodological issues created by the difference in victim interview rates and length of follow-up in several ways. First, we extended the basic Heckman selection model (Heckman, 1979) and produced a time-dependent latent-hazard selection measure. This approach used as its dependent measure the maximum length of time that the researchers tracked each victim during the study, rather than the traditional dichotomized measure of interview completion or noncompletion. For the 22% of victims who never were interviewed, their interview exposure time was set to one day. For the remaining victims with one or more interviews, their follow-up time was set to equal the number of days between the experimental incident and the date of their last interview. We then modeled the length of all 4,032 victim interview times as a function of the site and victim characteristics using a semiparametric maximum–likelihood Cox regression model. Using this process, we then produced a latent interview exposure rate for every victim. In our analyses of repeat offending, we used this measure as one means of addressing measured differences between the interviewed and noninterviewed victims, as well as to control for the different lengths of victim follow-up. This measure also permitted us to take advantage of the information about new victimizations gathered from all interviews regardless of the number or timing of interviews, rather than just those victimizations reported in the final interviews.

In the model predicting the length of victim interview follow-up, two of the seven measures tested, the site and the victim's age, predicted variation in the time covered by a victim's interviews. Dade County, Milwaukee, and Omaha had longer follow-up periods on average compared with Charlotte. In all sites, older victims also were observed over a longer follow-up period. The suspect's assigned treatment, the victim's relationship with the suspect, the victim's employment status, race, and the timing of any subsequent criminal offenses filed with the police involving the suspect did not significantly predict differences in whether the victim was interviewed or the average length of the follow-up period.

Outcome Measures

The SARP design called for collecting data that would permit the computation of the prevalence, frequency, and time-to-failure dimensions of the criminal career paradigm (Blumstein et al., 1986). In addition, the design called for computing each of these dimensions separately for violent offenses, property damage, and other types of offenses against the same victim, other victims, and any victim. This approach resulted in potentially hundreds of outcome measures derived from the official records and victim interviews. However, after review of the raw data and each site's data collection instruments and protocols, we found that not all of the data needed to calculate all of these measures were available for each of the five SARP experiments (see Maxwell, 1998 for details on the diversity and commonality of available measures in the archived data).

Using the available information in the victim interviews, we constructed composite outcome measures that capture incidents of subsequent assaults, verbal threats of assault, or property damage by the suspect against the original victim. From local law enforcement criminal history records, we constructed a measure that captured any reported offense against the same victim after the experimental incident. Using this measure, we then calculated a six-month prevalence rate, an annual incident rate, and a time-to-first-failure rate. From the victim interview data, we also calculated prevalence and six-month incident rates. Because sufficient information to determine the date of subsequent incidents reported in victim interviews was not always present in the victim interviews, we were unable to calculate a time-to-first-failure rate for all five sites. Both measures also are limited to incidents involving the offender and the victim identified in the original experimental incident. The interview measure captures threats, but police records typically do not include threats. Of course, many victims do not report offenses to the police (Bachman and Coker, 1995), and police do not always document all citizen complaints (Klinger and Bridges, 1997). Thus, we expected that victim interviews would identify more frequent victimization than would the official records. Therefore, we preferred the victim interview information over the official records for a measure of repeat offending and victim safety.

Multivariate Analytical Models

We estimated the effects of arrest on the recurrence of intimate partner violence in a series of models using (1) the treatment and site measures; (2) treatment, site, and the interview exposure measures; (3) treatment, site, interview exposure, and site by treatment interaction measures; and (4) treatment, site, interview exposure, and six suspect characteristics measurements thought to be associated with increased risk of re-offending. The choice of the appropriate estimation routine for the five outcome measures reflected the three measurement dimensions: The prevalence of any new victimization is a dichotomy, the rate of aggressive incidents is a count, and the time-to-first-offense is a righthand censored interval measure of days between the experimental incident and the first officially recorded offense. For dichotomous dependent measures of prevalence, models were estimated using logistic regression methods. To estimate the number of incidents, models were tested using Negative Binomial Regression.[6] We estimated the time-to-first-failure rates using the Cox semiparametric regression.[7] For each regression procedure, we report the unstandardized coefficients, the coefficient's standard errors, and the odds ratios. We use the odds ratio as a rough measure of the relative size of the effect of arrest.

RESULTS

Offenses and Victimizations Base Rates

Table 3 reports prevalence and mean incident rates of new incidents reported in the victim interviews and found in the official police records. In the official police records, 23.1% of the suspects in the research sample had one or more reported offenses after the experimental incident. The annual incident rate averaged 0.39 offenses per suspect. Among 3.149 victims interviewed at least once, 42.5% reported at least one new victimization by the suspect through the final victim interview. These same victims reported 9,009 incidents (an average of 2.86 incidents per suspect) during this period after the experimental treatment. Thus, similar to what was found in other domestic

Table 3 Base Rates of Failure by Treatment Assigned

	NON-ARREST		ARREST		TOTAL	
Official Record Sample	(N = 2,284)		(N = 1,748)		(N = 4,032)	
	%	N	%	N	%	N
Six-month prevalence of recidivism	21.1	481	25.7	450	23.1	931
		Chi-sqr. = 0.725				
Mean annual frequency of recidivism	0.32		0.48		0.39	
		F-value = 25.397 ***				
Mean survival time (days)	865		816		850	
		Log-rank = 15.8 ***				

	NON-ARREST		ARREST		TOTAL	
Victim Interview Sample	(N = 1,789)		(N = 1,358)		(N = 3,147)	
	%	N	%	N	%	N
Prevalence of victimization	42.3	756	42.9	583	42.5	1,339
		Chi-sqr. = 0.14				
Mean 6-month frequency of victimization	2.74		3.03		2.86	
		F-value = 1.075				

violence research (see Feld and Straus, 1989; Langan and Innes, 1986; Quigley and Leonard, 1996), analysis of the official criminal history records indicated no new offenses against three-quarters of all suspects, and almost three-fifths of the interviewed victims reported no new victimizations. However, when victims report at least one new incident, the average number of victimizations was 6.7, or greater than one victimization per month.

Effects of Arrest

With multiple outcome measures and sources, our criteria for judging across the five models for the existence of an effect for arrest are a combination of the consistency of direction, its relative size compared with other measures in the models, and its statistical significance. Among these three criteria, we place greater stock in the consistency of direction effects and in the size of effects, and we de-emphasize statistical significance tests. As other criminologists have noted, the use of statistical significance tests is technically not appropriate for nonprobability samples (Sampson and Laub, 1993), such as those used in the Minneapolis and SARP experiments. Nagin and Farrington (1992:519) similarly argue that "empirical regularities" such as the consistent direction of effects are the "grist for useful theory," rather than one or two tests for statistical significance. Yet, like Sampson and Laub (1993), we also report statistical significance tests to help avoid type I errors.

As reported in Table 4, arrest reduced the prevalence of new victimization by 25% and the incidents of victimizations by 30%. In the official criminal history data, arrest also was associated with reductions of 4% in the prevalence

Table 4 Multivariate Tests of the Effects of Arrest on Intimate Partner Violence

| | VICTIM REPORTS (N = 3,147) | | | | | | OFFICIAL REPORTS (N = 4,032) | | | | | | | | |
| | PREVALENCE[a] | | | 6-MONTH RATE[b] | | | 6-MONTH PREVALENCE[a] | | | ANNUAL RATE[b] | | | TIME-TO-FAILURE[c] | | |
Independent Variable:	B	S.E.	Exp(B)	B	S.E.	Exp(B)	B	S.E.	Exp(B)	B	S.E.	Exp(B)	B	S.E.	Exp(B)
Arrest	-0.28	0.08	0.75 ***	-0.35	0.08	0.70 ***	-0.04	0.08	0.96	-0.08	0.07	0.92	-0.03	0.06	0.88
Site (Charlotte)															
Colorado Springs	-0.97	0.13	0.38 ***	-0.49	0.15	0.61 ***	0.28	0.12	1.33 *	-0.02	0.13	0.98	-0.02	0.10	0.76 **
Dade Co.	-0.49	0.14	0.61 ***	-0.01	0.16	0.99	0.64	0.13	1.89 ***	0.64	0.12	1.89 ***	0.35	0.11	1.61 ***
Milwaukee	0.48	0.13	1.61 ***	0.96	0.16	2.62 ***	0.23	0.13	1.26	0.67	0.12	1.96 ***	0.16	0.11	1.10
Omaha	0.42	0.17	1.52 *	-1.01	0.20	0.36 ***	-0.54	0.19	0.58 **	-0.60	0.19	0.55 ***	-0.80	0.16	0.39 ***
Interview exposure	0.86	0.11	2.36 ***	-0.55	0.09	0.58 ***	0.54	0.09	1.71 ***	0.08	0.10	1.09	0.26	0.07	1.28 ***
Suspect's															
Age	-0.39	0.15	0.68 **	-0.83	0.14	0.44 ***	-0.50	0.15	0.61 ***	-0.32	0.13	0.72 *	-0.41	0.13	0.71 **
Use of intoxicant	-0.01	0.08	0.99	0.36	0.07	1.43 ***	0.21	0.08	1.23 **	0.10	0.08	1.10	0.14	0.06	1.12
White	0.23	0.08	1.26 **	0.30	0.07	1.35 ***	-0.39	0.08	0.68 ***	-0.36	0.07	0.70 ***	-0.33	0.07	0.74 ***
Married	0.04	0.09	1.05	0.11	0.07	1.11	-0.01	0.08	0.99	0.10	0.08	1.10	-0.03	0.07	0.74 ***
Prior arrest	0.45	0.08	1.56 ***	0.11	0.09	1.12	0.92	0.08	2.50 ***	0.86	0.08	2.36 ***	0.78	0.07	3.34 ***
Employed	0.02	0.09	1.02	-0.23	0.08	0.79 ***	-0.06	0.09	0.94	-0.16	0.07	0.85 *	-0.07	0.07	0.94
Constant	0.20	0.53		3.98	0.47	***	-0.07	0.52		-0.11	0.46	***			
Negative binomial scalar				5.02	0.17					2.12	0.13				
Initial likelihood	4292.51			-20158.7			4735.61			-4224.08			17656.49		
Final likelihood	3949.93		***	-5537.95		***	4476.31		***	-3618.03		***	17384.65		***

a = Logistic Regression; b = Negative Binominal Regression; c = Cox Regression.
* = p < 0.05; ** = p < 0.02; *** = p < 0.001.

and 8% in the incidence of recidivism, as well as a 12% reduction in the hazard rate. In other words, based on five outcome measures from two sources, there were consistently smaller rates of subsequent victimization and recidivism among the suspects assigned to the arrest treatment versus the nonarrest interventions.

For the two outcome measures based on victim interview data, these negative effects were statistically significant at the traditional $p < 0.05$ level.[8] Using the three outcome measures derived from the criminal history information, the arrest treatment also was associated with a reduction in the recidivism rates, but none of the differences between the two treatment groups were statistically significant.

The results reported in Table 4 also show that there were statistically significant differences in the base rates of failures across the five sites for all five outcome measures. We therefore tested to determine whether the effects of arrest were related to the site for any of the five measures, but did not find any evidence that was the case (see Maxwell, 1998 for detailed results of these tests). Thus, because the effects for arrest were in the same direction across all five measures and in the same direction in each of the five sites, as well as statistically significant in two of the five models, the results support the notion that, compared with nonarrest interventions, arrest provides additional safety to female victims of intimate partner assault. This finding is consistent with the specific deterrence hypothesis that these studies originally were testing.[9]

Effect of the Victim Interview Process

As mentioned above, we had to address the issue of missing victim interviews. We did so by including in the outcome models our interview exposure measure to assess the impact of the interview process on the outcome measures and on the effect of arrest. As reported in Table 4, we found higher victimization rates among those whose last interview occurred later in time after the initial experimental incident in four of the five comparisons. The one effect that was not significant was the relationship between exposure and failure measured by the victim's six-month victimization rate. This measure showed a negative association between the length of follow-up and the frequency of offenses reported by the victims.

Because our approach to controlling for missing victim interviews and time covered by the interviews was innovative, we also tested for relationships between arrest and our five outcomes without specifying the victim interview exposure measure. For the five models reported in Table 4, the exclusion of the exposure measure did not change the direction or statistical significance of either the treatment or site measures and the size of the arrest coefficients increased by an average of 3%. As an additional test of the interview selection process, we then modeled the criminal history data using only the suspects that had at least one victim interview ($n = 3,147$). The substantive results were similar to those reported in Table 4 for the full sample. Among this subsample, arrest led to a 7% reduction in the odds of any subsequent recidivism, but again this reduction was not significant ($p = 0.44$). The timing of the first subsequent incident ($b = 0.001$; $p = 0.988$) and the difference in the incident rates between the arrest and nonarrest groups were also not significant ($b = -0.01$; $p = 0.839$). Lastly, we compared the prevalence and incident rates of re-offending among those with and without a victim interview and found that suspects with noninterviewed victims have significantly smaller rates of recidivism across all three measures. This finding is contrary to our concern that noninterviewed victims in the SARP experiments might have had higher rates of repeat victimizations. From these results, we conclude that discrepancies in the size and statistical significance of the arrest coefficients from the victim interviews and from the official records were due less to differences in the interviewed and noninterviewed samples, and more to the ability of the victim interviews to capture subsequent victimizations not included in official police reports.

Effects of Suspect Characteristics

In Table 4, we also included statistical tests for the suspect's age, use of intoxicants at the experimental incident, race, marital status, prior arrest record, and employment status. Older suspects were less likely to aggress against their female intimate partners (cf., Farrington, 1986:7). Intimate partner aggression is perhaps also resistant to low-cost legal sanctions: Having one or more prior arrests for any offense against any victim was consistently associated with greater quantity of incidents, and this relationship was statistically significant in four of our five regression models (cf., Moffitt et al., 2000). The size of the relationship between prior arrest and new incidents ranged from about a 12% increase in the odds of a new victimization to a 234% increase in the odds for the time-to-first-failure in the official criminal history records. Alcohol use increased the risk of intimate partner aggression: The use of intoxicants at the time of the experimental incident was similarly associated with increased failures in four out of five outcome measures, and two of these positive relationships were statistically significant (the prevalence of victimization and the prevalence of recidivism) (cf., Fagan and Browne, 1994:3; Kantor and Straus, 1987).[10]

The suspect's race had a substantial and statistically significant relationship to subsequent failures, but the direction of the association depended on whether the data came from the victim interviews or official records. Based on victim interview data, victims were more likely to report new offenses if the suspect was white. Based on the criminal history information, white suspects were less likely to recidivate compared with all other suspects. The sizes of these relationships was substantial, from a 35% increase in the odds of victimization to a 30% decrease in the odds of recidivism. The role of the suspect's marital relationship with the victim also varied in size and direction by outcome measure. By three outcome measures, married suspects were more likely to fail, and by two measures, they were less likely to fail. However, only for the prevalence of new victimization was the increase statistically associated with married suspects. This one relationship was nearly a 5% increase. Finally, in four out of five models, employed suspects were less likely to commit additional incidents (cf., Sherman et al., 1992a). Two of the four negative relationships were statistically significant and ranged from 15% to 21% decreases in the odds of new incidents.

The results regarding the additional covariates suggest that the preventive effect of arrest was modest relative to the size of the relationships between suspect and victim characteristics and failure rates. We base this assessment primarily on comparing the sizes of Menard's (1995) standardized logistic regression coefficients, which corresponds to a one standard deviation increase in the independent measure for every b standard deviation change in logit (Y). The standardized coefficients based on the official criminal history data were arrest = -0.01; interview exposure = 0.09; prior arrest = 0.19; white = -0.08; age = -0.05; intoxication = 0.04; employed = 0.01; and married = 0.00. The standardized coefficients for the victim interview data were arrest = -0.06; interview exposure = 0.15; prior record = 0.10; arrest = -0.06; age = -0.05; white = 0.05; married = 0.01; intoxication = 0.00; and employment = 0.00.

DISCUSSION AND CONCLUSION

The design and implementation of the Spouse Assault Replication Program approaches the standards for criminological research put forth by the National Academy of Sciences (Blumstein et al., 1978; Sechrest et al., 1979). The five experiments used a common protocol that included random assignment of treatment after selecting incidents, documentation of suspect and victim characteristics, collection of outcome data from multiple sources, and data elements that allowed for the construction of multiple dimensions of subsequent offending. Earlier efforts to synthesize the SARP results have failed to capitalize on these important characteristics. Instead, these earlier syntheses relied on qualitative methods (Schmidt and Sherman, 1993), tested models using data from only a few sites (Sherman et al., 1992a), modeled just one outcome from one data source (Berk et al., 1992), or relied on published results (Sugarman and Boney-McCoy, 2000). To address these shortcomings, our research integrated original data from all five experiments, standardized cases according to the nature of incidents, employed three dimensions of outcomes, controlled for natural variation between suspects and incidents, used multiple sources of information about outcomes, and controlled for variability in victim interview rates and timing.

Policy Implications

Our findings of a consistent reduction in the incidents of victimization due to arrest, independent of other criminal justice sanctions and individual processes, support the continued use of arrests as a preferred law enforcement response for reducing subsequent victimization of women by their intimate partners.[11] Although the size and statistical significance of the effect of arrest varied depending on whether victim interviews or law enforcement records measured the suspect's subsequent aggression, in all five measures, arrest is associated with fewer incidents of subsequent intimate partner aggression. This finding exists during the first several days after the experimental incident as well as beyond one year. Thus, our research does not find that arrest will eventually increase the risk for violence against women.

In several ways, the results we generated from the Spouse Assault Replication Program provide stronger support for pro-arrest policies than do the results from the Minneapolis Domestic Violence experiment. First, our findings stem from five jurisdictions with a total sample of more than 4,000 male suspects, whereas the Minneapolis findings were based on 314 incidents collected in one jurisdiction. Second, the random assignment procedures used in SARP were more rigorous than the one used in Minneapolis. Third, SARP researchers interviewed almost 80% of the female victims, whereas only about 60% were interviewed in Minneapolis. Finally, our analyses control for missing victim interviews, the variability in timing of victim interviews, and suspect characteristics. Sherman and Berk's (1984b) published findings consider only the assigned treatment effects.

In addition, our data and methods may underestimate the current empirical support for arrest for a number of reasons. First, although Sherman and Berk's (1984b) Minneapolis results provide strong support for the deterrent effect for arrest, we could not incorporate cases from Minneapolis into our analyses. If the archived Minneapolis data were sufficiently complete and similar to SARP's common data, their use would likely enhance the evidence for the effectiveness of arrest. Second, our analyses compared cases assigned to arrest with those cases not assigned to arrest. However, the police arrested about 10% of the cases assigned to an informal treatment. Thus, the comparison between the arrest and the nonarrest treatments is diluted. Had the treatment assignment been implemented perfectly, the size of our reported deterrent effect might have been even larger.

On the other hand, because the size of the deterrent effects found in our analyses is smaller than those reported in the Minneapolis experiment, and because the results from our analyses of the official criminal history data do not reach statistical significance, our findings provide weaker support for pro-arrest policies than the Minneapolis findings provided. Nevertheless, on balance, we believe that the predominate weight of the empirical regularities favors a conclusion that arrest has a modest preventive effect on intimate partner violence.

Unlike most criminological research, the Minneapolis Domestic Violence Experiment and SARP were part of a continuing program of research that focused on a theory-driven policy addressing an important social problem. The results of these efforts have identified some benefits of arrest, specifically, the reduction of victimization of female intimate partners. However, as extensive as this program was, it does not provide a complete basis for a systematic examination of the costs and the benefits of the use of arrest to address violence against women. For instance, some academics (e.g., Stark, 1993) have argued for arresting batterers no matter its deterrent benefits because the forced separation provides immediate, presumably incapacitative, protection for the victims. Others have pondered whether arrest may create negative outcomes when other effects on the victims, the suspects, and their families are considered. Binder and Meeker (1992) suggest that arrest may have both positive and negative collateral consequences on children in the household, the likelihood that a spouse will call the police in the future, the stability of the marriage, and the suspect's employment status (see also Berk and Sherman, 1985; McCord, 1992). In addition, both fiscal and resource expenditures are attached to arresting suspects as well as possible reductions in expenditures due to law enforcement agencies responding to fewer subsequent encounters with suspects. However, neither SARP nor other systematic research has generated evidence about other possible costs or benefits of arrests. Although this type of assessment is routine in the development of environmental, health, and safety regulations (Cohen, 2000), we are unaware of any attempt to address the question of whether the benefits we find outweigh the cost of arrest to society. Therefore, a more thorough assessment of a policy promoting or mandating arrest needs to capture both the major costs and benefits of arrest.

The findings from the SARP experiment also suggest real limitations in the effectiveness of arrest in reducing violence against women. The evidence from this study shows that regardless of the treatment assigned and irrespective of the data source, most victims reported no subsequent victimization by their male partner during follow-up periods that ranged from six months to more than two years. The mere physical presence of a police officer may redefine the parameters of the violence from an interpersonal struggle for power to one that now involves, formally or informally, outsiders. Although the presence of an outsider may last from a few minutes to an hour, it may be enough to convince many suspects that the victim and the police mean business. In other words, the threat of arrest may suffice as the best specific deterrent for most suspects.[12]

However, victimizations also persisted for about 40% of victims. We estimate that the average suspect with at least one subsequent incident had committed about an average of seven new incidents of aggression against the same victim within just the first six months of follow-up. Apparently, some women continue to be victimized multiple times by their intimate partners, even after the police have responded to a request for help. For these reasons, the SARP experiments show that arresting suspects, although effective on average, is not a panacea for all victims of intimate partner violence. This suggests that other policies, either replacing or enhancing the use of arrest, that focus on identifying potential repeat offenders and either treating, sanctioning, or incapacitating them might produce larger reductions in intimate partner violence.

The challenge is twofold: developing plausible policies and carrying out a long-term, systematic research program that rigorously tests the underlying theories of those policies.

Testing Theory

Sherman (1980) designed the Minneapolis Domestic Violence Experiment as a test of specific deterrence theory. Its apparent impact on public policy might be a coincidence or a single example that illustrates a point—successful efforts at policy relevance need not be atheoretical. We believe that the use of theory in the Minneapolis and SARP experiments should enhance their policy relevance because the theoretical framework provides a basis for generalizing the results beyond a few jurisdictions at one point in time. However, the theoretical formulation used in the Minneapolis and SARP experiments was not fully developed. It merely asserted that there would be some reduction in criminal behavior with use of a formal sanction. This simple formulation makes specific deterrence theory infallible; because with any contrary finding, researchers can assert that the sanction was not swift, certain, or severe enough.

With our research, the field now has systematic evidence about how much reduction in subsequent violence is associated with arresting suspects for intimate partner violence. However, we agree with Lempert (1989) that additional sanctions need to be tested in ways that experimentally compare variations in the certainty, celerity, and severity across a variety of offenses, offenders, and victims. SARP contributes to this kind of theory-testing effort by examining one sanction for one offense in a variety of contexts. One of our concerns is that others might instead overgeneralize our results to support the use of more severe sanctions, particularly to control intimate partner violence, despite other research reporting no gains for domestic violence victims from more punitive practices such as prosecution (Davis et al., 1998; Ford, 1991; Steinman, 1990; Thistlethwaite et al., 1998). For these reasons, we advise against simple extrapolations of the preventive effects of arrest to other criminal justice sanctions, such as the restraining orders or incarceration of batterers without further systematic research and evaluation.

In addition, we suggest that future research obtain measurements of the offender's immediate and long-term cognitive reactions to sanctions and treatments. Subsequent research also would be stronger if it measured secondary outcomes like changes in offenders' employment status and familial relationships, or the victims' and children's welfare.[13] These measurements could further our understanding of the "black box" of specific deterrence (Manning, 1993:641) and permit an assessment of whether there are unintended consequences of sanctions on those not directly punished. As McCord (1992:233) argued, further research on domestic violence needs to go beyond the concept of deterrence by also assessing whether sanctions lead to outcomes like "loss of support for children or loss of shelter." Except for interviewing some arrestees in Milwaukee (Sherman et al., 1990), the SARP experiments did not measure the suspects' attitudes and perceptions and therefore cannot address the variety of underlying mechanisms suggested by Gibbs (1975) that might account for the association between increased sanctions and reduced offending found here. At this time, the available research can only estimate the amount of subsequent aggression reduced because of arrest. We need further research to understand more completely why and when sanctions deter and whether secondary consequences of arrest exist.

Suspect Characteristics

Several suspect characteristics are significantly related to the prevalence, frequency, and timing of the first new incident of victimization and recidivism. For instance, the odds of new victimization were 30% to 60% less for each additional year of age. Also, according to the official data, suspects with prior arrests for any offense are from 250% to 330% more likely to commit new acts of intimate partner violence. Unlike the consistent effects for suspect's age and prior record, the contradictory findings regarding their race in victim interviews and official records present a conundrum for this and subsequent research. From official records, white suspects are less likely to re-offend after the experimental incident. The effect size is large, with a 30% reduction in the odds for both the frequency and timing of an officially recorded failure. However, the victim interview data yielded the opposite result: White suspects are 30% more likely than are nonwhite suspects to continue victimization. There are several plausible explanations for this contradiction, including race interactions with the severity of violence, the different treatments, or the willingness of victims to report incidents to the police.[14] Future research will need to address these possibilities to unravel the complex role of race and should also incorporate the suspect's age and arrest record.

DISCUSSION QUESTIONS

1. How was the Spouse Assault Replication Program (SARP) research design different from the Minneapolis experiment's research design? Are aspects of one more effective than the other?
2. What did the results of Maxwell and Fagan's study show about the effects of arrest on the reoccurrence of intimate partner violence?
3. Which suspect characteristics had significant effects on intimate partner violence?
4. What policy implications can be taken from the results of Maxwell and Fagan's study?

NOTES

1. In Omaha, victims were to be interviewed three times over a year. In Colorado Springs, three-quarters of the victims were to be interviewed every two weeks for the first three months, and all were interviewed at six months. In Milwaukee, 25% of victims were not interviewed until six months after the experimental incident. For more details about the SARP designs, see Maxwell (1998) and Garner and Maxwell (2000).

2. The idea for this design was originally proposed by Albert J. Reiss, Jr. and Robert F. Boruch.

3. The majority of decisions to avoid the random assignment (78% of misdelivered treatments) involved suspects who were randomly assigned to nonarrest treatments but were arrested. Officers chose not to arrest when arrest was assigned in 59 (22%) of all misdelivered treatments.

4. A logistic regression model found that the only suspect characteristics that predicted misdelivery of treatment are intoxication ($b = 0.57$; $p < 0.001$) and unemployment ($b = 0.30$; $p < 0.05$).

5. The Colorado Springs design called for interviews in the first and sixth month for 25% of the cases and for monthly interviews for 75% of the sample. The archived data from this site did not identify the actual date of any interview. To avoid losing the Colorado Springs data, we used the dates the interview was scheduled to occur.

6. We compared a poisson regression with a negative binomial regression, but in every instance, there was too much overdispersion to justify using the results based on the Poisson Regression model. This result is consistent with what has been found with other criminal justice data of similar format (Land et al., 1996).

7. We tested the Cox regression assumption of equal or proportional hazards by introducing a time-dependent covariate that indicates whether the effect of arrest is dependent on the passage of time. While controlling for site effects, we found that the time-dependent covariate is not significantly associated ($b = 0.00$; $p = 0.08$) with the hazard rate.

8. We report findings from the models that include controls for suspect characteristics because we believe these provide the most precise estimate of the effect of arrest.

9. In addition to arrest, some suspects received additional criminal justice sanctions or controls, such as restraining orders, conviction, probation, fines, or incarceration. In the Milwaukee experiment, the researcher found that 60% of the suspects appeared at the prosecutor's office for charging, 3.2% were charged, and 2.7% were required to attend counseling. The researchers also asked the victims about the presence of restraining orders and found that 12% reported having one against the suspect (Bousa et al., 1990). In the Charlotte site, about 25% of the suspects either pled guilty or were found guilty regardless of their assigned treatment. The Omaha and Colorado sites also collected data on court disposition, but no disposition information was collected in Dade. Although it may have been valuable to include measures of additional sanctions, there were several reasons we could not do so in our multisite analysis. First, these subsequent treatments were not randomly assigned. Thus, any analysis would be confounded with selection biases. Second, we do not know the timing of subsequent sanctions so we would not know whether re-offending started before or after the sanction. Third, although some of the experiments collected and archived data about some of these issues, these items were not common data elements in the SARP design.

10. The high correlation between victim and suspect demographics precluded us from including both in the same model.

11. One alternative explanation for our findings is that arrest does not change suspect offending as much as it changes the victim's willingness to report offenses to the police and to interviewers. Two recent empirical studies do not support this speculation. Using data from SARP's Metro-Dade County Experiment, Hickman (2000) found that the use of arrest in the experimental incident was not related to reporting subsequent incidents to the police. Felson and Ackerman (2001), using NCVS data, found that the existence of prior domestic assaults increased the respondent's willingness to sign a police complaint.

12. The argument that there is desistance from calling the police is consistent with Bowker (1984) and Dutton et al.'s (1991) claim that social disclosure alone deters further domestic violence. Although these scholars were speaking about disclosure originating out of an arrest, the same effect seems likely to occur from just calling the police.

13. See, for instance, Paternoster and Brame's (1997) test of the effect of police procedural justice on recidivism using information from interviews of arrested offenders from the Milwaukee Domestic Violence Experiment.

14. Similar to our finding concerning the relationship between aggression and race, Bachman and Coker (1995) found evidence using the National Crime Victimization Survey that victimized African-American women were more likely to call the police compared with victimized white women. They also found that if the police were called to the scene, the officers were more likely to arrest the suspect if the victim and suspect were both African-American. Together, these two findings suggest an explanation for the relationship between the suspect's race and the likelihood of officially recorded failure found in SARP.

REFERENCES

Armitage, Peter (1996). The design and analysis for clinical trials. In Subir Ghosh and Calyampudi Radhakrishna Rao (eds.), *Design and Analysis of Experiments, Vol. 13, Handbook of Statistics*. Amsterdam: Elsevier.

Bachman, Ronet and Ann L. Coker (1995). Police involvement in domestic violence: The interactive effects of victim injury, offender's history of violence, and race. *Violence and Victims* 10:91–106.

Berk, Richard A. (1993). What the scientific evidence shows: On the average, we can do no better than arrest. In Richard J. Gelles and Donileen R. Loseke (eds.), *Current Controversies on Family Violence*. Newbury Park, Calif.: Sage.

Berk, Richard A. and Lawrence W. Sherman (1985). Data collection strategies in the Minneapolis domestic violence experiment. In Leigh Burstein, Howard E. Freeman, and Peter H. Rossi (eds.), *Collecting Evaluation Data: Problems and Solutions*. Beverly Hills, Calif.: Sage.

Berk, Richard A., Alec Campbell, Ruth Klap, and Bruce Western (1988). Police responses to family violence incidences: An analysis of an experimental design with incomplete randomization. *Journal of the American Statistical Association* 83:70–76.

Berk, Richard A., Alec Campbell, Ruth Klap, and Bruce Western (1992). The deterrent effect of arrest in incidents of domestic violence: A Bayesian analysis of four field experiments. *American Journal of Sociology* 57:698–708.

Binder, Arnold and James Meeker (1988). Experiments as reforms. *Journal of Criminal Justice* 16:347–358.

Binder, Arnold and James Meeker (1992). Arrest as a method to control spouse abuse. In Eve S. Buzawa and Carl G. Buzawa (eds.), *Domestic Violence: The Changing Criminal Justice Response.* Westport, Colo.: Greenwood.

Blumstein, Alfred, Jacqueline Cohen, and Daniel Nagin (eds.) (1978). *Estimating the Effects of Criminal Sanctions on Crime Rates.* Washington, D.C.: National Academy Press.

Blumstein, Alfred, Jacqueline Cohen, Jeffrey A. Roth, and Christy A. Visher (eds.) (1986). *Criminal Careers and "Career Criminals."* Washington, D.C.: National Academy Press.

Boffey, Philip M. (1983). Domestic violence: Study favors arrest. *New York Times* (5 April): Cl.

Bousa, Dominick, Sherman, Janell D. Schmidt, Dennis Rogan, and Patrick Gartin (1990). *Codebook and Frequencies for the Milwaukee Domestic Violence Experiment: The Criminal Justice Processing File.* Washington, D.C.: Crime Control Institute.

Bowker, Lee N. (1984). Coping with wife abuse: Personal and social networks. In Albert R. Roberts (ed.), *Battered Women and Their Families.* New York: Springer.

Chalk, Rosemary A. and Patricia A. King (eds.) (1998). *Violence in Families: Assessing Prevention and Treatment Programs.* Committee on the Assessment of Family Violence Intervention, Board on Children, Youth, and Families, National Research Council and Institute of Medicine. Washington, D.C: National Academy of Science.

Clark. Jacob R. (1993). Where to now on domestic-violence? Studies offer mixed policy guidance. *Law Enforcement News* (30 April):1,17.

Cohen, Mark A. (2000). Measuring the Costs and Benefits of Crime and Justice. David Duffee (ed.). *Criminal Justice* 2000,4, no. NCJ 182411. Washington, D.C.: U.S. Department of Justice, Office of Justice Programs, National Institute of Justice.

Cooper, Harris and Larry V. Hedges (1994). Research synthesis as a scientific enterprise. In Harris Cooper and Larry V. Hedges (eds.), *The Handbook of Research Synthesis.* New York: Russell Sage.

Davis, Robert C., and Barbara Smith (1995). Domestic violence reforms: Empty promises or fulfilled expectations? *Crime & Delinquency* 41:541–552.

Davis, Robert C., Barbara E. Smith, and Laura B. Nickles (1998). The deterrent effect of prosecuting domestic violence misdemeanors. *Crime & Delinquency* 3:434–442.

Dutton, Donald G., Stephen G. Hart, Leslie W. Kennedy, and Kirk R. Williams (1991). Arrest and the reduction of repeat wife assault. In Eve Buzawa and Carl Buzawa (eds.), *Domestic Violence: The Changing Criminal Justice Response.* Westport, Conn.: Greenwood.

Fagan, Jeffrey A. (1996). The Criminalization of Domestic Violence: Promises and limits. Presented at the Conference on Criminal Justice Research and Evaluation. Washington, D.C., National Institute of Justice.

Fagan, Jeffrey A. and Angela Browne (1994). Violence against spouses and intimates. Panel on the Understanding and Control of Violent Behavior, Committee on Law and Justice, Commission on Behavioral and Social Science and Education, National Research Council. In Albert J. Reiss, Jr. and Jeffrey A. Roth (eds.), *Understanding and Controlling Violence,* Vol. 3. Washington, D.C.: National Academy Press.

Farrington, David P. (1986). Age and crime. In Michael Tonry and Noval Morris (eds.), *Crime and Justice: An Annual Review of Research, Vol. 7, Crime and Justice.* Chicago, Ill.: University of Chicago Press.

Feld, Scott L. and Murray Straus (1989). Escalation and desistance of wife assault in marriage. *Criminology* 27:141–161.

Felson, Richard B. and Jeff Ackerman (2001). Arrest for domestic violence and other assaults. *Criminology* 39: 655–675.

Ford, David (1991). Prosecution as a victim power source: A note on empowering women in violent conjugal relationships. *Law & Society Review* 25:313–334.

Frisch, Lisa A. (1992). Research that succeeds, policies that fail. *Journal of Criminal Law & Criminology* 83: 209–216.

Garner, Joel H. and Christopher D. Maxwell (2000). What are the lessons of the police arrest studies? *Journal of Aggression, Maltreatment & Trauma* 4(1):83–114.

Garner, Joel H., Jeffrey A. Fagan, and Christopher D. Maxwell (1995). Published findings from the Spouse Assault Replication Program: A critical review. *Journal of Quantitative Criminology* 11:3–28.

Gibbs, Jack P. (1975). *Crime, Punishment and Deterrence.* New York: Elsevier.

Heckman, James J. (1979). Sample selection bias as a specification error. *Econometrica* 47:153–161.

Heckman, James J. and Richard Robb (1986). Alternative methods for solving the problem of selection bias in evaluating the impact of treatment outcomes. In Howard Wainer (ed.), *Drawing Inferences from Self-Selected Samples.* Papers from a conference sponsored by Education Testing Services. New York: Springer-Verlag.

Hickman, Laura Jean (2000). Exploring the impact of police behavior on the subsequent reporting of domestic violence victims. Ph.D. dissertation, University of Maryland at College Park.

Hirschel, J. David and Ira W. Hutchison III (1991). Police-preferred arrest policies. In Michael Steinman (ed.), *Women Battering: Policy Responses,* Vol. 3. Highland Heights, KY and Cincinnati, Ohio: Anderson Publishing Co. and Academy of Criminal Justice Science.

Kantor, Glenda K. and Murray A. Straus (1987). The "drunken bum" theory of wife beating. *Social Problems* 34: 213–321

Klinger, David A. and George S. Bridges (1997). Measurement error in calls-for-service as an indicator of crime. *Criminology* 35:705–726.

Land, Kenneth C., Patricia L. McCall, and Daniel S. Nagin (1996). A comparison of Poisson, negative binomial, and semiparametric mixed regression models with empirical applications to criminal careers data. *Sociological Methods and Research* 24:387–442.

Langan, Patrick A. and Christopher A. Innes (1986). *Preventing Domestic Violence Against Women, Special Report.* Washington, D.C.: U.S. Government Printing Office.

Lempert, Richard (1984). From the editor. *Law & Society Review* 18:505–513. (1989). Humility is a virtue: On the publication of policy relevant research. *Law & Society Review* 23:145–161.

Lerman, Lisa G. (1992). The decontextualization of domestic violence. *Journal of Criminal Law & Criminology* 83:217–240.

Manning, Peter K. (1993). The preventive conceit: The black box in market context. *American Behavioral Scientist* 36:639–650.

Maxwell, Christopher D. (1998). The specific deterrent effect of arrest on aggression between intimates and spouses. Ph.D. dissertation, Newark, N.J.: Rutgers, the State University of New Jersey.

Maxwell, Christopher D., Joel H. Garner, and Jeffrey A. Fagan (2001). *The Effects of Arrest on Intimate Partner Violence: New Evidence from the Spouse Assault Replication Program.* Research in Brief. Washington, D.C.: U.S. Department of Justice, Office of Justice Programs, National Institute of Justice.

McCord, Joan (1992). Deterrence of domestic violence: A critical view of research. *Journal of Research in Crime and Delinquency* 29(2):229–239.

Menard, Scott (1995). *Applied Logistic Regression Analysis, Quantitative Applications in the Social Sciences.* 07–106. Michael S. Lewis-Beck (ed.). Thousand Oaks, Calif.: Sage.

Mitchell, David B. (1992). Contemporary police practices in domestic violence cases: Arresting the abuser: Is it enough? *Journal of Criminal Law & Criminology* 83:241–249.

Moffitt, Terrie E., Robert F. Krueger, Avshalom Caspi, and Jeffrey Fagan (2000). Partner abuse and general crime: How are they the same? How are they different? *Criminology* 38:199–232.

Nagin, Daniel S. and David P. Farrington (1992). The onset and persistence of offending. *Criminology* 30:501–523.

National Institute of Justice (1985). *Replicating an Experiment in Specific Deterrence: Alternative Police Responses to Spouse Assault.* Washington, D.C.: National Institute of Justice.

Pate, Anthony and Edwin E. Hamilton (1992). Formal and informal deterrents to domestic violence. *American Sociological Review* 57:691–697.

Paternoster, Raymond and Robert Brame (1997). Multiple routes to delinquency? A test of developmental and general theories of crime. *Criminology* 35:49–84.

Quigley, Brian M. and Kenneth E. Leonard (1996). Desistance of husband aggression in the early years of marriage. *Violence and Victims* 11: 355–370.

Sampson, Robert J. and John H. Laub (1993). Structural variations in juvenile court processing: Inequality, the underclass, and social control. *Law and Society Review* 27:285–311.

Schmidt, Janell D. and Lawrence W. Sherman (1993). Does arrest deter domestic violence? *American Behavioral Scientist* 36:601–610.

Sechrest, Lee, Susan O. White, and Elizabeth Brown (eds.) (1979). *The Rehabilitation of Criminal Offenders: Problems and Prospects.* Washington, D.C.: National Academy of Sciences.

Sherman, Lawrence W. (1980). Specific deterrent effect of spouse assault. Proposal submitted to the National Institute of Justice Crime Control Theory Program. U.S. Department of Justice, Washington, D.C.

Sherman, Lawrence W. (1992). *Policing Domestic Violence: Experiments and Dilemmas.* New York: Free Press.

Sherman, Lawrence W. and R.A. Berk (1984a). The Minneapolis Domestic Violence Experiment. Police Foundation Reports, No. 1. Washington, D.C.

Sherman, Lawrence W. and R.A. Berk (1984b). The specific deterrent effects of arrest for domestic assault. *American Sociological Review* 49:261–272.

Sherman, Lawerence W. and Ellen G. Cohn (1989). The impact of research on legal policy: The Minneapolis Domestic Violence Experiment. *Law and Society Review* 23:117–144

Sherman, Lawrence W., Douglas A. Smith, Janell D. Schmidt, and Dennis P. Rogan (1992a). Crime, punishment, and stake in conformity: Legal and informal control of domestic violence. *American Sociological Review* 57:680–690.

Sherman, Lawerence W., Janell D. Schmidt, Dennis P. Rogan, Douglas A. Smith, Patrick Gartin, Ellen G. Cohen, Dean J. Collins, and Anthony R. Bacich (1992b). The variable effects of arrest on crime control: The Milwaukee Domestic Violence Experiment. *Journal of Criminal Law & Criminology* 83:137–169.

Sherman, Lawrence W., Janell D Schmidt, Dennis P. Rogan, Patrick R. Gartin, Dean J. Collins, Anthony Bacich, and Ellen G. Cohn (1990). *The Milwaukee Domestic Violence Experiment. Final Report*. Washington, D.C.: Crime Control Institute.

Stark, Evan (1993). Mandatory arrest of batterers: A reply to its critics. *American Behavioral Scientist* 36:651–680.

Steinman, Michael (1990). Lowering recidivism among men who batter women. *Journal of Police Science and Administration* 17:124–132.

Sugarman, David B. and Sue Boney-McCoy (2000). Research synthesis in family violence: The art of reviewing the research. *Journal of Aggression, Maltreatment & Trauma* 4:55–82.

Thistlethwaite, Amy, John Wooldredge, and David Gibbs (1998). Severity of disposition and domestic violence recidivism. *Crime & Delinquency* 3:388–398.

U.S. Attorney General's Task Force on Family Violence (1984). *Attorney General's Task Force on Family Violence. Final Report* Washington, D.C.: U.S. Government Printing Office.

Violence Against Women Grants Office (1996). Grants to Encourage Arrest Policies Programs. Proposed Regulations No. 28 CFR Part 90 [OJP No. 1019] RIN 1121–AA35. Washington, D.C.: Office for Justice Programs, U.S. Department of Justice, 13.

Wilson, James O. (1977). Forward. In Police Foundation (ed.), *Domestic Violence and the Police*. Washington, D.C.: Police Foundation.

Zimring, Franklin E. (1989). Toward a jurisprudence of family violence. In Lloyd Oblin and Michael Tonry (eds.), *Family Violence, Vol. 11, Crime and Justice: A Review of Research*. Chicago, Ill.: University of Chicago Press.

Zorza, Joan and Laurie Woods (1994). *Analysis and Policy Implications of the New Police Domestic Violence Studies*. New York: National Center on Women and Family Law.

8

✦

Militarizing the
Police

Peter Kraska

This work examines the blurring distinctions between the police and military institutions and between war and law enforcement. In this article, the author asserts that understanding this blur, and the associated organizing concepts militarization *and* militarism, *are essential for accurately analyzing the changing nature of security, and the activity of policing, in the late-modern era of the twenty-first century.*

S implicity is comforting. Modernity's basic dichotomies such as fact/ value, private/public, and national/international simplify our thinking and lull us into intellectual complacency. Police academics in the United States, with only a few exceptions, have been quite comfortable with the military/police dichotomy. The US military handles external security through the threat and practice of war. The civilian police handle internal security through the enforcement of federal and local laws. Most assume that studying the police and military is a mutually exclusive undertaking. Taking this dichotomy for granted is understandable given that the clear demarcation between the police and military has been considered a preeminent feature of the modern

Source: Peter Kraska, "Militarization and Policing–Its Relevance to 21st Century Police," Policing, vol 1:4. Copyright © 2007 Oxford University Press. Reprinted with permission.

nation-state (Giddens, 1985). The failure of a government to clearly demarcate the two is usually seen as an indicator of repressiveness and lack of democracy.

My research and writing has been challenging this dichotomy since the late 1980s. Its central thesis has remained steadfast, and may be viewed at this point in history as an obvious point to the keenly observant: we have been witnesses to a little noticed but nonetheless momentous historical change–the traditional distinctions between military/police, war/law enforcement, and internal/external security are rapidly blurring. Over the past 15 years, I have researched and traced the evolution of two interrelated trends that embody this blur: the militarization of US police and crime control, and the policeization of the US military. Empirical indicators of these converging trends include the following:

- the significant erosion of the 1878 Posse Comitatus Act by the United States, which previous to the early 1980s prohibited the military involvement in internal security or police matters, except under the most extreme circumstances, leading to an unprecedented level of US armed forces' involvement in internal security matters;

- the advent of an unprecedented cooperative relationship between the US military and US civilian police at both the highest and lowest level of organization, including technology transfers, massive military weapons transfers, information sharing between the military and police targeted at domestic security, a close operational relationship in both drug control and terrorism control efforts, and a high level of cross-training in the area of special weapons and tactics team (SWAT) and counter-civil disturbance, counterinsurgency, and antiterrorism exercises;

- the steep growth and normalization of police special operations units (e.g. SWAT teams) that are *modeled after* (not identical to) elite military special operations groups;

- a growing tendency by the police and other segments of the criminal justice system to rely on the military/war model for formulating crime/drug/terrorism control rationale and operations; and a redefining of criminality to 'insurgency' and crime control to 'low-intensity conflict'—requiring counter-insurgency measures carried out by both the US military and civilian police.

This article submits that understanding this blur, and the associated organizing concepts *militarization* and *militarism*, are essential for accurately analyzing the changing nature of security, and the activity of policing, in the late-modern era of the 21st century. Police leaders, in particular, will have to be increasingly cognizant and wary of the implications and potential consequences of this convergence, and the attendant social forces of militarism and militarization. The aim of this article, then, is to expose and sensitize the reader to what we might call a martial theoretical orientation. The idea here is to employ this orientation as a type of conceptual lens, or interpretive construct, which when peered through, will help us assess and accurately make sense of current trends in the police institution, the activity of policing, crime control, and warfare.

THE MILITARISM/MILITARIZATION CONCEPTUAL LENS APPLIED TO THE POLICE

The concepts in which I have centered the bulk of my work are 'militarization' and 'militarism.' Despite these terms' pejorative undertones for some, they are most often used in academe as rigorous organizing concepts that help us to think more clearly about the influence war and the military model have on different aspects of society.

Assessing whether a civilian police force, for example, is becoming 'militarized' should not be viewed as an antipolice or an antimilitary pursuit. Evaluating police militarization is a credible and important endeavor, and it can be accomplished through empirical evidence and rigorous scholarship. Of course, the integrity of this endeavor hinges on the clarity of our concepts.

Militarism, in its most basic sense, is an ideology focused on the best means to solve problems. It is a set of beliefs, values, and assumptions that stress the use of force and threat of violence as the most appropriate and efficacious means to solve problems. It emphasizes the exercise of military power, hardware, organization, operations, and technology as its primary problem-solving tools. *Militarization* is the implementation of the ideology, militarism. It is the process of arming, organizing, planning, training for, threatening, and sometimes implementing violent conflict. To militarize means adopting and applying the central elements of the military model to an organization or particular situation.

Police militarization, therefore, is simply the process whereby civilian police increasingly draw from, and pattern themselves around, the tenets of militarism and the military model. As seen in Figure 1, four dimensions of the military model provide us with tangible indicators of police militarization:

- material—martial weaponry, equipment, and advanced technology;
- cultural—martial language, style (appearance), beliefs, and values;
- organizational—martial arrangements such as 'command and control' centers [e.g. (COMPSTAT)], or elite squads of officers patterned after military special operations patrolling high-crime areas (as opposed to the traditional officer on the beat);
- operational—patterns of activity modeled after the military such as in the areas of intelligence, supervision, handling high-risk situations, or war-making/restoration (e.g. weed and seed).

It should be obvious that the police since their inception have been to some extent 'militarized.' After all, the foundation of military and police power is the same—the state sanctioned capacity to use physical force to accomplish their respective objectives (external and internal security) (discussed further in Kraska, 1994). Therefore, the real concern when discerning police militarization is one of degree—or put differently, the extent to which a civilian police body is militarized.

To militarize means adopting and applying the central elements of the military model to an organization or particular situation. Police militarization, therefore, is simply the process whereby civilian police increasingly draw from, and pattern themselves around, the military model. The figure below illustrates the four central dimensions of the military model that constitute tangible indicators of militarization.

Because the police have always been "militaristic" to some degree throughout their history, any analysis of militarization among civilian police has to focus on where the civilian police fall on the continuum and in what direction they are headed. This assessment will vary considerably when viewing not only different police forces around the world, but even different police agencies with a decentralized system such as in the U.S.

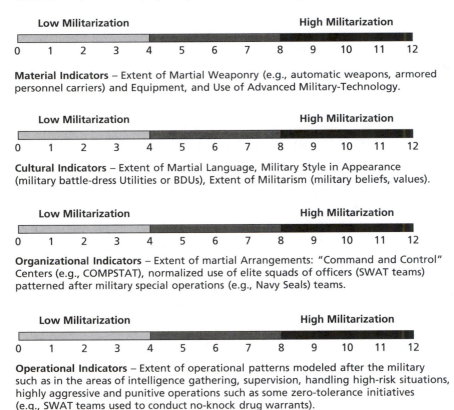

Low Militarization   **High Militarization**

0   1   2   3   4   5   6   7   8   9   10   11   12

Material Indicators – Extent of Martial Weaponry (e.g., automatic weapons, armored personnel carriers) and Equipment, and Use of Advanced Military-Technology.

Low Militarization   **High Militarization**

0   1   2   3   4   5   6   7   8   9   10   11   12

Cultural Indicators – Extent of Martial Language, Military Style in Appearance (military battle-dress Utilities or BDUs), Extent of Militarism (military beliefs, values).

Low Militarization   **High Militarization**

0   1   2   3   4   5   6   7   8   9   10   11   12

Organizational Indicators – Extent of martial Arrangements: "Command and Control" Centers (e.g., COMPSTAT), normalized use of elite squads of officers (SWAT teams) patterned after military special operations (e.g., Navy Seals) teams.

Low Militarization   **High Militarization**

0   1   2   3   4   5   6   7   8   9   10   11   12

Operational Indicators – Extent of operational patterns modeled after the military such as in the areas of intelligence gathering, supervision, handling high-risk situations, highly aggressive and punitive operations such as some zero-tolerance initiatives (e.g., SWAT teams used to conduct no-knock drug warrants).

FIGURE 1 Assessing Police Militarization Using Continuums*

*A version of this figure can be found in Kraska and Neuman's (2008) *Criminal Justice and Criminology Research Methods*. Prentice-Hall.

Police militarization, in all countries and across any time in history, must be conceived of as the degree or extent of militarization. Any assertion that the police are or are not militarized is simply misguided. This is a nuance easily overlooked by police analysts who react defensively to using these organiz- ing concepts (Kraska, 1999). They reason that because a police paramilitary squad such as a US SWAT team retains key attributes of civilian police—for example not being allowed to indiscriminately kill—the concepts of 'mili- tarization' or 'militarism' do not apply. This encourages a one-dimensional conceptual lens which sees police as either being militarized or not. The point here is that any analysis of militarization among civilian police has to focus on where the civilian police fall on the continuum—culturally, organizationally, operationally, and materially—and in what direction they are currently headed (Kraska, 1999).

It is worth noting that beyond the police, militarism and militarization can operate as powerful theoretical lenses to make sense of many issues and trends in society—particularly those societies such as the United States that place a premium on military superiority. In fact, many analysts see these as dominant influences in foreign policy and increasingly domestic policies when it comes to issues of security.

For example, the US government has been rapidly redefining what constitutes a threat to national security by turning its gaze inward, thereby militarizing to a significant degree its domestic security efforts (referred to as the 'national security syndrome') (Sherry, 1985; Klare, 1980). Scholars such as Tonry (2004); Christie (2000) and Ericson and Carriere (1994) have illuminated the role that martial rhetoric has in this process—focusing specifically on the militarization of US domestic crime-control initiatives (and increasingly in other countries as well). Metaphors such as the war on drugs, crime, and terrorism play a powerful role in the construction of reality: they shape discursive practices, clarify values and understanding, and guide problem-solving processes. Framing the crime, terrorism, and drug problems using militaristic language, thus, will likely result in thoughts and actions which correspond with the war/military paradigm (Kraska, 2001).

Another useful insight came from Dwight D. Eisenhower's (retired US Army general and former US President) thinking about the growing influence of the military paradigm. He dedicated his farewell speech to warning against the growing influence of militarism in US society. He coined the phrase, 'military-industrial-complex' (M.I.C.) in an attempt to raise the public consciousness about the undue influence of militarization in US society. Contemporary militarization in his view benefited not the public good, but politicians, bureaucrats, and corporations; a charge often heard today from those critical of the US-led war against Iraq. Similarly, several academics have argued that the crime-control enterprise operates as an analogous industrial complex—complete with political, governmental, and private-growth pressures (Christie, 2000; others found in Kraska, 2004). This essay raises the distinct possibility that we are witnesses to a growing overlap between military and criminal justice complexes.

DETAILING THE POLICE/MILITARY BLUR

A large body of literature documents the extent to which US police agencies have recently relied more heavily on the military model for various functions (Kraska, 2001; Maguire and King, 2004). A less well-developed literature has attempted to extend this thesis internationally (Lutterbeck, 2004; McCulloch, 2004). Likewise, both academic scholars and leading military analysts recognize the growing law-enforcement role and function of the US armed forces (Dunlap, 2001; Haggerty and Ericson, 2001; Dunn, 2001; Kraska, 2001; Zimmerman, 2005). The following, therefore, is a brief review of some of this work and its thinking.

Militarizing American Police

I began inquiring into the contemporary role the military model has on the US police when conducting a 2-year long ethnography of multijurisdictional SWAT teams (Kraska, 1996). Spending hundreds of hours training and going on actual deployments, I learned a great deal about police paramilitary units (PPUs) at the ground level, and especially police paramilitary culture. I first learned that PPUs derive their appearance, tactics, operations, weaponry, and culture to a significant extent from military special operations units (e.g. Navy Seals). (It is important to reiterate that PPUs are only closely modeled after these teams—clearly there are also key differences between a PPU and a military special operations unit—this is why they are referred to as police *para* military.)

With BDUs, heavy weaponry, training in hostage rescue, dynamic entries into fortified buildings, and some of the latest military technology, it became clear that these squads of officers fall significantly further down the militarization continuum—culturally, organizationally, operationally, and materially—than the traditional, lone cop-on-the-beat or road-patrol officer.

I also learned that the paramilitary culture associated with SWAT teams is highly appealing to a *certain segment* of civilian police (certainly not all civilian police). As with special operations soldiers in the military, members of these units saw themselves as the elite police involved in real crime fighting and danger. A large network of for-profit training, weapons, and equipment suppliers heavily promotes paramilitary culture at police shows, in police magazine advertisements, and in training programs sponsored by gun manufacturers such as Smith and Wesson and Heckler and Koch. The 'military special operations' culture—characterized by a distinct techno-warrior garb, heavy weaponry, sophisticated technology, hypermasculinity, and dangerous function—was nothing less than intoxicating for its participants.

I most importantly learned that my micro-level experience might have been indicative of a much larger phenomenon. I decided to test empirically my ground-level observations by conducting two independently funded national-level surveys. These surveys of both large and small police agencies yielded definitive data documenting the militarization of a significant component of the US police (Kraska and Kappeler, 1997; Kraska and Cubellis, 1997). This militarization was evidenced by a precipitous rise and main-streaming of PPUs. As of the late 1990s, about 89% of police departments in the United States serving populations of 50,000 people or more had a PPU, almost double of what existed in the mid-1980s. Their growth in smaller jurisdictions (agencies serving between 25 and 50,000 people) was even more pronounced. Currently, about 80% of small town agencies have a PPU; in the mid-1980s only 20% had them.

While formation of teams is an important indicator of growth, these trends would mean little if these teams were relatively inactive. This was not the case. There has been an increase of more than 1,400 in the total number of police paramilitary deployments, or callouts, between 1980 and 2000. Today, an estimated 45,000 SWAT-team deployments are conducted yearly among those departments surveyed; in the early 1980s there was an average of about 3,000 (Kraska, 2001). The trend-line demonstrated that this growth began during the drug war of the late 1980s and early 1990s.

These figures would mean little if this increase in teams and deployments was due to an increase in PPUs traditional *and essential function*—a reactive deployment of high-risk specialists for particularly dangerous events already in progress, such as hostage, sniper, or terrorist situations. Instead, more than 80% of these deployments were for proactive drug raids, specifically no-knock and quick-knock dynamic entries into private residences, searching for contraband (drugs, guns, and money). This pattern of SWAT teams primarily engaged in surprise contraband raids held true for the largest as well as the smallest communities. PPUs had changed from being a periphery and strictly reactive component of police departments to a proactive force actively engaged in fighting the drug war.

As further evidence, a surprisingly high percentage of police agencies also deployed their teams to do routine patrol work in crime 'hot spots;' a strong indicator of PPU normalization. In fact, a number of US police departments are currently purchasing, through homeland security funding, military armored personnel carriers (APCs), some of which are being used for aggressive, proactive patrol work. The Pittsburgh police department, for example, purchased a $250,000 APC using homeland security grant money (Deitch, 2007). It is being used to conduct 'street sweeps' in high-crime neighborhoods. The personnel involved are SWAT officers outfitted with full police paramilitary garb and weaponry.

No-Knock/Quick-Knock SWAT Raids

What exactly is a no-knock or quick-knock raid? In essence, they constitute a proactive contraband raid. The purpose of these raids is generally to collect evidence (usually, drugs, guns, and/or money) from inside a private residence. This means that they are essentially a crude form of drug investigation.

A surprise 'dynamic entry' into a private residence creates conditions that place the citizens and police in an extremely volatile position necessitating extraordinary measures. These include conducting searches often during the predawn hours, usually in black military BDUs, hoods, and military helmets; a rapid entry into the residence using specialized battering rams or entry explosives; the occasional use of flash-bang grenades designed to temporarily disorient the occupants; a frantic room-by-room search of the entire residence where all occupants are expected to immediately comply with officers' urgent demands to get into the prone position; and hand-cuffing all occupants. If a citizen does not comply immediately more extreme measures are taken—these situations may involve non-lethal and lethal weaponry. Finally, the police aggressively search the entire residence for contraband.

I receive at least two phone calls per week from journalists, lawyers, or police departments reporting a new botched raid, generally where a citizen has been killed under highly questionable circumstances. I have recorded more than 275 instances of seriously botched SWAT raids on private residences. Botched PPU raids often devastate the communities and police departments involved, sometimes resulting in disbanded SWAT teams, laws being passed prohibiting or curtailing no-knock deployments, and expensive litigation judgments (Balko, 2006).

I received a call while writing this that involved a US Army Green Beret soldier—suffering from Post Traumatic Stress Disorder (PTSD) and despondent because he had just heard he was being redeployed to Iraq for the third time—who had been killed by a SWAT team under highly questionable circumstances. The state attorney general's investigation of this botched raid concluded,

> The tactics adopted by the Maryland State Police EST [SWAT team] can
> be best considered as progressively assaultive and militaristic in nature . . . .
> This office is not unaware of the mounting criticism throughout our
> nation over the use of paramilitary units employing overly aggressive
> tactics against our civilian population. As State's Attorney, I can think of
> no greater threat to the good relations existing in our community as it
> relates to police/citizen relations than to witness the unbridled use of overly
> aggressive tactics by a faceless and shadowy paramilitary police unit . . .
> (Fritz, 2007:12,15)

Only 20 years ago, forced investigative searches of private residences, using the military special operations model employed during hostage rescues, were almost unheard of and would have been considered an extreme and unacceptable police tactic. It is critical to recognize that these are not forced reaction situations necessitating use of force specialists; instead they are the result of police departments *choosing* to use an extreme and highly dangerous tactic, not for terrorists or hostage-takers, but for small-time drug possessors and dealers. Attempting to control the crime problem by conducting tens of thousands of paramilitary style raids on private residences is strong evidence that the US police, and the 'war on crime' in general, have moved significantly down the militarization continuum.

Of course, a militarized response is sometimes necessary and even unavoidable if done in self-defense or to protect lives in imminent danger. The crisis situation at Columbine High School is a solid example of the necessity of having a professional, paramilitarized response to a preexisting crisis. The bulk of US SWAT activity (no-knock/quick-knock raids and aggressive patrol work), however, constitutes a proactive approach. Numerous departments are choosing, based on political pressures, to generate on their own initiative high-risk events.

A central critique of this trend, therefore, does not focus on SWAT's traditional and vital reactive function. It instead concentrates on the inappropriate manner in which its function has been essentially turned on its head—normalizing itself into a range of proactive and mainstream police functions such as contraband raids. This is a strong example of the potentiality of the misplaced application of the military model in civilian policing.

Militarized Policing Versus Community Policing?

Interestingly the rise and normalization of PPUs occurred simultaneously with the community policing (CP) 'revolution.' These two trends—one representing militarization and the other democratization—seem to contradict one another. One obvious explanation for this incongruity might be that militarization flourished as a backstage phenomenon, operating as a form of resistance, or corrective, to the immense political pressures put on the American police to adopt CP reforms. This view would be consistent with criminal justice theories put forward by academics such as Garland (2001) and O'Malley (1999). They posit that in our late-modern era of declining state sovereignty and conflicting ideologies, we can expect to see these types of incongruities and incoherence in police rationales and policies. The militarization/democratization paradox is a sign of the late-modern state attempting to regain its legitimacy and power in a confused and incoherent manner.

While plausible, this explanation does not hold up to ground-level research evidence (DeMichelle and Kraska, 2001). Survey research and in-depth interviews with US police administrators revealed little incoherence between the expanding role and function of SWAT teams and CP reform efforts. When asked about the relationship, the following comment from a SWAT commander was typical:

> We conduct a lot of saturation patrol. We do terry stops and aggressive field interviews. These tactics are successful as long as the pressure stays on relentlessly. The key to our success is that we're an elite crime fighting team that's not bogged down in the regular bureaucracy. We focus on quality of life issues like illegal parking, loud music, bums, troubles. We have the freedom to stay in a hot area and clean it up—particularly gangs. Our tactical team works nicely with our department's emphasis on community policing.

Another quote from a police chief of a self-proclaimed CP department parroted the strategic mission of the US federal CP program known as 'Weed and Seed.'

> The only people that are going to be able to deal with these problems (drugs, guns, gangs, and community disorder) are highly trained tactical teams with the proper equipment to go into a neighborhood and clear the neighborhood and hold it; allowing community policing and problem oriented policing officers to come in and start turning the neighborhood around.

For these comments to make sense, we must remember that two compet-ing strands of CP were evident within this reform movement. Police reformers such as Louis Radelet and Robert Trojanowicz promoted the first strand. It emphasized community empowerment, cultivating constructive relationships with disenfranchised minority groups, and establishing partnerships between the public and police. In this strand of CP, the end goal was for the commu-nity to police their own communities.

The second strand was touted by James Q. Wilson and George Kelling. It focused on creating a climate of order in the community through highly proactive police work. The police were to aggressively police the neighbor-hoods they took ownership and pride in—eliminating those signs of disorder (broken windows), which acted to breakdown community controls. This strand of CP has in many instances transformed into a zero-tolerance policing model, where the police strictly enforce all infractions of law and order using an array of aggressive tactics such as street sweeps, proactive enforcement of not just the law but community order, and a proliferation of drug raids on private residences.

Police administrators using SWAT teams to aggressively patrol hotspots and conduct investigatory drug raids viewed this as wholly consistent with Wilson and Kelling's vision. These police agencies are integrating a military-model approach—occupy, suppress through force, and restore the affected territory—with second strand CP ideology, which emphasizes taking back the neighborhood, creating a climate of order, and aggressively enforcing minor law and order infractions; all in an effort to cultivate healthier communities. Consistent with the quote from the chief of police above, militarized police units and tactics do the weeding, thereby providing the opportunity for other programs to seed the community. (This of course is similar to the tact taken by the US military in the Iraq conflict).

Viewing these developments through the lenses of militarism and mili-tarization demonstrates that despite efforts to do away with the military-professional approach of the mid-1900s, the specter of the military model still haunts the real world of contemporary policing. Militarism is obviously an enduring and flexible presence that can adapt to changing external forces. We should also note the remarkable ability of police practitioners to maneuver through the tensions and pressures of external influences. It is not uncommon for them to have to amalgamate seemingly contradictory messages so that their real-world thinking and practice exhibit a level of coherence and harmony that makes sense to them.

Police-icizing the American Military

That the US military is currently operating more as a police force than a mili-tary one should be obvious to those familiar with the postinvasion conflicts in Iraq and Afghanistan. The bulk of its security work involves routine patrol operations, house-to-house searches (including no-knock contraband raids), and arresting law breakers. Its 'rules of engagement' (use of force policies) are more similar to police work than they are for warfare. Serious questions have been raised about the extent to which military soldiers trained for traditional warfare are capable of effectively enforcing domestic peace in a foreign land. As many security analysts predicted (and some strongly advocated for), the line between war and law enforcement efforts has blurred considerably. In conducting operations known in military circles as 'low-intensity conflict,' distinctions between police and military mean little.

What is less known is the long history—predating the terrorist event of 9/11—of the US military's mission of creeping into functions traditionally viewed as the purview of police (Dunlap, 2001). Elsewhere I have documented the history of the US military's high level of involvement, both abroad and domestically, in drug control efforts beginning in the mid-to-late 1980s (Kraska, 1993). This was an unprecedented shift in the role and function of the US military—an attempt to make the military more 'socially useful' by engaging in drug control efforts. Military officials initially resisted this change until it was clear that the post-Cold War era would provide few justifications for continued funding.

By 11 September 2001, then, the stage was thoroughly prepared for a rapid acceleration of the military-police blur. The mission sprint of the US military into law-enforcement functions involved entirely new levels of cooperation and collaboration between civilian police and the armed forces, and the military has become a central player in a host of homeland security and war-on-terror initiatives. With little objection or discussion, the US Congress passed legislation that established the military as a central feature of homeland security known as Northcom. Its most controversial role, besides establishing close operational and training ties with civilian police, is a surveillance and information program that is currently the largest federal domestic surveillance initiative outside of the Federal Bureau of Investigation (Pincus, 2005).

CONCLUSION: MARTIAL TRENDS AND ISSUES

The purpose of this article is to use the concepts of militarism and militarization to illuminate and make more accurate theoretical sense of some disquieting trends in contemporary police and policing. Before I conclude with some final observations, I want to concede upfront that the positive virtues the military model brings to the policing table have not been discussed. As I have written elsewhere:

> The debate on paramilitary policing in the British literature illustrates clearly that normative concerns play a central role in assessing its desirability (Jefferson, 1990; Reiner, 1992). This issue involves heartfelt beliefs, values, and morals. To many people, even among academics, the military model represents constraint, discipline, honor, control, competence, and a type of patriotism. To others it stands for tyranny, state violence, human rights abuses, war, and an ideology which sees social problems as being best-handled through state force (Kraska and Cubellis, 1997:627).

Please note that my analysis does leave room for the military model in policing (e.g. the original and essential reactive function of SWAT teams). This is unavoidable given that the foundation of police and military power is the same—the ability to threaten and use force, lethal if necessary, to accomplish State objectives. It would be foolish to take an either-or position. However, the cautionary tone is justified if we keep in mind the importance of what has been and should be a central tenet of democratic policing: strive to keep the police as far left on the militarization continuum as possible.

Whether these two converging trends outlined—the militarization of police and the police-ization of the military—are alarming to the reader or encouraging, they are real. We are in the midst of a historic transformation—one that both police practitioners and academics should acknowledge and remain cognizant of. Attempting to control the crime problem by routinely conducting police special operations raids on people's private residences is strong evidence that the US police, and crime control efforts in general, have moved significantly down the militarization continuum. Moreover, the normalization of PPUs into routine police work, the patrol function, and in so-called 'order enforcement campaigns,' points to an enduring internal militarization not likely to recede anytime in the near future.

Of course, these developments were occurring previous to the 9/11 tragedy. Two recent wars, and the security crisis in Iraq, signal the dawn of a new era of serious armed conflict. The eerie stability provided by the Cold War and the specter of the Vietnam War has vanished. The ongoing war on terrorism is accelerating dramatically the blurring distinction between the police and military, between internal and external security, and between war and law enforcement. Any broad-based academic analysis that relies heavily on these traditional demarcations will soon seem misplaced and obsolete.

In the midst of this perpetual war-footing, I think it is also plausible to assume that government officials entrusted to keep us secure from terrorism, will more readily gravitate toward the ideology of militarism—both for internal and external security threats—when problem-solving and administering justice. Processing crime, drug, and terrorism control through the filter of militarism will undoubtedly render a militarized response more appealing and likely.

A poignant example of this is the recent Hurricane Katrina catastrophe in the United States. The government's response to this disaster was far different than has been the norm for the past 50 years. Symbolic of the decline of the social welfare paradigm, and the ascendance of a militarized, governance model that revolves around crime and security, the central focus of the Department of Homeland Security (and its newly subsumed Federal Emergency Management Agency) was not humanitarian relief, but instead a massive security operation that included police paramilitary squads, Blackwater-incorporated private soldiers, and the US National Guard. By all accounts, the fixation on crime and insecurity and the militarized deployment delayed and complicated the humanitarian relief effort considerably.

What impact will this have on the future of US police militarization? It could be that the war on terrorism provides such strong justification for the existence of PPUs that they may cut back on proactive functions, returning to their original status: reactive units that primarily train for the rare terrorist or hostage incident. While I would welcome this development, I think we will still be left with the problem of the regular police—operating in the context of a society that places a high level of emphasis on militarism—being increasingly seduced by the trappings of paramilitary subculture. Paramilitarism could exert even a stronger influence on what the regular police decide on for uniforms (e.g. military BDUs), how they think, the weaponry and technology they employ, the organizational models they adopt (e.g. COMPSTAT), and the crime control solutions they devise. The CP reform movement's call for democratization may be increasingly drowned out by the drumbeats of high-technology militarization.

Whatever trajectory the future takes, keeping track of the movement of civilian police on the militarization continuum, and the extent to which the military becomes more enmeshed in police functions, will be increasingly important for our understanding of 'policing' in contemporary society.

DISCUSSION QUESTIONS

1. Discuss the consequences of military and police convergence.
2. Define police militarization and discuss what role the four dimensions of the military model play in its regard.
3. In what situation do the military and the police work together to protect and serve?
4. List two reasons why PPUs are popular in most smaller jurisdictions.
5. Briefly discuss the necessity of a paramilitary style raid and when deadly force is required.

REFERENCES

Balko, Radley. 2006. *Overkill: The Rise of Paramilitary Police Raids in America,* White Paper published by the Cato Institute (www.cato.org/pub display.php?pub id=6476).

Christie, Nils. 2000. *Crime Control as Industry: Towards Gulags, Western Style,* Routledge: New York.

Garland, David. 2001. *The Culture of Control: Crime and Social Order in Contemporary Society,* Chicago: University of Chicago Press.

Deitch, Charlie. 2007. "Military Police." *Pittsburgh City Paper* 1–3.

DeMichelle, Matthew and Kraska, Peter. 2001. "Community Policing in Battle Garb: A Paradox or Coherent Strategy?".

Dunlap, Charles J. 2001. "The Thick Green Line: The Growing Involvement of Military Forces in Domestic Law Enforcement." *Militarizing the American Criminal Justice System: The Changing Roles of the Armed Forces and the Police,* Boston, MA: Northeastern University Press.

Dunn, Timothy J. 2001. "Waging War on Immigrants at the U.S. Mexico Border: Human Rights Implications." In Kraska (ed.), *Militarizing the American Criminal Justice System: The Changing Roles of the Armed Forces and* the Police, Boston, MA: Northeastern University Press 65–81.

Ericson, Richard and Carriere, Kevin. 1994. "The Fragmentation of Criminology." In Nelken, D. (ed.), *The Futures of Criminology*, London: Sage.

Fritz, Richard. D. 2007. "Dean Death Investigation." *State's Attorney for St. Mary's County Investigative Report*, Maryland: Court House, Leonardtown.

Giddens, Anthony. 1985. *The Nation-State and Violence*, Berkeley: University of California Press.

Haggerty, Kevin D. and Ericson, Richard V. 2001. "The Military Technostructures of Policing." *Militarizing the American Criminal Justice System: The Changing Roles of the Armed Forces and the Police*, Boston, MA: Northeastern University Press.

Jefferson, Tony. 1990. The Case Against Paramilitary Policing, Bristol, PA: Open University Press.

Klare, Michael. 1980. "Militarism: The Issues Today." In Eide, A. and Thee, M. (eds), *Problems of Contemporary Militarism*, New York: St. Martin's Press.

Kraska, Peter B. 1993. "Militarizing the Drug War: A Sign of the Times." In Kraska, Peter (ed.), *Altered States of Mind: Critical Observations of the Drug War*, New York: Garland Publishing.

_____ 1994. "The Police and Military in the Post-Cold War Era: Streamlining the State's Use of Force Entities in the Drug War." *Police Forum* **4**(1): 1–8.

_____ 1999. "Questioning the Militarization of U.S. Police: Critical Versus Advocacy Scholarship." *Policing and Society* **9**(2): 141–155.

_____ 1996. "Enjoying Militarism: Political and Personal Dilemmas in Studying Police Paramilitary Units." *Justice Quarterly* 3, **13**: 405–429.

_____ 2001. *Militarizing the American Criminal Justice System: The Changing Roles of the Armed Forces and the Police*, Boston, MA: Northeastern University Press.

Kraska, P. B. 2004. *Theorizing Criminal Justice: Eight Essential Orientations*, Prospect Heights, Illinois: Waveland Press.

Kraska, P. B. and Cubellis, L. J. 1997. "Militarizing Mayberry and Beyond: Making Sense of American Paramilitary Policing." *Justice Quarterly* **14**(4): 607–629.

Kraska, P. B. and Kappeler, V. E. 1997. "Militarizing American Police: The Rise and Normalization of Paramilitary Units." *Social Problems* **44**(1): 1–18.

Lutterbeck, D. 2004. "Between Police and Military: The New Security Agenda and the Rise of Gendarmeries." *Cooperation and Conflict* **39**(1): 45–68.

Maguire, Edward R. and King, William R. 2004. "Trends in the Policing Industry." *The ANNALS of the American Academy of Political and Social Science* **593**(1): 15–41.

McCulloch, Jude. 2004. "Blue Armies, Khaki Police and The Cavalry on the New American Frontier: Critical Criminology for the 21st Century." *Critical Criminology* **12**(3): 309–326.

O'Malley, Pat. 1999. "Volatile and Contradictory Punishment." *Theoretical Criminology* **3**(2): 175–196.

Pincus, Walter. 2005. "Pentagon Expanding Its Domestic Surveillance Activity." *Washington Post* **11/27**: A06.

Reiner, Robert. 1992. The Politics of the Police, Toronto: University of Toronto Press.

Sherry, Michael S. 1995. *In the Shadow of War: The United States Since the 1930's*, New Haven: Yale University Press.

Tonry, M. 2004. *Thinking About Crime: Sense and Sensibility in American Penal Culture*, Oxford University Press New York.

Zimmerman, D. 2005. "Between Minimum Force and Maximum Violence: Combatting Political Movements with Third-Force Options." *Connections: The Quarterly Journal* **4**(1): 43–60.

9

⊕

Suspicion and Discretion: Decision Making During Citizen Stops

Geoffrey P. Alpert
John M. MacDonald
Roger G. Dunham

This study examines the influence of racial, demographic and situational variables on types of police suspicion and the ancillary decision to stop and question suspects. Data were drawn from an observational study of police decision making in Savannah, Georgia. Based on the literature, we hypothesized that minority suspects will be more likely to be viewed suspiciously by the police for nonbehavioral reasons. We also hypothesize that minority status will play a significant role in the decision to stop and question suspicious persons. The findings from this study provide partial support for these hypotheses. The results indicate that minority status does influence an officer's decision to form

Source: Geoffrey P. Alpert, John M. MacDonald, and Roger G. Dunham, "Police Suspicion and Discretionary Decision Making During Citizen Stops" Criminology Vol. 43:2 pp. 407–434. Copyright © 2005 by The American Society of Criminology. Reprinted by permission.

nonbehavioral as opposed to behavioral suspicion, but that minority status does not influence the decision to stop and question suspects. We discuss the implications of these findings for understanding race and its role in police decision making.

Current theory and research on the use of discretion and biased policing make few references to the situational processes through which police determine behaviors to be suspicious and which, consequently, initiate official police action. Research on police behavior and the exercise of social control typically focuses on police actions after a contact with a citizen has been initiated, and tends to examine the subsequent courses of action police officers take (for example, citizen stop, citation, arrest, use of force and the like) (see Harris, 1999; Mastrofski et al., 2000; Smith and Petrocelli, 2001; Lundman and Kaufman, 2003; Gould and Mastrofski, 2004). Prior to the encounter, and the ensuing series of decision making points through the maze of the criminal justice system, a police officer typically forms a suspicion that a suspect is engaged in, or about to be engaged in, illegal behavior. Consequently, it is this earliest stage, an officer's formation of suspicion before identifying and stopping a citizen, that has the most profound consequences for the citizens in the criminal justice system.

Interestingly, criminological literature offers no empirical assessments of the social processes through which police officers form suspicions. At the core of the controversy surrounding issues such as racial profiling (Wilson, Dunham and Alpert, 2004; Fagan and Davies, 2000), is a police officer's initial decision to suspect that someone is involved in illegal behavior. This is an important and neglected area of research, and one that we address in this study by examining and explaining the factors that influence this crucial stage in an officer's decision making process.

The majority of police-citizen encounters occur in the absence of any outside supervision, and police officers therefore have a great deal of discretion throughout the decision making processes (Walker, 1993). Fortunately, the substantive body of research on policing has produced information on the social processes through which the police exercise discretion in applying the law (see, for example, Black, 1976; Smith, 1984; Worden, 1989; Klinger, 1994; Mastrofski, Snipes, Parks and Maxwell, 2000). Most of the literature on police discretion is focused on the decision to stop, search, or arrest a suspect. It is important, however, to step back and examine what precedes those decisions. Prior investigations on police discretion indicate that a combination of preexisting attitudes, and the personality that a police officer develops through experiences on the job, partly explains how officers respond in interactions with citizens (Alpert and Dunham, 2004; McNamara, 1967; Skolnick, 1977; Gardiner, 1969). Research findings, however, note that personal attitudes only partly explain police behavior. In fact, empirical research indicates that police decision making is primarily driven by situational factors related to criminal behavior (for example, seriousness of offense, victim requests) and the administrative decision making model under which the officer works (Worden, 1989). A police officer's discretion to choose a course of action, such as to stop a citizen, typically begins when an officer observes a person appearing suspicious or violating the law.

This study systematically observes the processes through which police officers form suspicion and make investigative stops of citizens. Suspicion is measured by an officer's interest in a citizen or vehicle, while a stop is measured by an officer's formal action of stopping a citizen or vehicle. This investigation, therefore, speaks to the social aspects of police officer decision making prior to the application of formal social control. First, we briefly review the relevant research, then discuss the theoretical and legal bases involved in forming suspicion and then describe our methods and findings. Finally, we present the implications of these findings.

REVIEW OF LITERATURE

Because there is no empirical research directly assessing the formation of police suspicion, we present a brief review of the research findings that explain the behavior of police officers when they interact with citizens (see Riksheim and Chermak, 1993; Worden and Shepard, 1996; Mastrofski et al., 2000). Our discussion includes a review of the literature on the influence of organizational, legal, individual-level and environmental variables on police officer decision making in encounters with citizens.

Organizational and Legal Factors

Wilson's pioneering work on police behavior suggests that the type of agency where an officer works influences how he or she makes judgments before making the decision to invoke legal authority (1968:38). More recent research has reaffirmed his findings indicating that the bureaucratic characteristics of the police organization play a role in explaining officer behavior, and further, that variations in department management styles and culture explain a significant amount of the variation in the willingness of officers to exercise their decision to arrest suspects (Smith, 1984; Mastrofski, 1981). For example, if an agency emphasizes a service function, then its officers are less likely to arrest offenders for low-level crimes than officers in a legalistic-style agency. Mastrofski's study on the influence of formal and informal organizational characteristics regarding discretionary arrests in cases of drinking and driving found that, in larger departments, officers were more likely to base their decisions on informal departmental culture, whereas, in smaller departments officers were more likely to follow written departmental policy (Mastrofski, Ritti and Hoffmaster, 1987). Smith's (1984) analysis of observational data, on more than 1,000 police-citizen encounters in several different police agencies, found that officers working in agencies characterized by a high degree of legalistic criteria were more likely to arrest citizens compared to officers in other types of departments.

These and other studies on police decision making provide important information on the determinants of police officer behavior and tend to focus on the decision to apply formal aspects of legal control (for example, Smith, 1986). Some studies, however, indicate that departmental policies and organizational characteristics have only a minimal effect on officer behavior (Worden, 1990). First, it should be pointed out that minimal effects are still important, especially to the individuals being mistreated. However, a more important point is that racial profiling at the organizational level, through police deployment practices, can lead to discriminatory policing without individual-level discrimination. In his classic discussion of the ecological distribution of police work, Bittner (1996, originally published in 1967) pointed out that the deployment of personnel could be based on prejudices and perceptions about the relationship between race and crime. A systematic review of the literature indicates that in addition to the influences of the police organization, legal factors related to the seriousness of the alleged offense, and the strength of evidence as perceived by the officer, are the most important factors associated with a police officer's actions and the decision to invoke legal authority (National Research Council, 2003).

Individual and Environmental Factors

In contrast to the explanatory importance of organizational and legally relevant variables, extralegal factors, including environmental and individual variables, are clearly less important. These variables, including the area in which an encounter takes place, as well as the social class, race, age, gender, sobriety, physical size and demeanor of the suspect, by themselves play only a minor role in a police officer's decision to invoke the use of formal, legal control (National Research Council, 2003; Walker and Katz, 2002; Gottfredson and Hindeling, 1979; Lanza-Kaduce and Greenleaf, 1994; Mastrofski, Snipes and Supina, 1996; Riksheim and Chermak, 1993; Sherman, 1978). It is nonetheless important to understand the potential importance of their influence.

Research conducted more than 30 years ago suggests that an officer's experience is related to his or her conclusions as to how suspicious and prone to crime a suspect might be, as well as to a suspect's moral character (Werthman and Piliavin, 1967). Recently, research has shown that younger officers are more likely to be aggressive than older officers. At the same time, younger suspects are likely to show less respect and act more aggressively toward officers than older suspects, leading to a greater likelihood that officers will take official action (Reisig et al., 2004; Alpert and Dunham, 2004).

Race is perhaps the most important individual-level factor in police-citizen interactions (Sun and Payne, 2004; Weitzer and Tuch, 2002; Barlow and Barlow, 2000; Kennedy, 1997). As Rawls (2000) notes, there are divergent underlying expectations between racial groups, even in such simple behavioral tasks as conversation. These different behaviors can be interpreted improperly and can affect the likelihood that a police officer will arrest a suspect. How a police officer interprets a suspect's nonverbal behavior can be even more problematic. European social psychologists have looked at the influence of race on the interpretation of nonverbal communication in police–citizen encounters, and have identified specific behaviors that officers often misinterpret. Aldert Vrij and his colleagues (see Vrij and Taylor, 2003, Vrij, 1994a, 1994b, and Winkel, Koppelaar and Vrij, 1988) have concluded that there are black and white styles of nonverbal communication in police–citizen encounters. They report that in police–citizen encounters black suspects are more likely than white suspects to appear "fidgety and lively," to use a greater range of voice, to raise their pitch more frequently and to avoid looking directly at the officer (Vrij and Winkel, 1992: 1546–1547). They conclude that "negative treatment of blacks may thus be a consequence of nonverbal communication errors, that is, faulty interpretations of characteristically black nonverbal behavior" (Vrij and Winkel, 1992: 1547).

For example, a young black male who does not look in the eyes of an officer, or appears nervous when he is being questioned, may appear suspicious, while in reality, the youth avoids eye contact in an attempt to not be disrespectful, and is nervous just to be talking with an officer. In addition, the officer may not react the same way, or with the same level of suspicion, to similar behavior of a white youth. Over time, this type of response can develop into a formal stereotype. As Kennedy (1997) informs us, race is often used as a proxy for an increased risk of danger, criminality and victimization.

Research on Race, Arrest and Community

Observational research indicates that the positive association between minority status and the probability of arrest is attributable to a larger proportion of blacks residing in lower-status communities (Smith, 1984). Obviously, police deployment decisions can account for much of this relationship. The perception of high crime rates in certain communities leads to greater police deployment, which yields higher arrest rates, which, in turn, are interpreted as evidence of a higher crime rate. However, this research also indicates that police officers are more likely to arrest suspects when whites have been the victims of crime than when blacks have been the victims, an outcome suggesting that racial bias is generated by a concern for the legal protection of white victims. Subsequent research (Smith, 1986), analyzed police–citizen encounters in sixty neighborhoods and found that variations in police use of its legal authority in specific neighborhoods is linked to the racial composition of those neighborhoods (confirming Blalock's 1967 racial threat theory) and not simply to the race of the individuals confronted (see Stolzenberg, D'Alessio and Eitle, 2004). For example, the importance of minority status is heightened when a member of a minority group travels through a largely segregated and white community or location. This may explain why police behavior can be linked to neighborhood composition but not to an individual's race or ethnicity. Smith (1986) found that people in lower-class black neighborhoods were more likely to be arrested than suspects in more affluent neighborhoods.

However, it is interesting to note that the police were less likely to stop suspicious persons in high-crime neighborhoods.

Taken together, the research on race and police behavior indicates that minority status must be considered when evaluating police-citizen interactions. Additionally, the characteristics of the area in which the interaction occurs play an important role, which suggests that there may be a "threshold effect" where police only stop, search or arrest individuals in high crime areas when the level of the offense rises to a level of seriousness they cannot ignore. In such circumstances the police ultimately provide fewer and poorer services in low-income and nonwhite neighborhoods, a phenomenon that Barlow and Barlow (2000) call "under policing." Underpolicing may occur because the police undervalue the people or property in the area and are less motivated to protect them, but may do so because the citizens in these areas lack the power to force the police to provide the appropriate levels of service (Anderson, 1999). In general, however, research has provided mixed results concerning the influence of race on police discretion. It also shows mixed results on the influence of a suspect's race on a police officer's response, and on the influence of an officer's race on a suspect's reaction. For example, some studies indicate that black suspects are more likely than white suspects to be arrested and/or to be treated more harshly by the police (Powell, 1990; Smith and Visher, 1981; Smith and Davidson, 1984), while other studies report that a suspect's race has no individual-level effect (Klinger, 1996; Smith, 1986). Research is also mixed on the importance of race on the use of deadly force (Geller and Karales, 1981; Blumberg, 1981; Fyfe, 1980) and the use of nondeadly force (Dunham and Alpert, 2004; Alpert and Dunham, 2004). After an exhaustive review of the literature, the National Research Council (2003:3) concluded that there is a strong empirical basis for asserting the importance of legal variables, but that "more research is needed on the complex interplay of race, ethnicity and other social factors, in police-citizen interactions." Despite the lack of definitive conclusions regarding the importance of race in police decision making, race and police work are inextricably tied to one another and often form the basis for problematic police-citizen relationships in many communities.

Theoretical and Legal Basis of Suspicion

Although race is not a legitimate justification for an officer to take a formal action against an individual, both real-world experiences and theoretical reasons suggest that race is an important factor for police officers in forming suspicions (Kennedy, 1997). Historically, the police have used race as a reason to stop, search and arrest suspects (Fridell, Luney, Diamond and Kubu, 2001; Harris, 1999; Walker, Spohn and DeLone, 2000). Sociologically based theories, such as racial threat theory, critical race theory or conflict theory, suggest that the police specifically target minorities as an instrument of the political establishment to suppress the potential threat minorities pose on the hegemony of the white elite (Chambliss and Seidman, 1982). Blalock's (1967) theory of minority group relations suggests that as the relative size of the minority group increases, members of the majority group perceive a growing threat to their positions and will take steps to reduce the competition. The "state" will increasingly perceive blacks as a threat to whites' political power, and respond by intensifying the level of social control to maintain the dominant position of whites. Research indicates that the presence of minorities is associated with greater police expenditures (see Kane, 2003 for a review), however, there is insufficient research at the individual-level to suggest that the police specifically target minorities as a method of political control.

In addition to sociological explanations for the importance of race in police decision making, there are also psychological explanations for how race interplays in police-citizen interactions. Cognitive theorists, for example, acknowledge that learning is influenced by observations, and that the relative power of that learning varies according to the degree of familiarity, and repeated number of associations (see Good and Brophy, 1990). Research provides evidence that these schema form a mental representation (model) that plays a key role in predicting a person's responses to others, places and things, in future encounters or events (Grosset and Barrouillet, 2003; Brehm, Kassin and Fein, 2002; Bower, Black and Turner, 1979; Read, 1987; Craik, 1943). Once a mental model is formed, persons or places that have familiar characteristics or properties activate these cognitive schemas. In other words, police officers learn to respond to people, places and situations based on their experiences, including how they were trained and taught in the police academy, by field training officers, supervisors and others. In fact, these influences, among others, may and often do include racially prejudiced attitudes. It is therefore important to acknowledge that behaviors based on police experience suffer from the same misinformation and prejudices as the behavior of other citizens.

Training and experience provide the basis for the mental model of police officers and the cues or schema that trigger suspicion (Rubinstein, 1973). Police officers are taught to look for nonverbal indicators of deception in forming suspicion of criminal activities. Many of these are culturally normative for blacks, such as avoiding eye contact, speaking at a faster rate, and arm and hand movement (Vrij and Winkel, 1992). Not surprisingly, studies find that white police officers are more likely to form suspicion with regard to the nonverbal communication characteristics of blacks compared to whites (Vrij and Winkel, 1992; Winkel, Koppelaar and Vrij, 1998). Further, experience is the basis by which people form mental models of suspicion. Police officers may be more likely to form cognitive schemas of blacks as suspicious because of their experiences with criminals. For example, research from both arrest data and victim accounts indicates that black males are overrepresented in offending rates for personal crimes (rape, robbery, assault and personal larceny) (D'Alessio and Stolzenberg, 2003; Hindelang, 1981). Police officers are also more likely to be deployed in high-crime minority neighborhoods (Kane, 2003). As a result of the disproportionate number of offending of black males with respect to certain types of crimes, and deployment practices which lead to disproportionate scrutiny and arrest of some groups, officers develop a history of arresting black males and may learn to assume that blacks are likely to be criminally suspect. Obviously, this line of reasoning controverts the "under-policing" phenomenon.

Once a police officer identifies an individual or a group by association with an assumed role (for example, seeing black males as automatically criminally suspect), the stage is set for interpreting future actions—in other words, the officer has formed a mental model of the individual or group. These mental models are impressionistic and are based on perceptions that may or may not reflect the reality of a given situation. Additionally, such schema may or may not be legally justifiable, but are understandable and predictable in "real world" police-citizen interactions. The cognitive schema of police officers may therefore result in a higher percentage of innocent citizens being viewed suspiciously, and consequently, being stopped and questioned, because they are minorities rather than because they are behaving in a suspicious manner. This pattern could explain the disparate experiences of blacks and whites with respect to being stopped and questioned by the police (Lundman and Kaufman, 2003).

Police officers are trained to identify suspicious and threatening people, and to develop their own cues of suspicious behavior based on their individual experience. Research indicates that police officers are more likely than citizens to apply a "cognitive schema" that interprets unfamiliar actions or actions of uncertain intent as suspicious (Ruby and Bringham, 1996). Police officers are also more likely than citizens to become suspicious about people or actions they do not believe fit the environment or situation (for example, a car idling in front of bank). Once an officer has developed these cues for suspicion, he or she may act on them in a given situation and approach or confront a citizen. A well-trained officer can look at a scene and determine what looks correct and what "doesn't fit" (Miller, 2000.). For example, vehicles that appear "normal" in one setting may appear out of place in others. New expensive vehicles in known drug dealing areas may appear suspicious, whereas run-down cars in affluent residential neighborhoods may attract attention. In both of these examples there are logical reasons for suspicion, just as there may be reasonable explanations that negate the suspicion. While in many circumstances these cues are reasonable, they are often tied to issues of race and social status. It is important to recognize that these cognitive schemas provide a theoretical basis for understanding how particular individual and environmental cues are tied to issues of race in America. Clearly, the suspicion developed from a cognitive schema is a supposition and not necessarily tied to the actual behaviors or actions of minority citizens.

In an ideal world, the formation of suspicion and any resulting police action should be aroused by the actual behavior of suspects. However, The Supreme Court ruled in the 1968 case of Terry v. Ohio (392 U.S. 1) that police officers have the constitutional right to stop and search an individual based on "specific reasonable inferences he is entitled to draw from the facts in light of his experience" (27). The Court explained that police officers can legitimately form suspicion based on information collected during their observation or through their investigation of a suspect. To justify intrusive action (for example, stopping and searching a suspect) a police officer must be able to articulate her or his suspicion of a specific crime. The Court acknowledged three primary sources that police officers rely on in determining whether an action is suspicious: information received about a suspect from other sources; information gleaned about a suspect through observation (appearance and behavior); and, the time and place of the suspect's actions. To justify intervention, a police officer can evaluate the incongruity between observed and expected patterns of behavior using her or his knowledge of "normal" behavior patterns for a given time and place. He or she must be able to determine whether a person's observed behavior is "normal" and appropriate for the given situation and conditions, or if it is suspicious and therefore justifies a continued probe or formal intervention. An officer giving more than a passing glance at a person or situation is referred to in some police cultures as someone "putting the antenna up."

While a particular behavior may be reasonable and acceptable in some situations (congruent), it may be out of place (incongruent) in another environment or situation. The mere fact that a young white citizen is driving around a predominately black neighborhood suggests nothing improper per se, but if the area is known for drug sales and the youth acts nervously in front of the police, an officer's suspicions may understandably be aroused and justify him or her stopping and questioning the youth. While the Supreme Court acknowledged this as proper police procedure, critics have argued that the court decision allows officers to use race improperly and to the detriment of minority citizens (Romero, 2002; Delgado and Stephanic, 2001). It is important that neither the court nor social science research has fully explored or evaluated the process and criteria the police use in forming suspicion.

THE STUDY

Theoretically, police suspicion should be based on prior knowledge, observation, and the time and place of an incident. While legal decisions and prior research direct our attention to these categories, it is important to gain as much insight as possible from the observations of the police officers actually forming suspicion. This would permit an assessment of the relative importance of the various factors that lead to police suspicion and the invoking of official action. By design, this study is limited to discretionary police actions, because of the difficulties involved in collecting data on the people, behavior and events that did not arouse police suspicion. Due to the unlimited possibilities of such individuals and events, it would be extremely difficult, if not impossible, to collect data, though such information would allow calculations on actual racial disparities. Without it, however, we are unable to assess actual racial disparities as to whether officers were more likely to become suspicious of minority citizens than others. The focus of this research is on minority status as a factor in officers forming nonbehavioral as opposed to behavioral suspicion, and deciding to make an actual stop. We are interested, as previous studies have not been, in the formation and creation of types of cognitive suspicion as well as the formal actions undertaken by the police (for example, stops).

This study systematically observes police officers to examine how important race and other situational and individual-level factors are in forming suspicions and deciding to stop citizens. Where prior literature is inconclusive concerning the role of race in official actions taken by the police, we hypothesize that race plays an important role in the informal mechanisms that lead police officers to form nonbehavioral suspicion. The sociological theories of racial threat and psychological theories of cognitive schema both suggest that race will play an important role in whom the police view suspiciously for nonbehavioral reasons. Legally, officers are required to observe behavior that presents reasonable cause for action. However, research on racial profiling suggests that race has some significance in stops of suspicious persons, regardless of any related traffic violation (see Gibbons, 2004; Gross and Barnes, 2002; Novak, 2004). Therefore, we hypothesize that race will play a role in whom the police stop. To test these hypotheses, we use the following set of variables recorded from systematic observations of officers working in the field during the time they formed suspicions and made stops.

Data and Methods

Our methodology integrates quantitative and qualitative data collection techniques to provide an in-depth understanding of the police decision making process. The qualitative data were collected to enhance the quantitative information, using the general principles of protocol analysis (see Ericsson and Simon, 1984; Worden and Brandl, 1990). Cromwell, Olson and Avary (1991) used a similar method, labeled "Staged Activity Analysis," to assess the decision making processes burglars used. As Worden and Brandl (1990) argue, this procedure can be used to improve the quality of police research.

This study includes an examination of police officers in Savannah, Georgia, who were observed and debriefed after incidents when they formed suspicion either about an individual or a vehicle. According to the 2000 census, the City of Savannah has 131,510 residents: 57 percent are African American, 39 percent are white, 1.5 percent are Asian and 1.5 percent are categorized as other. At the time of the research, the Savannah Police Department (SPD) had approximately 400 sworn officers, with the majority assigned to the Patrol Bureau, which consisted of 31.8 percent black males, 6.4 percent black females, 51.2 percent white males, 4.8 percent white females, 4.8 percent other males and 0.4 percent other females. Officers were assigned by area, meaning that some areas had a larger distribution of minority officers than others. The distribution of sworn officers in patrol closely matched the percentage of officers observed in the study. Shortly after the data collection phase of the study concluded, the Savannah police department merged with Chatham County's to form the Savannah Chatham Metropolitan Police Department.

During the months of April through November 2002, trained observers accompanied randomly selected officers on 132 8-hour shifts, during which time they observed officers forming suspicion 174 times. The observers accompanied officers in each of the four precincts and on all three shifts. Observers were assigned to a precinct and a shift and then randomly assigned to an officer. This allowed for complete coverage of the City of Savannah. A formal instrument was developed to capture what officers were thinking and feeling when they made decisions and/or took action. Data were not collected during the initial ride along so that observers could build rapport with officers and train them to discuss their suspicions. After the initial introductory rides, observers averaged 3.25 ride-along tours with the same officer. The observers were trained to document the police officer's actions and reactions as well as any interactions that occurred with citizens (see Mastrofski et al., 1998). Observers were trained to document what they witnessed and to record the sequence in which the events unfolded. To document when an officer became "suspicious," officers were asked to think out loud when something or someone raised their suspicion. Also, observers were trained to make note of times when officers seemed to take notice of something, and whether they acted on it, and to question the officer about his or her thoughts and feelings about the observation. The observer could thus remind and prompt officers to "think out loud" so they, the observers, could identify when an officer became at all suspicious about a person or a vehicle. For example, if the observer noticed an officer do a "double-take," the observer would bring that to the officer's attention after the event and ask what he or she was thinking and feeling at the time. The observer would ask what caught the officer's eye and what prompted the officer to either continue his or her routine activities or take action.

"Forming suspicion" occurred any time an officer became doubtful, distrustful or otherwise troubled or concerned about an individual. Only proactive encounters were included in the study; that is, the observations did not involve cases in which officers were responding to calls for service or other calls from dispatch. In most of the cases, it was the behavior of the suspect(s) that concerned the officer. This concern or unease did not always result in an individual or vehicle stop. In some cases, officers realized that their initial suspicion was unwarranted and continued to go about their routine activities.

To examine the effects of minority status on an officer's decision making with regard to suspicion, we investigated the role of officer and suspect race and other demographic variables, the characteristics of an area and the mode of transportation. For example, an officer's view of a suspect would vary if a civilian were driving a car or walking. Specifically, we assess whether the officer's race, level of education and tenure on the police force affected the way they formed suspicion. Additionally, we assess the relationship between the type of suspicion, the suspect's race, the racial makeup of the neighborhood, the perception of the neighborhood's level of dangerousness, the type of action in which a suspect was engaged, and the mode of transportation. Drawing on the literature on police behavior, we developed a set of independent variables that measured the individual attributes of officers and suspects as well as the demographic characteristics of the area being policed.

Dependent Variables

The focus of our study is on the type of suspicion formed by the police and any resulting action the police take. There were a total of 174 incidents in which police officers were observed forming a suspicion. For the purposes of this analysis we were interested in examining the influence of race and other predictor variables on the type of suspicion a police officer formed, and, additionally, whether the suspicion formed ultimately resulted in a stop. Consequently, we divided suspicion into behavioral and nonbehavioral categories. Behavioral criteria included specific actions by citizens that were either illegal or interpreted by the officer as suspicious. One example is observing a traffic offense. Obviously, not all police officers stop all traffic violators, but an observed traffic violation justifies an officer making a stop.

Nonbehavioral criteria included officer concern about an individual's appearance, the time and place, and descriptive information provided to an officer. Suspicions based on nonbehavioral criteria do not necessarily provide a clear justification for a stop. Suspicions initiated by BOLO (be on the look out) information were included in the nonbehavioral category for several reasons. While BOLO cases may be based on behaviors previously undertaken by suspected criminals, the description provided to officers is based on appearance and not behavior. It is important to bear in mind that many BOLO descriptions are vague and can apply to any number of individuals in a community or within a demographic group (for example, "be on the look out for a young black male wearing a red jacket and blue jeans"). BOLO descriptions may still justify suspicion in some cases, but they are typically not behaviorally based. In addition, the point of this study was to investigate factors related to the formation of behavioral and nonbehavioral suspicion for the individual officers being observed. As a result, our model cannot speak to events that preclude systematic social observation. For example, research suggests that officers acquire visual cues for suspicion based on experience and training and also that experience and training may also be behaviorally based. Based on past behavior they have witnessed, an officer may form a cue that individuals who wear specific clothing or spend a lot of time in a specific area are more inclined to be criminal. However, during the current formation of suspicion, the police officers were relying on nonbehavioral identifiers (clothing, race, location, for example). Therefore, stops based on nonbehavioral criteria are especially interesting and are in need of elucidation. Nonbehavioral suspicions were coded to equal 1 and behavioral suspicions were coded to equal 0. Stops of citizens were coded to equal 1 if the citizen was stopped and 0 for all other outcomes. As the dependent variables in this study are dichotomous we model the process using logistic regression.

Independent Variables

As noted, the literature suggests that demographic characteristics of police officers and citizens are important factors in the police decision making process (National Research Council, 2003). We therefore included measures of race, level of education, and number of years in-service for each observed officer. The race of the officer was dummy-coded to equal 1 if the officer was white. An officer's education was coded into the dummy variable with 1 equaling some level of college education (for example, associates, bachelors, or masters degree); we chose to do this because prior research suggests that education plays some role in police officer behavior (Sherman, 1978; National Research Council, 2003; Walker and Katz, 2002). The number of years an officer had worked for the police department was included as a continuous variable. Research also suggests that the racial characteristics of suspects and the racial composition of an area the police are patrolling are important ingredients in an officer's decision making process (Smith, 1986). We therefore included a dummy measure of the race of the suspect that equals 1 if the suspect were black. In terms of neighborhood composition, we included a dummy variable that equals 1 if the neighborhood were perceived by the officer as predominately black and 0 if this was not the case. These neighborhood racial categories were based on police officer perceptions of the area being patrolled. We also included a measure of each officer's individual perception of the neighborhood, which indicated whether the area appeared to be "troubled." We included this measure because prior research suggests that the police patrol differently in areas that they view as having a high crime rate (Klinger, 1997). Troubled neighborhoods were coded to equal 1 and 0 otherwise. Because the mode of transportation may influence whether an officer can see suspects and/or form a suspicion, we included a dummy variable coded to equal 1 if the suspect was driving an automobile.

Finally, there may be some concern that suspicions that result in traffic tickets are different from other suspicions because they are strictly behaviorally based. This is, however, not always the case. First, there are situations when an officer becomes suspicious of a person/vehicle because of nonbehavioral criteria and only witnesses a traffic infraction because of the continued observation. Indeed, some police officers have concluded that if you follow just about anyone for a time, you will observe a traffic infraction. In this case, the suspicion would be nonbehavioral while the stop would be behavioral. Second, it is common for police officers not to respond to every traffic infraction they observe. To do so would monopolize their time. Therefore, there is a subjective nature to selecting which traffic infractions they choose to ignore or respond to. Our criteria for nonbehavioral suspicion often provide the basis for these decisions. We thus concluded that suspicions that result in traffic tickets will have a range of behavioral and nonbehavioral reasons for suspicion, similar to other types of stops. However, to allow us to assess any statistical differences between stops resulting in traffic tickets and other stops, we included a measure of whether the suspect committed a traffic offense. Cases involving traffic offenses were dummy-coded to equal 1.

RESULTS

Table 1 includes the descriptive statistics for the dependent and explanatory variables of the sample of police suspicions. Thirty-four percent (N = 59) of the observations involved a nonbehavioral suspicion. Fifty-nine percent (N = 103) of the suspicions recorded involved stopping the suspect. Fifty-six percent of officers were white. Approximately 29 percent of the officers earned at least an Associate's degree. On average, police officers have 4.2 years of experience on the force. In approximately 41 percent of the cases, the officers indicated that the area was "troubled." Of all suspects, 71 percent were black and 70 percent were driving a car. In 47 percent (N = 82) of suspicions, the suspect committed a traffic offense and 57 percent were formed in predominately black neighborhoods. Two logistic regression models were estimated to examine the sequential relationship between the explanatory variables, nonbehavioral suspicions, and stops. Results from the logistic regression model predicting nonbehavioral suspicion are presented first, followed by the results from the logistic regression model of citizen stops.

Table 2 presents the results from the logistic regression model predicting nonbehavioral suspicion. The results indicate that suspect and officer demographic variables did not play an important role in forming nonbehavioral suspicion, with the exception of the suspect's race. Officers were significantly more likely to form a nonbehavioral suspicion when the suspect is black (b = 1.49; $p < .05$), the odds being more than four times (4.4) greater if the suspect were black. There was no relationship between the race of an officer and the likelihood of forming a nonbehavioral suspicion. These results are consistent with other studies on police behavior, indicating that the suspect's race is more important than the officer's (National Research Council, 2003, Walker and Katz, 2002). In this analysis, however, we are examining the thought processes of police officers prior to their engaging in any actual "behavior."

Table 1 Descriptive Statistics of Variables

Variable	Mean	SD	Min	Max
Nonbehavioral suspicion	.339	.474	0	1
Stops of citizens	.591	.492	0	1
Traffic offense	.471	.500	0	1
Black citizen	.709	.455	0	1
White officer	.563	.497	0	1
College degree (officer)	.298	.459	0	1
Suspect in car	.70	.459	0	1
Troubled neighborhood	.405	.492	0	1
Black neighborhood	.567	.496	0	1
Officer's years in service	4.224	4.233	1	21

Table 2 Predictors of Nonbehavioral Suspicions

Variable	Odds Ratio	z value	95% Confidence Interval
Traffic offense	.004*	−5.627	.0044–.004
Black citizen	4.447*	2.134	1.129–17.516
White officer	.418	−1.457	.129–1.351
College degree (officer)	1.992	1.138	.607–6.529
Suspect in car	8.073*	2.999	2.061–31.613
Troubled neighborhood	1.090	.141	.324–3.664
Black neighborhood	.711	−.543	.208–2.427
Officer's years in service	1.112	1.670	.981–1.261
Pseudo R2	.487		

* p < .05 (two-tailed)

The results are consistent with our predictions that minority status would be an important predictor of the type of suspicion raised by officers. In this context, the findings suggest that officers are more likely to view minority suspects suspiciously because of their appearance or other nonbehavioral factors. Also, the longer the officers had been on the police force, the more likely they were to form nonbehavioral suspicions (b = .100; p < .10). This finding is not significant at the .05 level, but is close enough to be noteworthy given our small sample size. These findings may indicate that as an officer gains experience he or she forms certain cues or "cognitive schemas" wherein people appear suspicious for reasons that are not behavioral. Due to the significance level of this finding, further research is needed to justify confidence in it. If a suspect were in a car, it was more likely that a police officer would form a nonbehavioral suspicion (b = 2.08; p < .05). That is, when a citizen is in a car, officers were eight times more likely to form a nonbehavioral suspicion. These findings suggest that automobiles may have certain appearances that generate nonbehavioral suspicions. Further, if a suspect were observed committing a traffic offense (behavior), then the initial suspicion was significantly less likely to be formed for nonbehavioral reasons (b = −5.40; p < .05). The racial composition of the neighborhood and the perception of it being troubled had no influence on the type of suspicions formed (behavioral vs. nonbehavioral). This finding differs from research on actual police behavior that suggests neighborhood composition is an important determinant of the use of legal authority (Smith, 1986). Here, however, we were examining incidents prior to any actual police action. The discrepancies between these findings and those generated by actual police behavior may also be the result of differences in the measurement of neighborhood characteristics. In general the findings from this analysis suggest that minority status plays an important role in explaining the types of suspicion that police officers form, and that blacks are more likely than whites to be viewed suspiciously for nonbehavioral reasons, when compared to behavioral reasons.

To provide an additional interpretation of the results we calculated a series of predicted probabilities for the average case. For the average case, the probability of nonbehavioral suspicion was .18. If a suspect were black and an officer were white then the probability of a nonbehavioral suspicion was .19. If both a suspect and an officer were black the probability of a nonbehavioral suspicion increased to .36. The probability of a nonbehavioral suspicion was only .05 if the officer and suspect were both white. These findings clearly illustrate that nonbehavioral suspicions are most common when a suspect and an officer are both black, and least common when both officer and suspect are white.

Next, we turn our attention to the actual behavior of police officers once they have formed a suspicion. Specifically, we examine the same set of predictor variables with regard to officers stopping and questioning suspects. The results from this model of stop behavior are displayed in Table 3. In contrast to the results for forming nonbehavioral suspicion, a suspect's race did not play a role in explaining stops of suspicious persons by the police. In fact, the only variable that significantly predicted stopping suspicious persons was the commission of a traffic offense (b = 2.35; $p < .05$), a behavior that can always justify a stop. Predictably, the risk of being stopped was more than ten times (10.5) as likely if a suspect committed a traffic offense. These findings suggest that race plays a minimal role in the actions of officers once a suspicion has been formed. Interestingly, we find no evidence that black suspects are more likely to be stopped and questioned by the police once they have been identified as a suspicious person. As with previous research on police behavior (see for example, Smith, 1984) these results may indicate that there is an informed threshold for making a stop. In other words, officers must actually see a violation of the law occur before stopping and questioning a suspect, even if they already think the person appears suspicious.

Table 3 Predictors of Citizen Stops

Variable	Odds Ratio	z value	95% Confidence Interval
Traffic offense	10.551*	4.342	3.642–30.563
Black citizen	.919	−.187	.379–2.226
White officer	1.269	.544	.537–2.995
College degree (officer)	.692	−.804	.282–1.696
Suspect in car	.503	−1.324	.182–1.390
Troubled neighborhood	1.531	.938	.628–3.732
Black neighborhood	.710	−.761	.293–1.716
Officer's years in service	1.023	0.459	.925–1.133
Pseudo R2	.170		

* $p < .05$ (two-tailed)

To provide an additional interpretation of the effect of a traffic offense on the likelihood of being stopped and questioned, we calculated predicted probabilities for the average case. The results indicate that the probability of being stopped was .87 if the suspect committed a traffic offense, and only .39 if not, holding all other variables constant at their mean value. These findings clearly illustrate that the factors that lead to forming a nonbehavioral suspicion are different from those that lead police officers to stop suspicious persons. In fact, it appears that officers often form nonbehavioral suspicions of individuals for reasons that do not result in stopping and questioning them.

The findings from the two sets of analyses suggest that race plays a role in the type of suspicion police officers form, but that it has little impact on actions taken by police officers (see Gould and Mastrofski, 2004: 341). These results, however, give us little contextual understanding of the actual mechanisms that lead to the formation of nonbehavioral suspicion and the decision to stop an individual. In an attempt to provide some contextual understanding we apply the results from the logistic regression models that predicted nonbehavioral suspicions and stop decisions on cases with high-ranked probabilities of each event occurring. First, we examine the narrative description of the criteria for an officer's formation of nonbehavioral suspicion for incidents where the predicted probability from the logistic regression model ranked in the ninetieth percentile or above, or in cases where there was a 90 percent or greater chance that the officer formed a nonbehavioral suspicion. There were thirteen cases that met this criterion. The narrative descriptions of the reasons that caused officers to form suspicions in these cases are informative. For example, in one case the officer formed suspicion because the suspect was driving a motor vehicle that matched the description of a "G-ride" (ghetto ride), a type of car with heavily tinted windows, custom rims, or flashy paint job. Four of the thirteen cases involved vehicles that matched a BOLO ("be on the lookout") call. One involved a suspect who was in the vicinity of a robbery and shooting that had recently taken place. Two involved suspects who appeared to be out of place to the officers when they pulled up next to their cars. One involved a woman observed in the shadows of an area known for prostitution. The narrative descriptions of each of these indicate that the probability of nonbehavioral suspicion was greatly influenced by a number of factors, such as officers having prior information on a suspect or on criminal activity in a specific area, or where civilians appeared to be nervous when the police approached. It is worth noting here, however, that none of these cases involved actual behaviors that one could say were suspicious or illegal.

Next, we select cases that met the criteria for having at least a 90 percent chance of being stopped by the police, as indicated by the logistic regression model. There were a total of ten cases that met this criterion. The narrative descriptions of these cases show that "traffic offenses" were the predominant reason for stops. Eight of the ten cases involved stops based on traffic offenses. There were two exceptions: a case in which a citizen who matched a description of a robbery suspect was stopped and another in which a citizen was "hanging around a locked trailer in a parking lot." Three cases involved individuals stopped for speeding. The other cases involved running red lights, stop signs, and expired or altered vehicle tags. The narrative descriptions of these cases indicate that the probability of stopping a citizen was greatly influenced by officers having observed citizens committing traffic related offenses. These narratives offer further evidence that the rationale for forming nonbehavioral suspicion differs from the reasons for deciding to stop citizens.

CONCLUSIONS

These results support the argument that race is an important factor in the type of suspicion—behavioral versus nonbehavioral—the police form, but is not predictive of official police action. What these data do not tell us, however, is the extent to which suspicions are warranted by citizen behavior. Research suggests that official police reactions to juvenile delinquency are biased against minorities (Sampson, 1986). This study cannot address the issue because no information on nonsuspicious citizen behavior was recorded.

Nonetheless, we found that the race of a suspect significantly affected inferences the police made about suspicion, although these types of inferences did not play a significant role in their decision to stop a citizen. Consequently, this study suggests that police officers are more likely to form nonbehavioral suspicions for individuals who are members of a minority group. This finding is consistent with psychological theory of cognitive schema in suggesting that blacks are more likely to be viewed suspiciously by the police for reasons that appear innocuous. The results also suggest that the relationship between minority status and nonbehavioral suspicion appears to fit a pattern in which suspects or vehicles match descriptions that officers are supposed to be looking for. However, this does not influence the ultimate decision to stop and question suspects. Instead, it appears that police officers require a clearer prompt, such as a suspect committing a traffic offense, or matching a reported description of a suspect in a crime, before they decide to exercise their discretion to stop a suspicious person or vehicle. The quality of an officer's decision making process, in terms of objectivity and consistency, is beyond the scope of these observational data, however, criminologists would be naive to think that mental images of criminals inextricably linked to race in American culture (Russell-Brown, 1998) do not exist among police officers working in urban areas. At the same time, one can imagine officers that retain race-conscious views of criminality and act objectively and neutrally, stopping citizens and questioning them only for objective and tangible reasons. The results from the present study suggest such a process may operate among the observed officers. As Kennedy (1997) notes, we must distinguish between officers who use race as a guide in decision making and those officers who use race as a discriminatory tool. We must be careful to make such distinctions on reliable data and not on faulty or inappropriate information or hunches.

Throughout this study we focused on the role of race in explaining the type of police suspicion formed. However, we want to emphasize that this research does not address the question of police fairness. Additionally, because of research limitations, this study may generate more questions than it answers—a cliché, but true of most social science research. The findings from this study are important in that they provide the first empirical evidence that race is an important predictor of the type of suspicion formed by the police in actual street-level encounters with citizens. One may wonder, for example, to what extent unmeasured social cues, such as dress or place, explain the race findings. Further inquiry is needed to examine how social cues are interpreted by the police when they form suspicion and, additionally, how these social cues coincide with or differ from public perceptions of what is or is not suspicious. Getting inside the "heads" of police officers and understanding how nonbehavioral visual cues associated with being black influence what looks suspicious is an important process to study in the future. Consequently, it is important for future research to focus on this neglected, yet critical, stage in a police officer's decision making process. While this study relied on observations of officers and their self-reported reasons for becoming suspicious, future research should create a control group of people, behavior and events that police do not find suspicious. The problem of creating a valid control group is complex, but may be overcome by employing simulated events in an experimental design. While the use of an experimental methodology would yield information on actual racial disparities, it necessarily would rely on simulated events. Whatever future methodological direction is taken to examine police officer suspicion, this study demonstrates the importance of this type of research and is a strong foundation on which future research can build.

DISCUSSION QUESTIONS

1. What is racial profiling? Why has it become an issue in policing today?
2. What is it about racial profiling that most people find unacceptable? Describe a situation in which law enforcement need to use racial profiling to apprehend a targeted suspect.
3. Discuss civil liability and how it is associated with policing. How can civil liability be reduced?
4. What innovative steps can a police department take to reduce or eliminate corruption?

REFERENCES

Alpert, Geoffrey and Roger Dunham. 2004 *Understanding Police Use of Force*. New York: Cambridge University Press.

Anderson, Elijah. 1999 *Code of the Streets: Decency, Violence and the Moral Life of the Inner City*. New York: W. W. Norton.

Barlow, David and Melissa Barlow. 2000 *Police in a Multicultural Society: An American Story*. Prospect Heights, IL: Waveland Press.

Bittner, Egon. 1967 *The Functions of Police in Modern Society*. Washington, DC: National Institute of Mental Health.

Bittner, Egon. 1996 Popular conceptions about the character of police work. In Steven Brandl and David Barlow (eds.), *Classics in Policing*. Cincinnati, OH: Anderson Publishing.

Black, Donald. 1976 *The Behavior of Law*. San Diego, CA: Academic Press

Blalock, Herbert. 1967 *Toward a Theory of Minority-Group Relations*. New York: Capricorn Books.

Blumberg, Mark. 1981 Race and police shootings: An analysis in two cities. In J.J. Fyfe (ed.), *Contemporary Issues in Law Enforcement*. Beverly Hills, CA: Sage Publications.

Bower, Gordon, John Black and Terrence Turner. 1979 *Scripts in text comprehension and memory*. Cognitive Psychology 11: 177–220.

Brehm, Sharon, Saul Kassin and Steven Fein. 2002 *Social Psychology*, 5th ed. Boston, MA: Houghton–Mifflin.

Chambliss, William and Robert Seidman. 1982 *Law, Order and Power*. Reading, MA: Addison-Wesley.

Craik, Kenneth 1943 The Nature of Explanation. Cambridge: Cambridge University Press.

Cromwell, Paul, James Olson and D'Aunn W. Avary. 1991 *Breaking and Entering: An Ethnographic Analysis of Burglary*. Newbury Park, CA: Sage Publications.

D'Alessio, Stewart and Lisa Stolzenberg. 2003 Race and the probability of arrest. *Social Forces* 81: 1381–1397.

Delgado, Richard and Jean Stefanic. 2001 *Critical Race Theory: An Introduction*. New York: New York University Press.

Dunham, Roger and Geoffrey Alpert. 2004 The effects of officer and suspect ethnicity in use-of-force incidents. In Karen Terry and Delores Jones-Brown (eds.), *Policing and Minority Communities: Bridging the Gap*. Englewood Cliffs, NJ: Prentice Hall.

Dunham, Roger, Geoffrey Alpert, Meghan Stroshine and Katherine Bennett. 2005 Transforming citizens into suspects: Factors that influence the formation of police suspicion. *Police Quarterly* 8.

Ericsson, Anders and Herbert Simon. 1984 *Protocol Analysis: Verbal Reports as Data*. Cambridge, MA: MIT Press.

Fagan, Jeffrey and Garth Davies. 2000 Street stops and broken windows: Terry, race and disorder in New York City. *Fordham Urban Law Journal* 28: 457–504.

Fridell, Lorie, Robert Lunney, Drew Diamond and Bruce Kubu. 2001 *Racially Biased Policing*. Washington, DC: Police Executive Research Forum.

Fyfe, James, 1980 Geographic correlates of police shootings: A microanalysis. *Crime and Delinquency* 17: 101–113.

Geller, Richard and Kenneth Karales. 1981 *Split Second Decisions: Shootings of and by the Chicago Police*. Chicago Law Enforcement Study Group.

Gibbons, Mary 2004 Profiling—more than a euphemism for discrimination: legitimate use of a maligned investigative tool. In Delores Brown and Karen Terry (eds.), *Policing and Minority Communities: Bridging the Gap*. Upper Saddle River, NJ: Pearson–Prentice Hall.

Good, Thomas and Jere Brophy 1990 *Educational Psychology: A Realistic Approach.* White Plains, NY: Longman (1990).

Gottfredson, Michael R. and Michael J. Hindelang. 1979 A study of the behavior of law and theory and research in the sociology of law. *American Sociological Review* 44: 3–18.

Gould, Jon and Stephen Mastrofski 2004 Suspect searches: Assessing police behavior under the U.S. Constitution. *Criminology & Public Policy* 3: 315–361.

Gross, Samuel and Katherine Barnes. 2002 Road work: Racial profiling and drug interdiction on the highway. *Michigan Law Review* 101: 651–754.

Grosset, N., and Barrouillet, Pierre 2003 On the nature of mental models of conditional: The case of If, If then, and Only if. *Thinking and Reasoning* 9 (4): 289–306.

Harris, David 1999 The stories, the statistics and the law: Why driving while black matters. *Minnesota Law Review* 84: 1–45.

Hindelang, Michael 1981 Variations in sex-race-age-specific incidence rates of offending. *American Sociological Review* 46: 461–475.

Kane, Robert. 2003 Social control in the metropolis: A community-level examination of the minority group-threat hypothesis. *Justice Quarterly* 20: 265 – 295.

Kennedy, Randall. 1997 *Race, Crime and the Law.* New York: Pantheon Books.

Klinger, David A. 1994 Demeanor or crime? Why hostile citizens are more likely to be arrested. *Criminology* 32: 475–493.

Klinger, David A. 1996 More on demeanor and arrest in Dade County. *Criminology* 34:61–82.

Klinger, David A. 1997 Negotiating order in patrol work: An ecological

theory of police response to deviance. *Criminology* 35 (2): 277–306.

Lanza-Kaduce, Lonn and Richard Greenleaf. 1994 Police citizen encounters: Turk on norm resistance. *Justice Quarterly* 11: 605–623.

Lundman, Richard J. and Robert L. Kaufman. 2003 Driving while black: Effects of race, ethnicity, and gender on citizen self-reports of traffic stops and police actions. *Criminology* 41: 195–220.

Mastrofski, Stephen. 1981 Policing the beat: The impact of organizational scale on patrol officer behavior in urban residential neighborhoods. *Journal of Criminal Justice* 9: 343–358.

Mastrofski, Stephen D., Richard R. Ritti and Debra Hoffmaster. 1987 Organizational determinants of police discretion: the case of drinking and driving. *Journal of Criminal Justice* 15: 387–402.

Mastrofski, Stephen, Jeffrey Snipes and Anne Supina. 1996 Compliance on demand: The public's response to specific police requests. *Journal of Research in Crime and Delinquency* 33: 269–305.

Mastrofski, Stephen, Jeffrey Snipes, Roger Parks, and Christopher Maxwell. 2000 The helping hand of the law: Police control of citizens on request. *Criminology* 38:307–342.

Mastrofski, Stephen, Roger Parks, Albert Reiss, Robert Worden, Christina DeJong, Jeffrey Snipes and William Terrill. 1998 *Systematic Observation of Public Police: Applying Field Research Methods to Policy Issues.* Washington, DC: National Institute of Justice.

Miller, Joel. 2000 *Profiling populations available for stops and searches.* Police Research Series, Paper 131. London: Home Office.

National Research Council. 2003 *Fairness and Effectiveness in Policing: The Evidence.* Washington, DC: The National Academies Press.

Novak, Kenneth. 2004 Disparity and racial profiling in traffic enforcement. *Police Quarterly* 7(1): 65–96.

Powell, David D. 1990 A study of police discretion in six southern cities. *Journal of Police Science and Administration* 17: 1–7.

Rawls, Anne. 2000 Race as an interaction order phenomenon. *Sociological Theory* 18: 241–274.

Read, Stephen J. 1987 Constructing causal scenarios: A knowledge structure approach to causal reasoning. *Journal of Personality and Social Psychology* 52: 288–302.

Reisig, Michael, John McClusky, Stephen Mastrofski and William Terrill. 2004 Suspect disrespect toward the police. *Justice Quarterly* 21: 241–268.

Riksheim, Erik C. and Steven M. Chermak. 1993 Causes of police behavior revisited. *Journal of Criminal Justice* 21: 353–382.

Romero, Victor C. 2002 Critical race theory in three acts: Racial profiling, affirmative action, and the diversity visa lottery. *Albany Law Review* 66: 325–341.

Rubinstein, Jonathan. 1973 *City Police.* New York: Farrar, Strauss and Giroux.

Ruby, C.L. and John C. Bringham. 1996 A criminal schema: The role of chronicity, race and socio-economic status in law enforcement officials' perceptions of others. *Journal of Applied Social Psychology* 26: 95–112.

Russell-Brown, Katheryn. 1998 *The Color of Crime: Racial Hoaxes, White Fear, Black Protectionism, Police Harassment and Other Macro-Aggressions.* New York: New York University Press.

Sampson, Robert J. 1986 Effects of socioeconomic context on official reaction to juvenile delinquency. *American Sociological Review* 51: 876–885.

Sherman, Lawrence. 1978 *The Quality of Police Education.* San Francisco: Jossey-Bass.

Smith, Douglas. 1984 The organizational aspects of legal control. *Criminology* 22: 19–38.

Smith, Douglas and Laura Davidson. 1984 Equity and discretionary justice: The influence of race on police arrest decisions. *Journal of Criminal Law* 75: 234–249.

Smith, Douglas and Christy Visher. 1981 Street level justice: Situational determinants of police arrest decisions. *Social Problems* 29: 167–178.

Stolzenberg, Lisa, Stewart D'Alessio and David Eitle. 2004 A multilevel test of racial threat theory. *Criminology* 42(3): 673–698.

Sun, Ivan and Brian Payne. 2004 Racial differences in resolving conflicts: A comparison between black and white police officers. *Crime & Delinquency* 50: 516–541.

Vrij, Aldirt. 1994a Behavioral correlates of deception in a simulated police interview. *The Journal of Psychology* 129: 15–28.

Vrij, Aldirt. 1994b The impact of information and setting on detection of deception by police detectives. *Journal of Nonverbal Behavior* 21: 87–102.

Vrij, Aldirt and Rachel Taylor. 2003 Police officers' and students' beliefs about telling and detecting little and serious lies. *International Journal of Police Science and Management* 5: 41–49.

Vrij, Aldirt and Frans Winkel. 1992 Cross-cultural police-citizen interactions: The influence of race, beliefs and nonverbal communication on impression formation. *Journal of Applied Social Psychology* 22: 1546–1559.

Walker, Samuel. 1993 *Taming the System: The Control of Discretion in Criminal Justice, 1950–1990.* Oxford: Oxford University Press.

Walker, Samuel and Charles Katz. 2002 *Police in America.* Boston: McGraw-Hill.

Walker, Samuel, Cassia Spohn and Miriam DeLone. 2000 *The Color of Justice: Race, Ethnicity and Crime in America*. New York: Wadsworth.

Weitzer, Ronald and Steven A. Tuch. 2002 Perceptions of racial profiling: Race, class, and personal experience. *Criminology* 40: 436–456.

Werthman, Carl and Irving Piliavin. 1967 Gang members and the police. In David Bordua (ed.), *The Police: Six Sociological Essays*. New York: John Wiley & Sons.

Wilson, George, Roger Dunham and Geoffrey Alpert. 2004 Prejudice in police profiling: Assessing an overlooked aspect in prior research. *American Behavioral Scientist* 47: 896–909.

Wilson, James Q. 1968 *Varieties of Police Behavior*. Cambridge: Harvard University Press.

Winkel, Frans W., Leendert Koppelaar and Aldirt Vrij. 1998 Creating suspects in police-citizen encounters: Two studies on personal space and being suspect. *Social Behaviour* 3: 307–318.

Worden, Robert E. 1989 Situational and attitudinal explanations of police behavior: A theoretical reappraisal and empirical assessment. *Law and Society Review* 23: 667–711.

Worden, Robert E. 1990 A badge and a baccalaureate: Policies, hypotheses, and further evidence. *Justice Quarterly* 7: 565–592.

Worden, Robert E. and Robin Shepard. 1996 Demeanor, crime, and police behavior: a reexamination of the police services study data. *Criminology* 34: 83–105.

Worden, Robert and Steven Brandl. 1990 Protocol analysis of police decision making: Toward a theory of police behavior. *American Journal of Criminal Justice* XIV No. 2: 297–318.

10

❂

Policing Immigration: Federal Laws and Local Police

Scott H. Decker

Paul G. Lewis

Doris Marie Provine

Monica W. Varsanyi

Some local governments are asking their police departments to enforce federal immigration law more aggressively. However, there is little research or policy guidance available to assist police in balancing local immigration enforcement with the norms of community-oriented policing. This paper presents results from a national survey of municipal police chiefs. The survey responses indicate substantial differences in the way that police departments are approaching unauthorized immigration. The highly varied nature of policing practice on this issue is a function of the lack of clear policy guidance and models for local enforcement of immigration law.

Source: Scott H. Decker, Paul G. Lewis, Doris Marie Provine, and Monica W. Varsanyi, "Policing Immigration: Federal Laws and Local Police" in Khashu, A. (ed.) The role of local police: striking a balance between immigration enforcement and civil liberties. Copyright © The Police Foundation. Reprinted with permission.

INTRODUCTION/STATEMENT OF THE PROBLEM

Unauthorized immigration has become a primary domestic issue in the United States, and a major concern for law enforcement and the criminal justice system. Some estimates place the number of unauthorized immigrants at 12 million (Passel 2006). Many immigrants are settling in new locations unaccustomed to immigration and bring their families, hoping to integrate more fully into American society (Zuniga and Hernandez-Leon 2005; Massey 2008; Singer *et al.* 2008). State and local jurisdictions have responded with a patchwork of ordinances, policies and proclamations, many of which are designed to discourage settlement (Ramakrishnan and Wong 2007; Hegen 2008; Varsanyi 2008). Some local governments are asking the police to work directly with federal authorities to apprehend unauthorized immigrants, or to check legal status in the course of routine law enforcement.

Throughout the history of the United States, local and state law enforcement has played varying roles in the enforcement of immigration law. During the first century of U.S. history, which legal scholar Gerald Neuman (1996) calls the "lost century of American immigration law," state and local governments held primary responsibility for the formulation and enforcement of immigration law. However, starting in the latter decades of the nineteenth century and throughout the twentieth century, the federal government held plenary authority in this area, reserving to itself decisions about whether to initiate enforcement and what procedures to employ (Aleinikoff 2002). Immigration was a civil matter under federal law, not a prosecutable crime under local jurisdiction. Local and state police participated in immigration enforcement during this time (see Vogel *et al.* (this volume) and McDonald 1997b), but their participation was ad hoc and often marked by conflicting mandates.

In 1996, the authority of local and state law enforcement to engage in civil immigration enforcement became more clearly defined with the adoption of two federal statutes, the Anti-terrorism and Effective Death Penalty Act (AEDPA), which gives local police authority to arrest previously deported non-citizen felons, and the Illegal Reform and Immigrant Responsibility Act (IIRIRA), which authorizes training of local and state police to enforce federal immigration laws. Although local police and sheriff departments did not immediately avail themselves of this training opportunity, they began signing on for training in 2002 and have continued to do so in increasing numbers. As of August 2008, 55 agreements had been signed between local and federal officials, providing local authority either to identify suspects already in custody or to participate in enforcing immigration laws, with another 80 localities on a waitlist (Sullivan 2008). Even without this special training, local police departments are developing new links with federal immigration authorities, often at the encouragement of city and state officials.

The emerging picture is one of blurred responsibilities for immigration control, with a constantly evolving recalibration of relationships between local and federal authority (Spiro 1997; Huntington 2007). There is little firm policy guidance for police departments coming from local or federal authorities, including the courts. It is unclear how police departments are responding to this situation, a serious gap in knowledge that is relevant to scholars and policy makers alike. To begin to address this issue, we present key results from a national survey of municipal police chiefs. The survey responses indicate substantial differences in the way that police departments are approaching unauthorized immigration. We argue that the highly varied nature of policing practice on this issue is a function of the lack of clear policy guidance and models for local enforcement of immigration law.

LITERATURE REVIEW

The devolution of immigration policing authority from the federal to local governments is occurring within a broader context of diffusion of governmental responsibility to more local levels and away from traditional centers of power (see e.g. Berman 2003). This movement lacks clear parameters, which poses a dilemma for police departments. Decisions in the realm of immigration are high stakes, not just for immigrants, but for the communities in which they live, and the police charged with the provision of public safety. The existing practices contain contradictions, with unfortunate results in some instances. Romero and Serag (2005) describe how local police engaged in racial, cultural, and class profiling in the notorious 1997 "Chandler Roundups" in Arizona, which resulted in the arrest of 432 suspected unauthorized immigrants, many of whom were, in fact, legal residents.

Community policing is another area where law enforcement faces new challenges. The scholarly literature has surprisingly little to say about the relationship between community policing and immigration enforcement (see e.g. Herbert 2006; Katz and Webb; 2006; Skogan, 2006), yet the potential for conflict is obvious. Community policing seeks to mobilize the community and the police in public safety partnerships aimed at reducing fear, crime, disorder and distrust of one another. These partnerships link resources across many public and private agencies, focusing on "quality of life" issues (Greene 2001; and see Crank 1994).

This partnership approach may not be compatible with aggressive efforts to root out unauthorized immigrants. As the Immigration Committee of the Major Cities Chiefs (2006, p. 3) observed, "Local enforcement of federal immigration laws raises many daunting and complex legal, logistical and resource issues for local agencies and the diverse communities they serve." While stopping short of endorsing one approach for local law enforcement in the debate over how best to respond to unauthorized immigration, the recommendations highlight the many challenges to local law enforcement in carrying out its primary function, including loss of trust among immigrant groups, lack of resources, complexity of federal laws, lack of local legal authority for intervention, and risks of civil liability. A more recent report on immigration enforcement by the International Association of Chiefs of Police (2007) identifies eight specific areas of conflict between communities, their elected officials, and federal and local law enforcement.

Many of these challenges emerge from the precarious position in which local law enforcement finds itself regarding immigration enforcement. Communities are often divided, or hold views divergent from those of the police regarding the appropriate activities to take with regard to persons without legal status. In this politically volatile situation, departments are inevitably tempted to refrain from entering the fray, and may thus fail to develop their own clear-cut policies. But without internal procedures and policies, and without training, officers must make their own ad hoc decisions in the field. The inevitable result is a lack of overall coherence in the local police response to immigration, and a lack of transparency and democratic accountability in police operations.

These challenges occur within a law-enforcement context that is already rife with uncertainty, a normal condition in police work because of its highly discretionary character (Bittner 1979). The complexity of the job also increases levels of uncertainty. Kelling (1999) identifies two sources of complexity in police work: the complexity of the situations encountered by police, and the complexity of responses available. His analysis focuses not on the relatively rare instances of major crimes, but on the more common realm of less-serious offenses, such as panhandling or loitering. Bayley's study (1986) is similar. He describes thirty-three separate categories of intervention for domestic violence and fourteen possible responses to motor vehicle stops.

Manning (2003) describes the police role as an "impossible mandate" that arises from unclear or conflicting expectations from the communities that police serve and from misunderstandings that arise in the course of law enforcement. Information flows between police departments and communities tend to be constricted, and police officers tend to be socially isolated from the larger community they serve, in part because of the nature of their work (Wilson 1968; Skolnick 1994). Police engagement in immigration-control efforts creates a higher-than-usual sense of uncertainty because it is controversial, and because it is on the frontier of traditional policing responsibilities.

The volatility of the immigration issue in American society is especially relevant in this context. Jenness and Grattet (2005) describe the impact of environment as "perviousness" to suggest the important role that the external environment plays in producing a pattern of police behavior. James Q. Wilson (1968) comes to a similar conclusion in his classic work. He identifies three distinct styles of policing—watchman, legalistic, and service—each reflecting a distinct composition of political structure, population composition, and police leadership style. It is reasonable to expect the environment to condition the response by local police to immigration enforcement.

The challenges that immigration enforcement—particularly civil immigration enforcement—creates for police departments involve more than conflicts between professional standards and political pressure, serious as those are. Expanding authority to engage in immigration enforcement also raises its own issues for policing. It is part of an expanding universe of crimes like bias or hate crime, terrorism, human trafficking, gangs and electronic crime that arise out of changed sensibilities, new technology, or revised legal definitions. New crimes generally provoke police to search for appropriate existing models or policies in developing a response. Jenness and Grattet (2005) found, for example, that hate crime legislation in California led to widespread borrowing of an available policy for use in the enforcement of hate crime. Katz and Webb (2006) suggest other problems that arise in these situations with their documentation of the struggles that local police have had in developing dedicated units to respond to gang crimes. These specialized units tend to be isolated from the mainstream department and not fully in step with its community policing principles. Non-enforcement or over-enforcement can also occur because the new crime type is not well defined. Farrell (this volume) notes that, despite increasing pressure and publicity, there have been fewer than 200 prosecutions of human trafficking cases since 2000 in the United States. She observes that the police lack a framework for categorizing and responding to such crimes, in many cases seeing victims initially as offenders.

In sum, new crimes and emerging areas of police responsibility such as immigration enforcement are on the frontier of traditional policing responsibilities. These offenses lack many of the usual trappings of criminal-justice practice, such as clear policy guidance, training opportunities, well-established statutory authority, and integration into the mission of the agency. These crimes also lack a firm basis in cultural or normative understanding, both among officers and in the public at large. This is highly problematic for law enforcement because, as research has shown, the effectiveness and perceived fairness of criminal justice processes depend on a shared set of norms and understandings about the characteristics of cases (Skolnick 1969; Skogan and Hartnett 1997).

Immigration enforcement, edging as it does into organizational niches held by federal law enforcement, creates unique pressures on law-enforcement agencies as organizations. These agencies, Jenness and Grattet (2005: 339) note, create "the 'law-in between'—organizational structures and policies that provide intermediary linkage between state statutes and officer discretion." This responsibility to translate legislative intent into action has important implications for our understanding of the role of local police in immigration enforcement. The situation is quite different from what have been dubbed by Sudnow (1965) and others as "normal crimes" that everyone involved in the enforcement process understands in normative and substantive terms. These crimes can be processed by prosecutors, judges, and defense attorneys in a consensual, rather than adversarial, manner because there is no controversy over their meaning, scope, and significance. For police, normal crimes offer what Skolnick (1994) called "a perceptual shorthand"—ways of responding that are unlikely to cause controversy within police ranks or in the community at large.

We argue that immigration enforcement lacks such an understanding among law enforcement about what its salient features are, what should trigger a response from the police, and how such cases are to be handled. In response, a number of large city governments (e.g., New York, Los Angeles, San Francisco) follow a strategy of limited cooperation with federal immigration authorities, citing *inter alia* expense and challenges to public safety as reasons for which they do not want to take on what has historically been defined as a federal responsibility. Other localities have responded in the opposite direction, proactively and aggressively enforcing immigration-status violations—even extending, in Maricopa County, Arizona, to unannounced, county sheriff-led immigration raids in incorporated municipalities.

DESCRIPTION OF DATA

This chapter presents results of a recent nationwide survey of police executives about immigration enforcement at the local level. The survey was directed to the chief of police (or equivalent position) in large and medium-sized cities across the United States. Our discussion of the results focuses on three areas of concern raised by immigration policing at the local level. The first is the extent of convergence or divergence between police departments and the local political leadership in the community in which they serve. To what extent are beliefs about immigration policing within departments at odds with those of the community they serve? Are local governmental officials satisfied with the approach their police department is taking to immigration enforcement? Second, we examine the extent to which communities have created specific policies for police, or departments have constructed their own policy and practice standards. Is there guidance for officers as they interact with and engage undocumented immigrants in their community? Are there training opportunities or requirements? Is there a memorandum of understanding in place with federal immigration authorities? More broadly, what are the parameters in which local police operate in this new area of law enforcement? Third, we attempt to determine from the survey responses how police officers in the field are responding to the policy guidance they are receiving.

The survey hit the field in November 2007. We asked 452 law-enforcement executives to participate. Chiefs could respond to the self-administered survey either by mail or on a secure website. We began with a list of all U.S. cities and towns that were included in the Census Bureau's American Community Survey (ACS) in 2005; the Census Bureau aimed to include in the ACS all localities of 60,000 or higher population, although a few communities had slightly lower populations. We dropped from this list several communities that do not have their own police departments (generally either townships or municipalities that contract with other local governments for police services). This yielded our 452-department list, and ultimately the 237 responses reported here (a response rate of 52.4%).

The communities surveyed are diverse in many respects, but most have substantial numbers of foreign-born residents. The average among communities surveyed was sixteen percent foreign-born residents as of 2005, according to ACS data. The share of immigrants in particular communities surveyed ranged widely, from 1% to 60% of the population.

FINDINGS

Congruence of Perspectives between Local Community and the Police

Our survey results suggest that there are significant differences between departments and communities in how they look at immigration control. We asked chiefs to compare views within their departments to those prevailing in the communities they serve. We found statistically significant differences in five of the six areas examined, as Table 1 indicates. Differences between police and local community views are particularly large in regard to whether unauthorized immigration is seen as controversial, and whether it is believed that determining legal status is easy. Only on the question of whether immigration enforcement is a drain on law-enforcement resources is there not a significant difference between the chiefs' perceptions of departmental and community views.

Despite these differences, a majority of police chiefs (59%) report that most elected officials in their community are satisfied with the department's current level of immigration enforcement. Significantly fewer perceive that local officials would prefer their department to become either more engaged (9%) or less engaged (4%) in immigration enforcement.

Policy Guidance from Outside or Inside the Department

While some local governments have received substantial media attention for adopting immigrant-related laws, our evidence suggests that, at least in the realm of immigration policing, most have not been very active. Forty-six percent of the chiefs responding reported that their local government has no

Table 1 Differences between Perspective of Department and Perspective of Locality, According to Chiefs

	Mean Score (on scale of 1 to 5)		
	. . . in my department	. . . in this locality	T-test prob.
Unauthorized immigration is a controversial topic . . .	2.92	3.60	.000
Victimization of immigrants is considered a significant problem . . .	2.82	2.69	.031
People believe that it is relatively easy to determine who is in this country without authorization . . .	2.55	3.29	.000
Gaining the trust of unauthorized immigrants is a priority . . .	3.54	2.92	.000
Immigration enforcement is considered the responsibility of the federal government . . .	4.07	3.68	.000
Issues surrounding unauthorized immigration are considered a drain on law-enforcement resources . . .	3.46	3.37	.209

Notes: Responses were scored from 1 ("strongly disagree") to 5 ("strongly agree"). Probability levels refer to a two-sided t-test of the difference in means between "in my department" and "in my locality." N = 237.

official policy in place relating to policing of unauthorized immigrants, while an additional 5% were unsure about this. Fifteen percent report that their locality has an *unwritten, informal* policy of "don't ask, don't tell" regarding unauthorized residents in the community. Another 18% note that the local government has developed, or is developing, some type of policy designed to encourage local police to participate in controlling certain kinds of crime associated with unauthorized immigration (e.g., human trafficking). Only a small minority of communities have taken a firm, comprehensive stand, with 4% declaring themselves "sanctuary" communities that will take no action against unauthorized immigrants unless they engage in criminal activities, and 12% taking a contrary position urging police to take a proactive role in deterring unauthorized immigration in all activities.

The situation within police departments is similar. Only 39% of chiefs report that they have a written departmental policy to guide officers in dealing with persons they encounter who they believe to be undocumented. An additional 9% state they have a policy, but that it is not in written form. A majority (51%) report that their department does not have either a written or unwritten policy, with a few (1%) unsure about this. Nor are departments heavily invested in training for their officers to handle incidents involving unauthorized immigrants. A majority (51%) report that they do not offer any training, while 45% state that they do (and 3% are not sure).

Relationships with federal authorities show a similar pattern: to the extent that there is a relationship, it tends to be informal and ad hoc. The vast majority of respondents (74 percent) state that they have no formal agreement with federal Immigration and Customs Enforcement (ICE); they contact ICE only when they are holding suspected unauthorized immigrants for criminal violations. Formal Memoranda of Understanding with ICE are rare. Only 4% report a formal agreement to provide training and cooperation in investigations, and 3% have a formal agreement to manage incarcerated immigrants. ICE agents are embedded in 8% of departments responding to the survey. Thus in the area of immigration enforcement, local police are largely without guidance either inside or outside of their own department. In this new area of responsibility for local law enforcement, there is little guidance of any kind to help structure discretion and decision making by individual officers.

The Impact of Policy Direction on the Policing of Unauthorized Immigration

We asked chiefs to describe what typically happens when officers encounter persons they think might lack the legal status to remain in the country. Seven commonly encountered law-enforcement scenarios were presented, ranging from traffic stops to arrests for a violent crime. Figure 1 suggests a pattern of response consistent with a normative evaluation that balances the seriousness of the crime against the likely consequences of reporting the incident to federal authorities. Of course, it is also possible that responses reflect a pragmatic evaluation of how federal immigration agents would respond to reports of various kinds of crime. In either event, there is clearly a weighing of the seriousness of the offense in these responses, with more serious offenses and actions (arrest for violent crime, parole violation or failure to appear in court, arrest for domestic violence) resulting in formal action to check immigration status or report to ICE.

Do the city and departmental policies, discussed earlier, influence the practices of officers "on the ground" in dealing with suspected undocumented immigrants? To investigate this question, we constructed a four-part typology of cities that is based on the type of policy direction that is offered to officers. Type 1 municipalities have an official city policy that is "supportive" of immigrants—that is, the city is either a self-identified sanctuary city or employs a "don't ask, don't tell" policy. Nineteen percent of cities fall into this category. Type 2 cities also have an official city policy, but it is enforcement-oriented—that is, it encourages local police to collaborate with federal authorities on immigration, or expects the department to be proactive in deterring unauthorized immigration in all its activities. This city type

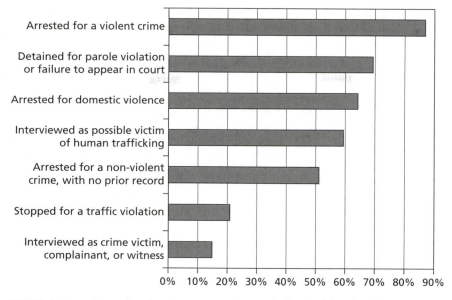

FIGURE 1 Percentage of police departments that typically check immigration status, contact ICE, or both, when encountering possible unauthorized immigrants in these situations

included 29% of communities in our sample. Type 3 cities are those that lack an official city government policy, but where the police department has its own written or unwritten policy regarding encounters with suspected unauthorized immigrants. This group includes 18% of all cities in our sample. (It is worth noting that Type 3 conflates two different types of approaches—that is, police departments may have developed policies that are supportive or are enforcement-oriented.) Finally, Type 4 cities have no official city government policy, and nor do they have a police department policy. This group comprises 32% of the sample. The remaining 2% of cities in our sample could not be classified due to one or more missing responses.

In Figure 2, we show how this typology relates to the number of situations in which (according to the chief) officers would typically inquire about immigration status or contact ICE, based on the tally of situations from Figure 1. In Figure 2, the vertical line for each type of city extends from the top quartile to the bottom quartile, giving a sense of the range of responses, and the square on each vertical line represents the mean for that type of city.

Not surprisingly, the variance across cities in enforcement practices is highest where the officers have less policy guidance. The standard deviation of the number of situations in which officers check status and/or contact ICE is 1.6 for Type 1 cities, 1.8 for Type 2 cities, 1.9 for Type 3 cities and 2.1 for Type 4 cities. Thus, where there is no policy guidance—either from local government or the departmental leadership—there is more variation in whether officers inquire about immigration status or report it to ICE. These results underscore

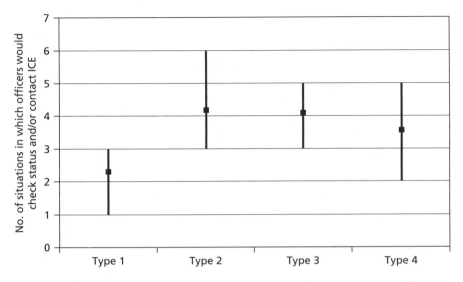

FIGURE 2 Differences in Aggressiveness of Immigration Enforcement among Cities with Four Different Types of Policy Approaches

the conclusion that officers <u>do</u> follow policies when they exist. This held true both for city policies that discourage asking about immigration status (Type 1 cities) and those that encourage officers to ask and report to federal authorities (Type 2 cities).

What city characteristics might help us predict whether a city is a Type 1, 2, 3, or 4? This question requires a detailed analysis that is beyond the scope of this chapter, but we can sketch some possibilities here. Using probit models, we examined the four dichotomous outcomes of whether a city falls into each of these categories. Potential predictor variables that we considered included the city's population size, its percentage of foreign-born residents, the partisan leanings (that is, percentage Republican or Democratic vote) in the 2004 presidential election, measured at the county level; and an indicator variable for whether the city is located in a Mexican-border state (California, Arizona, New Mexico, or Texas). Mirroring Ramakrishnan and Wong's (2007) recent analysis, the results suggest that local political leanings are of significant importance in distinguishing those communities with munici-pal policies relating to immigration enforcement, with the "immigrant-supportive" Type 1 cities tending to be in Democratic counties whereas the "enforcement-oriented" Type 2 cities tended to be in Republican coun-ties. None of our predictors helped to distinguish Type 3 cities (those with department-set policies) from the others, perhaps because that category may conflate two different tendencies. Type 4 cities—those with no policy guidance—tend to have smaller populations than the other cities, suggesting that they lack either the critical mass or policy capacity to devise an official response to unauthorized immigration.

CONCLUSION

These results suggest several important initial conclusions about immigration and local policing. Most significantly, as local police face a new responsibility in enforcing immigration laws, they find themselves without much guidance. City governments have not overtly committed themselves to immigration enforcement—nor to lack of enforcement—in large numbers, and there are relatively few police-department policies in place. Furthermore, only limited training for officers is occurring. Most departments have some relationship with ICE, but generally it is informal. The vast majority have no formal agreement, such as a 287g MOU.

These circumstances suggest that local police are often operating in something of a public policy vacuum regarding immigration law enforcement (see also Lewis and Ramakrishnan 2007). Based on the chiefs' description of typical local enforcement practices, local police appear to be resolving this dilemma by drawing distinctions in the seriousness of crimes, with less serious crimes less likely to be reported to federal authorities. Such judgments must often be made on an ad hoc basis. In this process, we suspect that informal norms about when to inquire about immigration status may be developing below the radar of police supervisors and independent of the wishes of the community or local political authorities. Our results also suggest that departments and communities differ on many issues related to immigration. Of course, it should also be noted that within communities there are often significant differences about what to do about unauthorized immigration, which may be why most local governments have not been active in creating policy directives for their police departments.

Significantly, we find that where policies *are* available, police behavior appears to be responsive to that policy. In cities mandating aggressive police action, a wider range of offense-related activity is reported to federal authorities. In cities where the policy is to focus elsewhere, fewer such instances are reported. Where there is no policy in place, either at the city or departmental level, responses are more varied. These results suggest that police discretion, inevitably great, is nonetheless conditioned by relevant public policy, when it exists.

It should not be surprising that political leaders and law-enforcement executives are at an early stage of the development of policies and training to respond to the presence of unauthorized individuals in their communities. The issues are complex and controversial. We have described immigration enforcement as on the frontier of traditional policing niches, a space between existing practices, tactics, and culture that calls for a new assessment of appropriate police responsibilities.

For police the issue is particularly complex. There is no easily accessible political consensus to consult. One of the salient features of the debate over immigration enforcement and local policing is the number of groups that seek to have an impact on what police do and how they go about doing it. The police have long found themselves between contending forces on a variety of enforcement issues, of course. What is new in the immigration debate is the active role of the federal government, particularly ICE and the Border Patrol, in offering enforcement partnerships—particularly partnerships that enable civil immigration enforcement—to state and local police departments. The infusion of traditionally federal concerns into the sphere of police and local government responsibility, and the generally contentious climate in which unauthorized immigration is occurring, raise significant questions for policy-makers at all levels about federalism, police discretion, community policing, and the environment within which policing occurs.

DISCUSSION QUESTIONS

1. What steps can local police departments take in order to implement a policy standard for dealing with illegal immigrants?
2. Discuss why a community would be against law enforcement cracking down on illegal immigration in that particular community.
3. Analyze the reason behind why immigration responsibilities have been relinquished to the local level of government.
4. Define the ICE and discuss why the local authorities reach out to them.

REFERENCES

Aleinikoff, T. Alexander. 2002. *Semblances of Sovereignty: The Constitution, the State, and American Citizenship.* Cambridge, MA: Harvard University Press.

Bayley, David. 1986. The tactical choices of police patrol officers. *Journal of Criminal Justice,* Volume 14, 4: 329–348.

Berman, David R. 2003. *Local Government and the States: Autonomy, Politics and Policy.* Armonk, NY: M.E. Sharp.

Bittner, Egon. 1979. *Functions of Police in Modern Society.* Westport, CT: Greenwood Press.

Crank, John M. 1994. "Watchman and Community: Myth and Institutionalization in Policing," *Law & Society Review* 28:2, pp. 325–52.

Farrell, Amy. 2008. State and Local Law Enforcement Responses to Human Trafficking (in this volume).

Grattet, Ryken and Valerie Jenness. 2005. "The Reconstitution of Law in Local Settings: Agency Discretion, Ambiguity, and a Surplus of Law in the Policing of Hate Crime," *Law & Society Review* 39, pp. 893–942.

Greene, Jack R. 2001. "Community Policing." In J. Homey (Ed.) *Criminal Justice 2000.* Washington, D.C.: National Institute of Justice.

Hegen, Dirk 2008 "State Laws Related to Immigrants and Immigration," National Council of State Legislatures, accessed at: http://www.ncsl.org/print/press/immigrationlegislationreport.pdf.

Herbert, Steve. 2006. *Citizens, Cops, and Power: Recognizing the Limits of Community.* Chicago: University of Chicago Press.

Huntington, Clare. 2007. "The Constitutional Dimension of

Immigration Federalism," *University of Colorado Law Legal Studies Research Paper No. 07-06*, accessed at http://ssm.com/abstract=968716

International Association of Chiefs of Police. 2007. *Police Chiefs Guide to Immigration Issues.* Accessed Jan. 3, 2008 from: http://www.theiacp.org/documents/pdfs/Publications/PoliceChiefsGuidetoimmigration.pdf.

Jenness, Valerie and Ryken Grattet. 2005. "The Law in Between: The Effects of Organizational Imperviousness on the Policing of Hate Crime," *Social Problems* 52, pp. 337–359.

Katz, Charles and Vince Webb. *Policing Gangs in America.* New York: Cambridge University Press.

Kelling, George. 1999. *"Broken Windows" and Police Discretion.* Washington, D.C.: National Institute of Justice.

Lewis, Paul G., and S. Karthick Ramakrishnan. 2007. "Police Practices in Immigrant-Destination Cities: Political Control or Bureaucratic Professionalism?" *Urban Affairs Review* 42:6, pp. 874–900.

Major Cities Chiefs. 2006. *M C.C. Immigration Committee Recommendations for Enforcement of Immigration Laws by Local Police Agencies.* Retrieved 3 Jan 2008 from http://www.houstontx.gov/police/pdfs/mcc position.pdf.

Manning, Peter K. 2003. *Policing Contingencies.* Chicago: University of Chicago Press.

Massey, D. (ed.) 2008. *New Faces in New Places: The Changing Geography of American Immigration.* New York: Russell Sage Foundation.

McDonald, William F. 1997a. "Crime and Illegal Immigration: Emerging Local, State and Federal Partnerships," *NIJ Journal* (June). Washington D.C.: National Institute of Justice.

———. 1997b. "Illegal Immigration: Crime, Ramifications and Control (The American Experience)." In William F. McDonald, ed., *Crime and Enforcement in the Global Village.* Cincinnati, OH: Anderson Publishers.

Passel, J.S. 2006. "The Size and Characteristics of the Unauthorized Migrant Population in the U.S.: Estimates Based on the March 2005 Current Population Survey." Retrieved 15 July 2007 from http://pewhispanic.org/files/reports/6l.pdf.

Ramakrishnan, S. Karthick and Tom (Tak) Wong. 2007. "Immigration Policies Go Local: The Varying Responses of Local Governments to Undocumented Immigrants." Unpublished paper, University of California. Retrieved from http://www.law.berkeley.edu/centers/ewi/Ramakrishnan&Wongpaperfinal.pdf.

Romero, Mary and Marwah Serag. 2005. "Violation of Latino Civil Rights Resulting from INS and Local Police's Use of Race, Culture, and Class Profiling: The Case of the Chandler Roundup in Arizona," *Cleveland State Law Review* 52, pp. 75–96.

Singer, Audrey, Susan W. Hadwick, and Caroline B. Brettell (eds.) 2008. *Twenty-First Century Gateways.* Washington, DC: Brookings Institution.

Skogan, Wesley. 2006. *Police and Community in Chicago: A Tale of Three Cities.* New York: Oxford University Press.

Skolnick, Jerome. 1994. *Justice without Trial: Law Enforcement in Democratic Society,* rev. ed. New York: McMillan.

Spiro, Peter. 1997. "Learning to Live with Immigration Federalism," *Connecticut Law Review* 9, pp. 1627–36

Sudnow, David. 1965. "Normal Crimes: Sociological Features of the Penal Code in a Public Defender Office," *Social Problems,* Vol. 12, No. 3, pp. 255–276.

Sullivan, Bartholomew. 2008. Blackburn knocks Homeland immigration enforcement effort. *Memphis Commercial Appeal,* August 1.

Varsanyi, Monica W. 2008. Immigration policing through the backdoor: City ordinances, the 'right to the city' and exclusion of undocumented day laborers. *Urban Geography,* Vol. 29, No. 1, pp. 29-52.

Wilson, James Q. 1968. *Varieties of Police Behavior: The Management of Order in Eight Communities.* Boston: Harvard University Press.

Zuniga, Victor, and Ruben Hernandez-Leon, eds. 2005. *New Destinations: Mexican Immigration in the United States.* New York: Russell Sage Foundation.

11

❂

Terrorism
and Local Police

Ronald V. Clarke
and Graeme R. Newman

It is becoming clear that the police have an important role in preventing terrorism. They are in a good position to learn about and investigate local terrorist threats, and they can work to ensure that vulnerable targets in their jurisdictions are protected. Filling the first of these functions, investigation of terrorists, will require police to extend their normal community policing activities and improve their handling of information. Filling the second function, protecting vulnerable targets, will require greater adjustments. They will need to become more expert in crime prevention and security matters, and they will have to develop partnerships with businesses and a wide range of public and private agencies. However, these changes are consistent with current best practices in policing.

INTRODUCTION

It has been said that the 9/11 attacks in the United States changed everything and this is certainly true for the police. It has become increasingly clear that national security agencies can no longer work alone in preventing future attacks. They must work in partnership with other public and private agencies, most importantly with local police. The police can identify potential terrorists living or operating in their jurisdictions, help to protect vulnerable targets and they can coordinate the first response to terror attacks. These are heavy new responsibilities that significantly expand the workload of already busy police forces. Many forces welcome the challenge of meeting these responsibilities, but in any case they cannot be shrugged off because elected officials and the public will increasingly expect that their police are prepared.

The case for the essential involvement of local police in counter-terrorism has been made in the United States by Kelling and Bratton (2006): They have argued that local police play a critical role in defeating terrorism, which they claim is not much different from other crime. They go on to argue that: 'Counter-terrorism has to be woven into the everyday workings of every department. It should be included on the agenda of every meeting, and this new role must be imparted to officers on the street so that terrorism prevention becomes part of their everyday thinking' (Kelling and Bratton, 2006: 6). This is a tall order. We know that terrorist attacks are extremely rare events—much rarer even than murders, for example. And many police jurisdictions, particularly in the United States, would be unlikely to attract the terrorists' attention. But Kelling and Bratton are correct to this extent: local police cannot risk the lives of people in their community. They have been, and will be held responsible should a disaster occur. It makes sense, therefore, for them to plan ahead for terrorism, and even better sense to fold these plans into everyday police practice.

But what should they actually do? In brief, we think they must: (a) collect intelligence about possible terrorist activity; (b) ensure that vulnerable targets are protected; and (c) be ready to respond in the event of an attack. The last of these is uncontroversial and will not be discussed here. Rather, we will discuss the first two tasks, both of which, in their different ways, are focused on prevention. We welcome this focus. Because of the devastating conse-quences of terrorism, prevention assumes far greater importance than for other crimes where bringing perpetrators to justice may be equally important. But there is another general point to be made about prevention—police should guard against devoting the bulk of their efforts to gathering intelligence at the expense of effort on protecting targets. Gathering intelligence about potential terrorists might be congruent with their usual business, but devoting their efforts exclusively, or even predominantly, to 'taking out' terrorists is likely to be unproductive for reasons that we will discuss. Devoting effort to protecting targets, on the other hand, is a less familiar role for police and, in fact, will require them to develop new skills and expertise. But assuming that terrorism will always remain a threat, communities must develop long-term plans to protect their most vulnerable targets, and these plans ought to be led by the police. We will be giving some pointers to how they must set about this task.

'TAKING OUT' THE TERRORISTS

Regular police practice, too, often assumes that arresting offenders is the same as preventing crime, when in fact this is not the case. Despite the best efforts of police, currently only a tiny proportion of crimes are followed by arrest and it is unclear how this proportion could be significantly increased (Heaton, 2000). In